The Fall of the South

The Vietnam Experience

The Fall of the South

by Clark Dougan, David Fulghum,
and the editors of Boston Publishing Company

Boston Publishing Company/Boston, MA

Boston Publishing Company

President and Publisher: Robert J. George
Vice President: Richard S. Perkins, Jr.
Editor-in-Chief: Robert Manning
Managing Editor: Paul Dreyfus
Marketing Director: Jeanne C. Gibson

Senior Writers:
    Clark Dougan, Edward Doyle, David
    Fulghum, Samuel Lipsman, Terrence
    Maitland, Stephen Weiss
Senior Picture Editor: Julene Fischer
Researchers:
    Jonathan Elwitt, Sandra W. Jacobs, Mi-
    chael Ludwig, Anthony Maybury-Lewis,
    Carole Rulnick, Nicole van Ackere, Rob-
    ert Yarbrough
Picture Editors:
    Wendy Johnson, Lanng Tamura
Assistant Picture Editor: Kathleen A. Reidy
Picture Researchers:
    Nancy Katz Colman, Robert Ebbs,
    Tracey Rogers, Nana Elisabeth Stern,
    Shirley L. Green (Washington, D.C.),
    Kate Lewin (Paris)
Archivist: Kathryn J. Steeves
Picture Department Assistant:
    Karen Bjelke
Historical Consultants:
    Lee Ewing, H. D. S. Greenway, Colonel
    Harry G. Summers, Jr.
Picture Consultant: Ngo Vinh Long
Production Editor: Kerstin Gorham
Assistant Production Editor:
    Patricia Leal Welch
Editorial Production:
    Sarah E. Burns, Pamela George, Dalia
    Lipkin, Elizabeth Campbell Peters,
    Theresa M. Slomkowski
Design: Designworks, Sally Bindari
Design Assistant: Sherry Fatla

Business Staff:
    Amy Pelletier, Amy P. Wilson
Special Contributor to this volume:
    Mary Jenkins (picture editor)

About the editors and authors

Editor-in-Chief *Robert Manning*, a long-
time journalist, has previously been editor-in-chief of the *Atlantic Monthly* magazine and its press. He served as assistant
secretary of state for public affairs under
Presidents John F. Kennedy and Lyndon B.
Johnson. He has also been a fellow at the
Institute of Politics at the John F. Kennedy
School of Government at Harvard University.

Authors: *Clark Dougan*, a former Watson
Fellow and Danforth Fellow, has taught
history at Kenyon College in Ohio. He received his M.A. and M.Phil. at Yale University. *David Fulghum* has been a senior
writer with the *U.S. News & World Report*
Book Division. A veteran of the U.S. Navy,
he received his B.A. from Angelo State
University in Texas and has done gradu-
ate studies at Texas A&M and Georgetown
universities. Messrs. Dougan and Fulghum
have coauthored other volumes in *The
Vietnam Experience*.

Historical Consultants: *Lee Ewing*, editor
of *Army Times*, served two years in Vietnam as a combat intelligence officer with
the U.S. Military Assistance Command,
Vietnam (MACV) and the 101st Airborne
Division. *H. D. S. Greenway* is national-
foreign editor of the *Boston Globe*. He covered Vietnam for *Time* magazine and the
Washington Post from early 1967 until the
American evacuation of Saigon in 1975.
Colonel Harry G. Summers, Jr., is an infantry veteran of the Korean and Vietnam
wars and now holds the General Douglas
MacArthur chair of military research at
the Army War College. He is the author of
On Strategy and *The Vietnam War Alma-
nac*.

Picture Consultant: *Ngo Vinh Long* is a social historian specializing in China and
Vietnam. Born in Vietnam, he returned
there most recently in 1980.

Cover Photo: The South falls. On April 30, 1975,
ten years after the first American combat troops
entered Vietnam, a North Vietnamese tank
crashes through the gates of Saigon's presidential palace, symbolizing the Communists' final
victory.

Library of Congress Catalog Card Number:
85-071747

ISBN: 0-939526-16-6

10 9 8 7 6
5 4 3 2 1

Contents

Conditions So Perfect

Barely five feet tall, bespectacled and ever-smiling, Tran Van Tra bore no resemblance to the Western image of a fighting general. His untailored, dark-green uniform carried no wings, wreaths, or rows of ribbons, yet for thirty years this slim South Vietnamese man had carried the fight to the enemies of the Lao Dong party. Freed from a French prison along with many other Communists at the end of World War II, Tra joined the revolutionary army and rose through its ranks carrying with him the dream of someday returning to Saigon, the city of his youth, as a liberator. In 1968, after lengthy debates with the Politburo, Tra won permission to attack the capital. The reasoning for his choice of target, Tra believed, was irrefutable: If the capital fell, with it would fall the Thieu regime and the South Vietnamese army. But his assurances that a popular uprising would materialize to support the military effort proved humiliatingly wrong. Tactically the Tet assault resulted only in the exposure and

needless destruction of many carefully placed Communist cadres. Tra bore responsibility for the fiasco and, his judgment thus blemished, lost the chance to join the Politburo. The general and his dream, however, survived.

Now in late 1974, as a member of the Communist party Central Committee and lieutenant general in command of the Communist military forces in the lowlands-Mekong Delta region, he once more made plans for the conquest of Saigon. With the American troops gone, U.S. financial support of the South Vietnamese government (GVN) waning, and the Army of the Republic of Vietnam (ARVN) stretched to the breaking point, the general knew that time and circumstance had joined logic as his allies. A bold strike at Saigon could end the long, costly war.

The summons north

To give substance to this dream required more troops, heavy artillery, tanks, and ammunition than the Central Office of South Vietnam (COSVN) and its combat arm, the B-2 Front, possessed. Since coming south to fight in 1959, Tra had chafed under the knowledge that the North Vietnamese generals fighting in the central highlands and along the demilitarized zone (DMZ) received the newest equipment and mountains of artillery shells while he often made do with captured arms. To obtain a full share for COSVN required a persuasive argument to the parsimonious high command in Hanoi, whose members would recall Tra's promises and failure of 1968. But Tra would have a chance to make his case in person because today, November 13, marked the start of a journey north; the Politburo had summoned all the regional commanders in the South to Hanoi to discuss future military operations.

In the morning coolness, Tra walked down the steps of his thatched bachelor's quarters still tucked in the shade of a copse of trees and climbed into the front passenger seat of a Russian-built GAZ69. Already in the back of the canvas-topped field car sat COSVN's chairman, Pham Hung. Chunky, with pouches of perpetual worry under his eyes, Hung stood fourth in influence among the eleven members of the Politburo and topped even Tra as the highest-ranking Communist in the South. Followed by several other light vehicles carrying staff members, the GAZ moved along a few kilometers of plank road to the intersection with Route 13 in nearby Loc Ninh.

Route 13 began in Saigon some 100 kilometers to the south where it served as the main artery for supplies and reinforcements from the big GVN storage depots at Bien Hoa and Tan Son Nhut. The traffic was destined for the ARVN garrisons at Lai Khe, Chon Thanh, and An Loc that made up the defense line north of the capital. But north of

An Loc the country belonged to the North Vietnamese Army and the remnants of the Vietcong.

Loc Ninh stood where the vast French rubber plantations finally gave way to hardwood forests, home for some of the rarest orchids in the world. Piles of rubble and badly damaged buildings marked the former GVN district capital, now perhaps the most important South Vietnamese town in the hands of the Communists. In addition to housing COSVN and the B-2 regional military headquarters—organizations that for so many years defied location and destruction by U.S. and South Vietnamese forces—Loc Ninh served as the capital of the Provisional Revolutionary Government (PRG) and the terminus of the new fuel pipeline from North Vietnam.

The PRG served as a figurehead government ostensibly for South Vietnamese rebelling against Saigon's Republic of South Vietnam, but the primary organization carrying on the war in the far south was COSVN. According to enemy propaganda COSVN was autonomous; in fact, it served as an intermediate organization between the Lao Dong party in Hanoi and the Communist troops in the southern half of South Vietnam. Politburo members referred to COSVN as the "southern branch of the [Communist Workers-Lao Dong] Party." By 1974 COSVN, run by Hung and Tra, shared only in planning the battles around Saigon and in the Mekong Delta, while the party's military committee and the NVA's General Staff in Hanoi directly controlled the fighting in the central highlands and the provinces south of the DMZ.

When the convoy with the two COSVN leaders reached Route 13 the vehicles turned north, and with studied contempt of the limited offensive threat of the South Vietnamese air force (VNAF) the group continued the trip in daylight. They knew fuel and aircraft shortages, coupled with the Communist missile threat, limited GVN air operations primarily to close support of ground fighting. Within an hour the group crossed the border into eastern Cambodia turning northwest to the banks of the Mekong River near Kratie, where they switched to motorized sampans. Far up the Se Kong branch of the great river, in southern Laos, the southerners transferred back to autos and continued along the Ho Chi Minh Trail, one branch of which was now a smooth four-lane highway of crushed white limestone and gravel, until Route 9 branched east back into South Vietnam just below the DMZ. At the port city of Dong Ha the convoy turned north into the DRV and the final leg of the trip to Hanoi.

Return to revolutionary violence

During the journey, Tra and Hung must have reflected on the momentous changes in the political and military situation in North and South Vietnam since the cease-fire in 1973: the failure of peace-keeping attempts, the inability to force a coalition government on the GVN, the growing

Communist strategists.
Above. Senior General Vo
Nguyen Giap, stricken by
disease, served only as a
figurehead chief of the
NVA in 1975. Below. Pham
Hung, COSVN head,
urged a quick thrust
against Saigon.

Left. Lieutenant General
Tran Van Tra, who re-
quested more arms and men
for his COSVN forces near
Saigon. Above. Senior General Van Tien Dung, NVA
chief of staff, who refused
Tra's request and instead
ordered an offensive in the
central highlands.

Above. Le Duan, Communist
party first secretary, supported a bold offensive. Left.
Le Duc Tho, an influential
member of the Communist
Politburo, advocated a conservative approach.

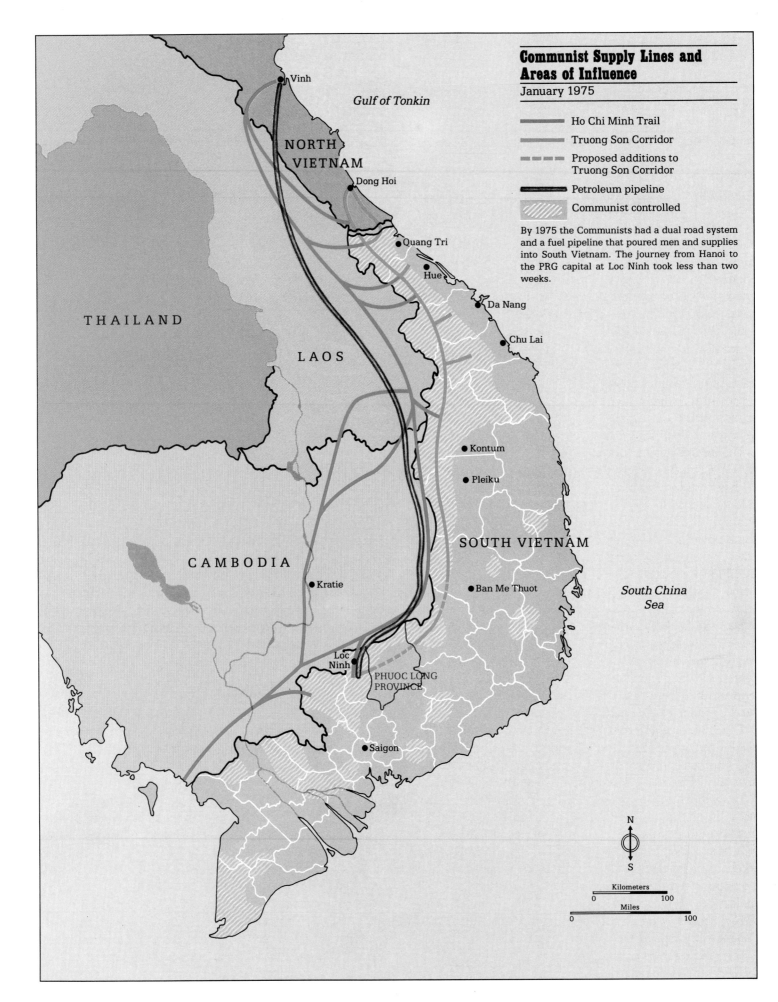

Communist Supply Lines and Areas of Influence
January 1975

Ho Chi Minh Trail

Truong Son Corridor

Proposed additions to
Truong Son Corridor

Petroleum pipeline

Communist controlled

By 1975 the Communists had a dual road system
and a fuel pipeline that poured men and supplies
into South Vietnam. The journey from Hanoi to
the PRG capital at Loc Ninh took less than two
weeks.

Gulf of Tonkin

NORTH
VIETNAM

Vinh

Dong Hoi

Quang Tri

Hue

Da Nang

Chu Lai

THAILAND

LAOS

Kontum

Pleiku

SOUTH VIETNAM

CAMBODIA

Kratie

Ban Me Thuot

South China
Sea

Loc
Ninh

PHUOC LONG
PROVINCE

Saigon

N

S

Kilometers
0   100

Miles
0   100

weakness of the Republic of Vietnam's Armed Forces (RVNAF), and the diminution of U.S. support.

First came the triple failure of the two-party Joint Military Commission (JMC), the International Commission of Control and Supervision (ICCS), and a negotiated political settlement. The JMC, made up of representatives from the GVN and PRG, proved itself powerless to ensure joint action in carrying out the terms of the Paris agreement concerning areas of control and prisoner exchange. The group never achieved the unanimity required for any action. The ICCS, consisting of delegates from Indonesia, Iran, Poland, and Hungary, also failed to produce unanimity as they attempted to assess guilt in cease-fire violations. Chances for a negotiated political settlement in South Vietnam through elections foundered when both sides entered negotiations with rigid and unrealistic positions. Saigon wanted a national referendum immediately while GVN influence remained strong. The PRG, however, demanded freedom of movement and expression throughout South Vietnam that would allow them time to regain influence through a series of local elections. Each side proposed a scenario that would maximize the prospects of its own electoral victory. As a result, the initial proposals remained virtually unaltered over the course of the talks.

The belligerents thus could neither decide on, nor their foreign advisers push them into, a new plan for cease-fire. With progress toward a peaceful resolution on the battlefield halted and the avenue for Communist political advantage through a coalition government blocked, it became obvious to the Politburo that they would once again have to turn to force of arms. The party's Resolution 21 and COSVN's Resolution 12, both formulated by mid-1973, ordered a return to "revolutionary violence" as the path to reunification of North and South Vietnam.

Despite the 1973 redeclaration of war, throughout 1973 and most of 1974 the North Vietnamese continued to concentrate on the reconstruction of an economy ravaged by years of war. Communist strategic planning remained formless until the effects of ARVN's growing weakness and the diminution of U.S. support became apparent.

The Communists had only to read the Western papers to follow the decline in U.S. support for the South Vietnamese, whether in dollars or public opinion polls. On May 22, 1974, the House of Representatives voted not to raise its $1.126 billion ceiling for Fiscal Year (FY) 1974 for military aid to South Vietnam even though the House Armed Services Committee recommended $1.4 billion. Funding for FY 1975, which began July 1, 1974, was even worse news for South Vietnam. On September 23-24 the House and Senate voted for an actual appropriation for Saigon of $700 million, including shipping costs to South Vietnam. Since public opinion was demanding the war be laid to rest, Congress seemed unlikely to reverse the trend.

The decline in aid produced a profound impact on the RVNAF when compounded by inflation, increasing world prices, and fewer U.S. dollars spent by American servicemen. The combined effects destroyed the ability of the average soldier to produce a subsistence living for his family even with a second job, or "moonlighting." Predictably, desertions soared and morale plummeted, producing a crisis for South Vietnam's President Nguyen Van Thieu, whose political support by late 1974 already rested almost entirely on the military. Hanoi's leaders, however, remained focused primarily on the material ramifications of South Vietnam's fiscal constraints, which they believed had forced ARVN to switch to a "poor man's war." Intelligence reports informed the Communists that air and artillery support for ARVN operations fell nearly "60 percent because of the shortages of bombs and shells" and that mobility had decreased by half because of shortages of aircraft, vehicles, and fuel. The General Staff surmised that the RVNAF retained the capacity to defend its positions but possessed only a limited ability to patrol aggressively and launch counterattacks.

It was thus a combination of factors that prompted Hanoi to renew its military offensive against the South. In October the Politburo and the Central Military Committee met to hear the military's General Staff confirm its new strategic combat plan: The NVA would conduct a two-year offensive. The 1975 objectives aimed at improving their battlefield position by destroying exposed outposts and completing supply corridors, while minor attacks kept ARVN tied to the defense of urban strongholds. The U.S. election year of 1976 would bring with it strong assaults against the cities and major garrisons of the South Vietnamese. The North gambled that their military efforts could either force the South to accept a coalition government or perhaps even gain a total military victory for the Communists. As a result, in late October the message went out to Hung, Tra, and the other regional commanders in South Vietnam to gather in Hanoi to discuss their plans for the new two-year campaign.

The road to Hanoi

Tra made the trip "faster and with less hardship" than the first time he traveled along Route 559, the original Ho Chi Minh Trail. In 1959 the general established the pathway as he went south to organize and command an insurgency against the GVN. Then the journey had taken him four months. This time it would take him only ten days. As the delegation moved along the river routes and paved highways, their path paralleled strings of telecommunications lines and the petroleum pipeline that "crossed streams and climbed mountains." The staff pointed out to each other the pumping stations, machine shops, headquarters, and maintenance parks for the 10,000 Chinese- and Russian-made trucks that punctuated the trail. They also keenly eyed the 500-man units of soldiers, moving in the opposite direction by truck. They were new recruits from

Corridor 613

The North Vietnamese opened a second supply corridor into the South to support the 1975 offensive. The route followed the Truong Son mountain range through South Vietnam and ended less than 100 kilometers from Saigon. (Much of the old route, the Ho Chi Minh Trail, wound through Laos and Cambodia.) Down the new roads carved out by soldiers and Vanguard Youth units poured the tanks, artillery, troops, and supplies that allowed the Communists to concentrate overwhelming numbers against the South Vietnamese defenders.

Left. *In the days of American bombing attacks, NVA movement south took place only at night. Now, troops moved in broad daylight down roads in South Vietnam itself. Above. North Vietnamese flatten a new section of road. Right. NVA troops, including a command section with portable radio gear, move south.*

the North earmarked as replacements to flesh out Communist units to full strength before the new campaigns began. Between the troop convoys moved columns of Ural375 and Zil131 trucks towing large-caliber antiaircraft guns, batteries of 122MM and 130MM long-range field guns, scores of T54 heavy tanks, and a leavening of powerful SA-2 antiaircraft missiles on mobile launchers.

Even more reassuring for the southern Communists, they knew that about 160 kilometers east of the route they traveled, on the opposite side of the Annamite (Truong Son) mountain range inside South Vietnam, a new strategic supply corridor paralleling the Ho Chi Minh Trail neared completion after two years of work. To meet the early 1975 construction deadline, 30,000 troops and uncounted numbers of young men and women members of volunteer Vanguard Youth units labored on the route, which was called Corridor 613. They prepared the way, observed Senior General Van Tien Dung, NVA chief of staff, for the "massive amounts of tanks, armored cars, rockets, long-range artillery and AA guns" needed at the front lines.

The military committee and General Staff in Hanoi had been hoarding these supplies in North Vietnam since the big Soviet and Chinese resupply effort that came between the end of the 1972 offensive and the signing of the cease-fire. After the cease-fire, the amount of Soviet military aid decreased, reflecting changes in the thinking of both the Soviets and the North Vietnamese.

Heavy military losses and the destruction of North Vietnamese industry brought on by the Communists' 1972 invasion of the South and allied retaliatory bombings brought the Politburo "doves" into ascendancy, led by Truong Chinh, Pham Van Dong, and Le Duc Tho. During 1973 and early 1974 the nation's efforts were directed at strengthening the North and alleviating some of the wartime strains on the citizenry. The DRV asked the Soviets for an increase in nonmilitary aid to rebuild roads, railroads, communications, and industry.

Requests for economic assistance fit in well with Soviet goals that aimed at restraining Hanoi's war-making capacity in the interests of Soviet-American détente. While seeming to placate the Americans but without abandoning their Communist allies, the Russians simply lessened military shipments while increasing nonmilitary economic aid. Henry Kissinger, in maneuvering Moscow to support the U.S. cease-fire efforts as national security adviser, had promised the Soviets most-favored nation status for trade purposes. Such an arrangement would allow the Russians opportunity for expanded commerce with the West, a goal the Soviet Union urgently sought to prop up a sagging socialist economy.

But in late 1974, with Politburo power moving back into the hands of the "hawk" faction led by party First Secretary Le Duan, who had moved from a moderate position, and Senior General Vo Nguyen Giap, Hanoi's leadership

began planning new offensives. To support them the supplies held in the North were finally released to build the NVA's striking power.

Moving rapidly past the heavy traffic headed south, Hung and Tra arrived in Hanoi on November 22, three weeks before the official beginning of the Politburo meeting at which the offensive plans would be finalized. Members of the southern delegation quickly began sounding out their friends and allies in the various bureaus and committees for information useful in their quest for more troops and to solicit support for their own scheme of conquest of the South.

COSVN's plan

From the moment the Politburo notified Tra and Hung of the planned offensives to end the war, the pair started designing a two-part campaign for COSVN. They saw their command as the most critical theater in South Vietnam but placed in the anomalous position of being the most poorly supplied. Although the 1975 offensive was planned as a fight preparatory to the main event in 1976, Tra wanted enough strength to strike hard in the first year to prevent the ARVN from rallying and counterattacking "with the support of superior U.S. air and naval power." Under heavy attack, they reasoned, the South Vietnamese forces would withdraw into enclaves around the major cities of Saigon in the lowlands and Can Tho in the Mekong Delta. "In such an event," Tra declared in his memoirs, "the B-2 theater would, by itself, have to launch the final attack on the enemy's headquarters lair and conclude the war." But to execute such a coup de grâce demanded that Hanoi release three or four of the strategic reserve divisions in North Vietnam to COSVN as insurance for victory "in the final battle."

A bold strike at Saigon constituted COSVN's strategic goal, but in addition it planned a quick tactical maneuver in December that also needed approval from the high command. Before the main offensive they needed to eliminate a GVN salient in Phuoc Long Province. It would serve both political and military purposes. Five key outposts stood northeast of Saigon near the Cambodian border. If the ARVN garrisons could be destroyed, stretches of new road and highway captured in 1972 would be linked, giving the Communists for the first time a corridor inside South Vietnam to carry tanks, troops, and fuel from the DMZ to Loc Ninh and beyond. The early attack would also serve to tie down ARVN forces, leaving no mobile reserves to strike at the vulnerable Communist supply lines and troop concentrations so necessary for success in the later battles. With a minor military investment the B-2 troops could keep the government soldiers off balance while allowing the NVA to husband its major units, heavy weapons, food, and munitions for 1975-76.

Politically, the capture of Phuoc Long would give the

Giap and Dung

A Change in Command

Throughout the French and American wars in Vietnam, General Vo Nguyen Giap was recognized as the commander and architect of the Communist armed forces. After the Vietminh's victory at Dien Bien Phu in 1954, Giap became a subject of international regard. He had proven to be a planning and logistical expert and had shown great tactical and organizational versatility in switching from guerrilla warfare to large-scale offensives. The general maintained his reputation for military genius through the years of fighting against the Americans, even though, as Giap admitted to reporter Oriana Fallaci, by early 1969 his methods had cost the North Vietnamese 600,000 men and an end to the war was not yet in sight.

Giap's successes were not entirely of his own making. In the commander in chief's shadow labored General Van Tien Dung, leader of one of the Vietminh's first divisions and the army's chief of staff since 1953. Like Giap, Dung had been exiled in China during World War II and, also like Giap, had been given by Ho Chi Minh the task of organizing the Vietminh military arm. The years of combat that followed made both generals firm believers in the thesis that while guerrilla tactics could prolong a war and limit losses, the key to victory was the use of regular army forces capable of waging major battles.

Dung, the only NVA four-star general besides the commander in chief, if not the actual author of Giap's plans was most responsible for carrying them out. He orchestrated battlefield maneuvers and marshaled the necessary supplies, arms, munitions, and men. He was also the prime mover in transforming the NVA into a modern military machine between 1968 and 1972. For his efforts, Dung became, at age fifty-six, the youngest full member of the Politburo in 1973.

After Giap was stricken with Hodgkin's disease in 1973, the commander in chief was relegated to mainly ceremonial tasks while actual command of the army fell to his protégé, Dung. In the two years after the Paris cease-fire, the chief of staff rebuilt the formidable North Vietnamese military machine. At the same time Dung put many of the North's soldiers to work improving and expanding an extensive network of roads leading from the supply depots of Hanoi to deep inside South Vietnam. The products of his efforts were a northern militia of 200,000 men to protect the home front and an expeditionary force of twenty-two divisions backed by hundreds of Soviet and Chinese tanks, long-range artillery, large-caliber antiaircraft guns, and a variety of missiles. Perhaps even more crucial than its sheer firepower and numerical strength was this force's mobility; it could strike anywhere in South Vietnam within a matter of weeks, perhaps even days.

After addressing the problems of logistics, arms, and manpower, Dung turned his attention to reorganization. In the 1972 Communist offensive, the North Vietnamese applied the lessons they had been taught in Soviet armor and artillery schools. North Vietnamese tanks, artillery, and antiaircraft units fought alongside the infantry but with each branch under its own independent command. As a result, the infantry sometimes had to attack without artillery preparation and the tanks without infantry support. The U.S. and South Vietnam took advantage of the lack of tactical coordination and inflicted heavy losses on NVA men and equipment.

Dung was determined not to repeat these mistakes. For the offensive planned for 1975–76, the general consolidated many of the independent regiments into divisions capable of fighting larger, longer battles. He then redesigned the chain of command to place infantry, artillery, tanks, and antiaircraft within the control of these divisional commands. A division or corps (two or more divisions) commander could now move all his units into the fight quickly and where most needed without having to go through a long and cumbersome chain of command for approval.

The first test for Dung and his newly organized army was to be the battles for Phuoc Long Province during the winter of 1974–75. Under Lieutenant General Tran Van Tra, the NVA 2d Corps, closely supported by well-trained tank and artillery units carefully parceled out by the General Staff, struck quickly into the ARVN defenses and overwhelmed them before reinforcements could arrive. These tactics were to be repeated on a larger scale in March, April, and May as the Communist armies swept south.

Communists control of their only GVN provincial capital and make mockery of President Thieu's policy of surrendering no territory to the enemy. If this bulwark of his policy were breached, the legitimacy of Thieu's other policies, such as no recognition, no cooperation, and no negotiation with the Communists, would also be shaken. Lastly, a limited attack so near Saigon would constitute one final test of the American will to respond before larger numbers of Communist forces were committed to an all-out offensive.

But soon after its arrival in Hanoi, the southern delegation discovered that severe obstacles stood in the way of its plans and hopes for the heavy reinforcement of COSVN. From the senior operations officer of the NVA's General Staff, Tra learned that weapons and ammunition, especially big guns and heavy tanks, remained in short supply. It appeared that most were slated for B-3 (central

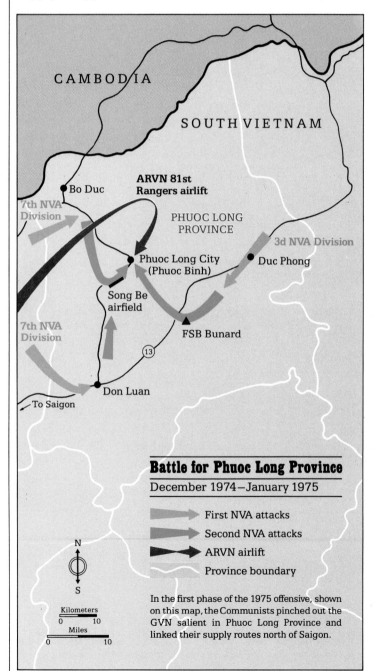

Battle for Phuoc Long Province

December 1974–January 1975

→ First NVA attacks
→ Second NVA attacks
→ ARVN airlift
— Province boundary

In the first phase of the 1975 offensive, shown on this map, the Communists pinched out the GVN salient in Phuoc Long Province and linked their supply routes north of Saigon.

highlands) and B-4 (DMZ area) theater forces, which were directly controlled by Hanoi. COSVN's B-2 Front, the delegation realized, would have to make do with the 105MM and 155MM howitzers and the M41 tanks and M113 armored vehicles captured from the South Vietnamese, instead of new Soviet equipment. Another unsettling discovery concerned the availability of troops. Hanoi's plans set aside 40 percent of COSVN's infantry for operations in the Mekong Delta. The General Staff intended to limit the southerners to minor attacks. COSVN's striking power was to be held in reserve for 1976.

"Anxious and worried," the military commander of COSVN realized that despite the ambitious rhetoric of the Politburo's October Resolution, his plans for vigorous attacks around Saigon were not those of the General Staff. Nor were they sanctioned by the chief of staff, Senior General Van Tien Dung, the protégé and successor to General Vo Nguyen Giap as the operational commander of the NVA. General Dung was, at fifty-eight, the youngest member of the Politburo and the only living member to have risen from peasant origins to power. Although he agreed with Le Duan that the Americans, now militarily out of South Vietnam, would be reluctant to "jump back in," the chief of staff planned to conduct a cautious offensive. Minor attacks by Tra's command around Saigon and in the Mekong Delta were to rivet ARVN's attention in the south while the NVA's main blows fell on the central highlands and just below the DMZ.

Disappointed by the General Staff's preliminary plan, COSVN's representatives began to lobby the Politburo members. But their efforts ran into an immediate rebuff when a personal appeal by Hung and Tra to Le Duc Tho failed. Tho told them that men, munitions, and equipment must be conserved for the final assault in 1976 since the Soviet Union continued to control the shipment of military supplies. "The situation abroad is very complicated," Tho diplomatically pointed out, therefore "we must limit the fighting in 1975."

Be certain of victory

After the interview with Tho, Tra discovered his difficulties with the General Staff included objections to his proposal for the already scheduled attack on Phuoc Long. While reading through a sheaf of messages forwarded from his headquarters in the South, the general discovered that General Dung had summarily ordered changes in COSVN's operational plans. Don Luan, the key town in the attack on the province, was not to be taken nor could tanks or heavy artillery be used in any of the assaults. In addition, Dung diverted the 7th Division and 429th Sapper Regiment, about half of Tra's assault force, to attack outposts in Quang Duc Province far to the northwest of COSVN's intended targets.

Tra quickly reported the situation to Pham Hung, and

the two of them enlisted the aid of Phan Van Dang, a member of the standing committee of COSVN, to demand a hearing before the General Staff and the military commission. On December 3 they were allowed to make a case for retaining the original Phuoc Long attack plans.

The trio's argument centered around the contention that ARVN, overextended and short on reserves, could counter the Communist move into Phuoc Long with no more than a single regiment. Furthermore, any large GVN counterattack would be tied to the roads because of the lack of air transport. Tra pronounced B-2's troops capable of stopping any such land-bound relief attempt. Tra then began to pressure his superiors by demanding not only that the 7th Division be returned to him but that additional forces be reassigned from the other theaters to apply heavy pressure on Saigon itself. Without mentioning the fact that southern-commanded troops would be allowed to capture the capital, Tra argued that the request was not inspired by COSVN parochialism; their plan was actually more faithful to the mandate of the October Resolution—"to exploit great opportunity"—than that of the General Staff.

Hung, Tra, and Dang made their points well enough that they regained control of the 7th Division. But the decision on the Don Luan attack, the most critical element of the Phuoc Long offensive, remained unresolved. Equally disturbing to the southerners, the military committee announced that during the 1975 offensive B-2 would conduct relatively minor attacks. The focus of the year's offensive would remain the northern half of South Vietnam.

The COSVN arguments for bold tactics engendered more interest among Politburo members than the southerners realized. Originally the DRV's eleven ruling officials had accepted the General Staff's conservative plans for what appeared to be sound reasons. In 1968 and 1972, all-out offensives had diverted resources from rebuilding the North and shattered major units of their army. More limited attacks to wear down the enemy appeared a less costly philosophy of war. It also made sense geographically and logistically to concentrate attacks on the northern provinces of South Vietnam since NVA supply lines were shortest there and the terrain offered ease of maneuver for tanks and heavy artillery. Yet the tactics advocated by the southern officers held out the possibility of a shortened war. The appeal of the strategy among the Politburo members was infectious. If not themselves convinced to go all out, the Politburo might at least let COSVN try out their audacious theories provided that the southerners also accepted all responsibility for failure.

A few days after the military commission meeting, the COSVN leaders were invited by party First Secretary Le Duan to meet at his home. After exchanging pleasantries, Tra straightforwardly asked Duan, a fellow southerner and past advocate of bold offensives, why the attack on Don Luan had been called off. Duan replied that he had been told by the General Staff that B-2's valuable main

forces would be thrown into the fight from the beginning. If these attacks turned into major battles the resulting losses in NVA men, munitions, and equipment might cripple COSVN's striking power for the main 1975 offensive and the big push in 1976. "To attack" Don Luan, Le Duan affirmed, "would not be appropriate."

Pham Hung and General Tra began to pound at the theme of ARVN weakness and the GVN's inability to reinforce the isolated outposts once the major roads of Phuoc Long were cut. Le Duan was apparently making a final test of their conviction since, to their amazement, the first secretary relented; the weeks of lobbying had paid off. As the voice of the Politburo, Le Duan said, "Go ahead and attack." But the first secretary also added the element of risk: Failure would not be accepted and their reputations would be at stake. "You must be certain of victory," he warned them.

Tra promptly drafted a message for COSVN ordering the regional command to carry out the attack as originally planned with the ARVN outpost of Don Luan as the first target. But Tra's frustrations were not over. The answer from his deputy carried the maddening news that the tanks and long-range artillery had been pulled out of Phuoc Long Province. The troops had also been told of Dung's order canceling the attack. To issue yet a third set of orders demanded an additional week of preparation; the attack could not begin before December 12. Undeterred, Tra ordered the attack forces reformed. "[We] recommend that our old plan," he wired the regional command, "be left unchanged."

The Russians and a spy

While the COSVN delegation fretted over launching its December attack, the preliminary meetings in Hanoi ended, and on December 18 the members of the Politburo began the 23d Plenum of the Central Committee of the Lao Dong party to endorse all the plans negotiated in the preceding weeks. In a surprise to many outside the Politburo, sitting down with them was General Viktor Kulikov, chief of the Soviet armed forces, who had just arrived from Moscow. The last time a high-ranking Soviet official visited Hanoi was on the eve of the 1972 offensive. The visit by Soviet President Nicolai Podgorny in October 1971 "turned on the taps" of Soviet military aid, which continued until the 1973 cease-fire. In 1974 Hanoi's leaders hoped for another such torrent. They needed ammunition to supplement only partly filled magazines as well as a reserve of tanks and missiles to exploit any unforeseen military breakthroughs.

Since mid-1973 leaders in Moscow and Peking had rejected North Vietnamese inquiries concerning large amounts of new military aid. But now, a year and a half later, luck again shifted to the DRV's side. The Soviets had grown furious with the U.S. because Congress had vetoed

Kissinger's agreement designating them, for trade purposes, a "most favored nation." When the trade bill came before Congress in the fall of 1974, a group of senators led by Henry Jackson, a presidential hopeful, attached an amendment linking approval of the bill to a relaxation of emigration quotas for Soviet Jews. Almost at the same time, amendments were put forward limiting loans to the Soviet Union. The bill, with amendments, would not be signed into law until January 3, 1975, but it was obvious well before then that the Soviets would not accept any manipulation of their internal affairs. As Secretary of State Kissinger pointed out, with classic understatement, "The Soviet Union was not induced to behave in a more reasonable manner."

General Kulikov arrived in Hanoi that December with encouraging words for the North Vietnamese. He not only endorsed the DRV's planned offensive but also thought that, since the U.S. Congress seemed unlikely to grant any additional economic or military assistance to Saigon, now was the time to strike. To back up his rhetoric, shipments of arms to North Vietnam quadrupled in January, February, and March.

Two days after Kulikov's appearance before the 23d Plenum, the North Vietnamese received a second windfall. A spy reported that on December 9-10 President Thieu and his military commanders met in Independence Palace to try and anticipate the Communist actions for the 1974-75 dry season. They judged the attacks would occur in the Mekong Delta and the central highlands but would not comprise an offensive on the scale of 1968 or 1972. They believed that the NVA remained too weak to take and hold large towns and cities. In the area around Saigon the GVN anticipated only an attack in the west near Tay Ninh not far from the Cambodian border. They predicted the attacks were to start just before or after Tet in early February and that they would continue sporadically until the monsoons began in June. The ARVN high command also decided not to reinforce the western highlands but to begin forming a strategic reserve for the defense of the Saigon area.

Unknown to the South Vietnamese, an agent of the North was either in the room or had access to the records of the meeting. In less than two weeks, on December 20, accurate accounts of the discussion and resulting decisions of the GVN leaders were in the hands of NVA General Dung. It is a great moment for any commander when he can determine his enemy's plans while keeping his own shrouded in secrecy. Now the Communists had such an advantage and with it they could define their still amorphous plans for the 1975 and 1976 offensives. But well before the Communists finished their twenty-day debate to hammer out the details for the next two years, they would also have the evidence from the battle of Phuoc Long Province, now already underway in South Vietnam, to consider.

The first move

The COSVN leaders, running the Phuoc Long offensive from Hanoi through their deputies, had launched the initial attacks on December 13. The five South Vietnamese outposts in the province were important because they lay across the east-west and north-south supply lines used by the NVA in the Saigon area. While an obstacle to the Communists, their location placed them far north of the main South Vietnamese defense line in Military Region 3. Major concentrations of COSVN infantry and special units, such as the M-26 Armor Command, bordered ARVN's position on three sides. The government soldiers had as their only links to outside help Route 14 to the south and an airfield big enough to land C-130 transports at the capital city of Phuoc Binh (also known as Song Be or Phuoc Long City) almost in the center of the province and about 110 kilometers northeast of the nation's capital (see map, page 11). The forces in the government salient kept enough ammunition stored for a week of intensive combat before they required resupply.

A week before the Phuoc Long attack, Tra struck in the west at Tay Ninh to attract any ARVN reserves away from his main battlefield. The move fulfilled ARVN expectations and focused attention far from their eastern flank. On December 13 (the date predicted by Tra's assistant), B-2's 7th and newly formed 3d Divisions struck hard, capturing Bo Duc and Duc Phong the next day. Don Luan, held by a Regional Force battalion of about 350 men, survived the initial assault, but Route 14 beyond the town was closed by the Communists. The ARVN forces at Phuoc Binh managed to launch a counterattack toward Bo Duc, but as they did so the NVA struck behind them capturing Firebase Bunard and its four 105MM howitzers. The South Vietnamese air force began flying in replacement artillery and taking out civilians, but soon NVA artillery fire destroyed a C-130, damaged a second, and closed the airfield at Phuoc Binh. By December 22 the remaining ARVN garrisons were cut off.

In Bien Hoa the III Corps commander, Lieutenant General Du Quoc Dong, newly appointed in November, weighed the attacks at Tay Ninh in the west against those at Phuoc Long to the northeast. With his major units tied to their defensive positions, and the Airborne and Marine Divisions, the nation's strategic reserve, still in I Corps, General Dong possessed only a few battalions of reinforcements. Dong decided that these had to be saved to defend the more important city of Tay Ninh, the keystone of Saigon's defense. He sent only one battalion to reinforce Phuoc Binh, a smaller force than even Tra had anticipated.

Nevertheless, the implications of losing a province capital, especially when the South Vietnamese were already discouraged by shrinking U.S. aid and support, was not wasted on General Dong. With his own III Corps reserves gone, he cornered President Thieu's assistant for security

affairs, Dang Van Quang, and insisted that to save Phuoc Long he needed at least part of the Airborne Division that currently was in the lines north of Da Nang.

Thieu's decision must have been an agonizing one. All the tactical and logistical weaknesses of the RVNAF had finally caught up with the president's policy of no retreat. Either he shifted some of his overextended troops to Phuoc Long, which would endanger the nation's military position somewhere else, or he allowed the province to fall, which would undermine his political position. On this occasion Thieu opted to preserve the precarious military situation around Saigon. The single group of Airborne Rangers remaining in the JGS reserve stayed in Saigon and the Airborne Division stayed in I Corps. According to Colonel William Le Gro, the senior U.S. intelligence officer in South Vietnam, Thieu wrote off Phuoc Long with the statement that "the Airborne was not available and that it could not be moved in time anyway."

ARVN soldiers in Phuoc Vinh manning the Saigon defense perimeter go on alert in January 1975 after the fall of Phuoc Long seventy kilometers north put them near the front line.

The "liberation" of Phuoc Long

The noose around Phuoc Binh closed a little more tightly when the NVA brought up tanks and unleashed a thousand-round artillery barrage on December 26 to overrun the stubbornly held town of Don Luan. At the end of the day only the garrison at Phuoc Binh remained. Since all the maneuvering had narrowed the campaign down to the final battle, both sides decided to raise their ante on January 5. The Joint General Staff (JGS) relented enough to send two companies of the 81st Airborne Rangers into the fight. The 250 Rangers, highly skilled in commando operations, moved in by helicopter early in the day and joined the survivors of the city's other units. But on the opposite side of the battle lines, Le Duan and the Politburo allowed Tra to commit more of the precious T54 tanks and 130MM field-gun batteries.

The attacking Soviet-built tanks were equipped with shields to neutralize the effects of armor-piercing shells. As one survivor described the phenomenon: "The enemy tanks had something new and strange. Our M-72 rockets were unable to knock them out. We hit them; they stopped for a while then moved on." Another ARVN combatant, Major Le Tan Dai, watched as his men, despite the NVA's four-to-one superiority of forces, climbed onto the backs of the buttoned-up tanks in brave attempts to throw hand grenades into the hatches. The defenders of Phuoc Binh destroyed at least sixteen tanks, but more appeared to continue the attack on the city. At midnight, with all their heavy guns and communications destroyed by NVA artillery and while under direct fire from Communist tanks, a few hundred survivors of the Rangers and Territorial Forces filtered out of their defensive positions into the jungle. Eventually 850 of the 5,400 soldiers of various types defending Phuoc Long returned to government lines.

A victory for Tra

Tra breathed a sigh of relief on the morning of January 6 as a wire was read to the members of the 23d Plenum still in session in Hanoi. The battle for Phuoc Long was over, the messenger read from the dispatch, the 4th Corps soldiers had "killed or captured all of the enemy troops and completely liberated Phuoc Long Province." The Central Committee members responded with applause and a round of handshaking. After a few minutes, Le Duan brought them back to order by elaborating on the ramifications of the newly won battles. For the first time the NVA had completely "liberated" a province. The conquest linked the new supply roads in western South Vietnam and considerably expanded the base areas around Saigon. But to Le Duan, "more clearly than anything else" the Communist victories pointed out the lack of "reaction of the [GVN], and especially the United States." The South Vietnamese did not have the troops to retake outposts, and, more importantly, the skies had remained empty of American bombers.

Le Duan concluded the Central Committee conference on January 8. In his closing statements he reiterated the leadership's belief that the U.S. would not return to fight in South Vietnam. Even so the NVA must be on guard. If the 1975–76 offensives did not succeed quickly, the first secretary warned, "the United States will intervene to a certain extent to save the puppets from total defeat," though as to when and in what way they were uncertain.

Troopers of South Vietnam's 81st Airborne Ranger Group prepare to fly to the relief of the embattled garrison at the city of Phuoc Binh on January 6.

As Comrade Pham Hung and General Tra drove back down Route 559 to COSVN headquarters in Loc Ninh, they garnered some satisfaction from their role in winning approval for the capture of all Phuoc Long Province. However, they also realized the fate of the 1975 offensive now rested in the hands of General Dung and the northern branch of the party. The southerners had not altered the General Staff decisions to launch the main attacks against the central highlands and northern provinces of South Vietnam. As the small convoy wound south their cars squeezed in among the trucks carrying the 316th NVA Division to the central highlands. The gray-haired officers were cheered and chanted at by the young soldiers, but the two elders of COSVN doubted they would have much to do with the next act of the great drama taking place in South Vietnam.

"Take Ban Me Thuot"

In Hanoi, the Central Military Committee started its meeting the day after the conclusion of the 23d Plenum and the departure of the regional delegations. These deliberations were to produce the detailed plans for the offensive. Conservative to a fault, the committee's tactical dispositions for the highlands assigned three divisions, heavy tank units, and a battalion of the long-range 130MM field guns to take the small border town of Duc Lap about fifty kilometers southwest of Ban Me Thuot, the capital city of Darlac Province. The General Staff advised that taking Duc Lap would lure ARVN forces into battle far from their main bases, making them easy targets for the NVA. The highlands attack, linked with other relatively minor territorial objectives south of the DMZ and in the Mekong Delta, constituted the General Staff strategy for the year. The move into the highlands would not be followed up until 1976 when assaults were scheduled on the traditional targets of Kontum and Pleiku. Underscoring a reluctance to innovate, the military had made at least one of these two cities a target of every major North Vietnamese offensive of the war.

But while the General Staff myopically detailed its pre-Phuoc Long plans, the members of the Politburo, led by Le Duan and Le Duc Tho, now united by COSVN's victory and new Soviet aid, were considering the changing situation that confronted their forces. With the completion of the Truong Son logistics corridor, troops and supplies moved swiftly toward the battlefields of South Vietnam, giving the NVA more tactical mobility than ever before. The ARVN, conversely, had proven themselves unable even to reinforce their outposts, much less recapture them once fallen. The loss of an entire province for the first time since the start of the Second Indochina War, whatever the rationale of the South, severely damaged both South Vietnamese morale and Thieu's status as protector of the nation. More important, the failure of the United States to respond to the crisis had undermined Thieu's role as the one South Vietnamese leader capable of eliciting American support.

Ironically, now that Tra had departed, his pleas for a more aggressive offensive were being heeded. As a result of their ruminations many of the Politburo members began informally to question the use of such a large force on an isolated subsector and a few small positions. Why not think on a grander scale and strike directly at Ban Me Thuot? They possessed intelligence that even though the city held strategic importance to both sides, ARVN regarded it as a safe, rear-area divisional and regimental base meriting only a weak defense. Besides offering the chance to capture a second province capital, they knew that the occupation of Ban Me Thuot would sever Route 21, leaving the government forces only the highly vulnerable Route 19 and the airfield at Pleiku as avenues for reinforcement or escape from the central highlands. The conquest of Ban Me Thuot in 1975 would make a victory at Pleiku in 1976—when the North Vietnamese had planned to continue the attack—much more likely.

The majority of the Politburo members decided to adopt the southerners' call for boldness. The meeting of the Central Military Committee had only begun on January 9 when Le Duc Tho walked in and sat down with the committee being chaired by the army chief of staff, General Dung. Tho told the general that the other Politburo members, including General Giap, felt "ill at ease" because the committee had produced no operational plans for an attack on Ban Me Thuot. Therefore, Tho had been sent to prod them into action by asking, "If we have nearly five divisions in the Central Highlands but can't take Ban Me Thuot, where are we?" Informally, members of the military committee had resisted changing their plans, but the Politburo's directive left them little choice. An assault on Ban Me Thuot was quickly made part of the 1975 offensive with the code name Campaign 275.

Dung immediately dispatched orders for the senior officers in the highlands to begin scouting Ban Me Thuot, but the Politburo spokesman held yet another surprise for the general. Perhaps to show solidarity among senior DRV officials or to assure wholehearted support of the campaign that initially lacked Dung's endorsement, Tho and Le Duan ordered the chief of staff to direct the operation personally. "On behalf of the Political Bureau, the Central Military Committee, and the General Command," Dung prepared to head south to lead from the battlefield, taking with him the final words of First Secretary Le Duan at the 23d Plenum: "Never have we had military and political conditions so perfect or a strategic advantage so great as we have now."

An NVA soldier directs a convoy on the Ho Chi Minh Trail toward battlefields in South Vietnam.

The Lull

During the second week of January, South Vietnam's senior military advisers on the Joint General Staff searched desperately for a solution to their dilemma. At the moment of crisis in the battle for Phuoc Long, their commander in chief's guiding strategy of "no retreat" had been cast aside and an entire province was allowed to fall to an ever-strengthening Communist foe. Although the loss demoralized the JGS, the implied change in policy was welcome. For years they had advised Thieu to adopt a more flexible defense; now at last it appeared such a change would be forced on the president. The weighing of the nation's options seemed to lead to but one inescapable conclusion: The RVNAF must fight a new style of war.

Yet to the JGS staff's surprise there came no summons for counsel from Thieu, no request for new plans. The silence was the result of Thieu's own quandary over his military and political goals, which had been compromised by a series

of increasingly chronic problems. Some of these matters, such as planning, leadership, and response to growing personal criticism, were within his power to control. Others, like the flow of manpower, supplies, and new U.S. aid, he could do little to change. But Thieu made his problems more difficult by circumscribing any potential solution with his pursuit of an ever more personal rule. Staying in power remained an important goal for the president, and this desire forced decisions that threatened the nation's very existence.

The crisis facing the military had been building since the American departure two years earlier. Manpower was part of the basic problem. Simply too few young South Vietnamese were coming of age to fill the ranks of a 1.1 million-man army that suffered from a high desertion rate and endured over 72,000 casualties in 1974 alone. By the beginning of January 1975 the RVNAF had shrunk to about 996,000 men, among them an undetermined number of "ghost soldiers" who existed only on paper. ARVN relieved some of the demand by shifting rear-echelon soldiers, military police, and guard troops into fighting units and by integrating Regional Forces into the regular army. These measures strengthened the existing formations, but there were still too few fully equipped units to fulfill Thieu's pledge to defend every foot of South Vietnam. That task required more well-trained ARVN regiments, Marine brigades, and Ranger groups backed by artillery and tanks. But the flow of military supplies from the U.S. was shrinking faster than the South Vietnamese army.

By 1975 it strained the RVNAF budget just to keep enough fuel and ammunition on hand to fight a sixty-day all-out war. Even if fuel and ammunition had been plentiful, the equipment on hand often broke down because the technicians and specialized tools required to keep them in operation proved insufficient for the task. The M48 tanks, 155MM howitzers, CH-47 helicopters, and C-130A transport aircraft provided the RVNAF with its muscle and mobility. But a limited ability to maintain the equipment curtailed their effectiveness and value in battle. Tank engines needed regular rebuilding, artillery recoil mechanisms required knowledgeable adjustments, and the helicopters would not fly without constant skilled attention. The early model C-130s available to the Vietnamese, discarded from U.S. reserve units, suffered from cracked wing spars, fuel leaks, and a shortage of spare parts.

The U.S.-taught philosophy of combat dictated a fast-moving, hard-hitting army with all its equipment operational that could counter an enemy thrust anywhere and overwhelm it with firepower. This method also suited Thieu who in his "Four No's" (no retreat from, no negotia-

tions with, no recognition of, and no coalition with the Communists) had proclaimed that not a foot of South Vietnam would be ceded to the enemy. His thinly stretched army needed every bit of mobility and striking power it could muster to defend the nation's long borders. While initially successful, by 1974 this hard-fighting approach had produced severe strains on the military. Strategists had warned that an attrition strategy would not work against a superior enemy force. As the battle for Phuoc Long had demonstrated, manpower, supply, and logistics demands had finally undermined Thieu's strategy. Still, even with shortages, sufficient resources remained to mount a stout defense if there was innovative planning from the JGS and inspired leadership from the senior field commanders. Events and indecision militated against such a solution.

A search for leadership

Thieu's most vocal critics had continued to accuse many of his most loyal government and military officials of corruption. To mollify the critics and to defuse growing discontent with his regime, the president had chosen in late 1974 to sacrifice some of these loyalists. Beginning in October, Thieu had sacked four cabinet ministers, including his cousin Hoan Duc Nha, moved three of his corps commanders to training and staff positions, and relieved 400 other senior officers. Unfortunately for Thieu and the fighting ability of the ARVN, at least two of the removed corps commanders, Lieutenant General Nguyen Van Toan of II Corps and Lieutenant General Nguyen Vinh Nghi of IV Corps, were proven leaders, popular with their troops, and versatile on the battlefield. Their replacements, while untainted by corruption, were militarily unproven. One of them was III Corps commander Lieutenant General Du Quoc Dong, whose ineffectual defense lost Phuoc Long, most of his troops, and at least twenty VNAF aircraft, including two of the precious C-130s. While Dong suffered from Thieu's intervention into command decisions during the defense, he made little effort even within his prerogatives to innovate tactics. Instead, he had mutely consented to Thieu's unexpected decision not to reinforce.

If Thieu or Dong had chosen to withdraw before the attack on Phuoc Long, the ARVN troops there could have been saved, albeit at the political expense of abrogating the Four No's. But the military decision neither to withdraw nor reinforce entailed both military and political sacrifices. The chairman of the JGS, General Cao Van Vien, later itemized the costs of not making a serious attempt to save the outposts: "People began to lose faith in the ability of the armed forces to protect the country. After Phuoc Long, many people became skeptical about the intent of the government and angry people engaged in talk about Phuoc Long being sold out to the Communists."

By going along with Thieu's decisions, Dong had sealed

his own fate. The president's immediate effort to avoid the onus of public criticism was a traditional one in the South Vietnamese army: General Dong was relieved of command. Then, with the encouragement of U.S. Ambassador Graham Martin, Thieu had recalled the recently fired General Toan from his training command to take on the defense of the South Vietnamese heartland. It was not without reservation that Thieu rehabilitated Toan. Thieu asked Martin whether the general's reputation for corruption might make for bad press. Martin replied, "Some ladies called on President Lincoln to complain about Grant's whiskey drinking. Lincoln said Grant won battles, he would have to find out what brand of whiskey Grant drank and send a barrel to all his other generals. What you need, Mr. President, are some victories. Since Toan will fight, maybe he can give you some."

Thieu's other hope for military salvation lay with the JGS, which numbered among its members some of the nation's best military minds. But Thieu's silence to the JGS after the fall of Phuoc Long confounded the group, which was designed to function only at the president's orders. So for all their talent and the frequently excellent intelligence of enemy intentions at their disposal, the JGS members could not issue orders to the corps commanders or even debate the president's decisions; they could merely advise, and then only when asked.

JGS takes the initiative

Despite this institutional weakness and Thieu's silence, the loss of Phuoc Long did spur the JGS into action of a sort. "In the absence of specific guidance by the president," said General Vien, "JGS took on itself the task of preparing for the next enemy move." They began discussing two critical issues: reconstitution of a national mobile reserve and a new plan of defense to replace the one-dimensional policy of "no surrender of territory," which had already proven fanciful.

To defend Saigon, the JGS first formulated a plan to assemble a brigade-sized group of infantry, armor, and artillery from the Mekong Delta forces supplemented by small units from the Ranger, infantry, and armor schools around the capital. The force could be in action within seventy-two hours. They made another decision about reserves that proved to be one of the most fateful of the war. The JGS members recommended, even demanded, of JGS Chairman Vien that I Corps be ordered to rearrange its forces so that "the Airborne Division could be moved [to Saigon] within [three days]." If adopted by Thieu the plan would mean the critical enclave that contained Quang Tri City, Hue, Da Nang, and Chu Lai could muster only four divisions for its defense instead of five, a critical difference in an area where the NVA could most easily mass.

Strategically, the JGS did flesh out some preliminary work on a plan to shorten defensive lines after agreeing

Two of Thieu's key military advisers, General Cao Van Vien (top), chairman of the JGS, and Lieutenant General Nguyen Van Toan, who commanded III Corps, including the troops defending Saigon.

among themselves that the armed forces stood a better chance if they had less territory to defend. According to the JGS chief of staff, Lieutenant General Dong Van Khuyen, the idea of "truncation"—the sacrificing of territory in order to withdraw to more defensible lines—"had been advocated by several South Vietnamese and foreign military authorities." Although the idea of defensive enclaves had been around since 1966, the JGS plan for truncation had as its most direct antecedent a report by Major General John Murray, the first head of the U.S. Embassy's Defense Attaché's Office (DAO), which had supplanted MACV in March 1973. A logistics expert, Murray had anticipated the crisis that would face Thieu if U.S. aid decreased. In a report on June 1, 1973, to his superiors in the Pentagon he declared, "You can roughly equate cuts in support to a loss of real estate." Ambassador Martin used Murray's report to warn Defense Department civilians in Washington of the dangers facing South Vietnam, although he considered such consolidation improbable. "It never occurred to me that [Thieu] would have the political courage to do this," Martin said in a postwar interview. "I myself didn't think a Vietnamese leader could do this and survive." Murray's figures were then passed on to the JGS, which drew up its own study and circulated it to senior members of Thieu's government. It obviously had an impact because in early August Prime Minister Tran Thien Khiem warned the I Corps commander that he might have to give up territory to buy time for the rest of the country. More significantly, recalled an embassy employee, "whenever an American Congressman passed through Saigon, [President Thieu] would unfurl it and proclaim sadly that 'this is what will happen if Congress is not more forthcoming.' " But the JGS committee went no further than to prepare a preliminary study. It never established formal contingency plans for the consolidation of South Vietnamese military forces.

The idea of giving up chunks of South Vietnam without a fight required a great deal of preparation, if only because of the inevitable political and psychological effects on the people and soldiers of the Republic. Thieu, though, remained unwilling to prepare the country for such a retreat. The president maintained his silence and therefore his de facto opposition to truncation. Two theories have been advanced as to why.

First, some of Thieu's intimates suggest he was so preoccupied with threats of a coup that he could not concentrate on the country's problems. This fear was surely fed by the memory of his own role in the coup against former President Ngo Dinh Diem in 1963. "During times of crisis," the president's special adviser, Bui Diem, said in a postwar interview, "his suspicion was centered on the possibility of an American-sponsored coup against him personally." General Murray of the DAO confirmed that Thieu's fears caused him to make some troop assignments with little concern for the nation's defense needs. Pointing

out that the CIA had bugged Independence Palace with listening devices, he recalled that at one cabinet meeting Thieu was "paranoiac about the coup business." The president asked his inner circle of officials which South Vietnamese general the Americans would support in the event of a coup. The ministers agreed it would be the I Corps commander, Lieutenant General Ngo Quang Truong. "I know this is the reason that Thieu kept those best divisions and the best commander up north," Murray said, "because he was afraid of a coup." General Tran Van Don explained that Thieu feared a coup that would cost him his life as had happened to President Diem. Air Vice Marshal Nguyen Cao Ky, without any command in 1975, said that Thieu slept in a different room every night in order to evade assassins; he anticipated an American hand in such an attempt. "He even said," Vice Marshal Ky recalled, " 'They may kill me at any time if I do something against them.' "

A second reason given for Thieu's failure to face the issue of truncation, however, was rooted, ironically, in a certain trust of the Americans. Contradictory as it may seem in light of his coup worries, according to Bui Diem, Thieu "held the belief that the Americans would never tolerate a takeover of South Vietnam by the Communists, at least not in the foreseeable future." Thieu had several reasons to believe this to be true.

Relying on the U.S.A.

On November 14, 1972, President Richard Nixon had written to Thieu, "You have my absolute assurance that if Hanoi fails to abide by the terms of this agreement it is my intention to take swift and severe retaliatory action." A second letter dated January 5, 1973, was even more explicit: "We will respond with full force should the settlement be violated by North Vietnam." Some U.S. Embassy insiders point out that even after Nixon's resignation, Ambassador Martin and other officials continued to maintain that the U.S. would provide more aid and perhaps intervene with armed forces if the North Vietnamese Army launched an all-out attack.

Influential American visitors also seemed to confirm Thieu's trust in U.S. support. Major General Homer Smith, Murray's successor as defense attaché, observed that, "In nearly every case when a high-ranking American visited Saigon, the message was the same; to wit, every attempt would be made to secure supplemental appropriations. . . . Hearing this, the Joint General Staff and other higher officers . . . believed that the chances were very good that [increased aid] would be forthcoming" in an emergency. Another boost to the president's confidence came from the Americans' habit of periodically taking senior South Vietnamese officers to the United States Support Advisory Group/7th Air Force headquarters in Nakhon Phanom, Thailand, where they were briefed on the latest contin-

As U.S. aid decreased and equipment shortages appeared, ARVN and Territorial troops were forced to draft civilians to haul supplies to remote outposts. Here young women and soldiers carry 81MM mortar rounds to a camp of the ARVN 22d Infantry Division in the hills around Bong Son near the coast halfway between Qui Nhon and Quang Ngai in January 1975.

gency plans for U.S. air attacks in the event of a North Vietnamese invasion.

Still another explanation of Thieu's unflagging faith in the Americans was later offered by PRG Minister of Justice Truong Nhu Tang, who understood it in light of the "ingrained Confucianism" of Vietnamese culture. "Among the very deepest feelings of one raised in a Confucian society," Tang wrote, "is the inhibition against betraying those with whom one enjoys a relationship of trust." While Thieu clearly was "betting on the American geopolitical investment in South Vietnam . . . a relationship of personal commitment had been created. Trapped in his Vietnamese habits of thought, Thieu imagined that this relationship must prevail, regardless of apparent political realities and logic."

While conservatives within the JGS counseled self-reliance and truncation, many South Vietnamese leaders believed that the U.S. would support them in a crisis even if it was unclear what provocation would be required before America would act. Whatever their views of American trustworthiness, most GVN officials were dismally ignorant of the realities of the U.S. legislative system. In South Vietnam President Thieu was the government; in the United States President Gerald Ford was not.

Had President Ford possessed Thieu's freedom from Congressional restraint, he could have moved a U.S. naval task force that included the nuclear carrier U.S.S. *Enterprise* into position off the coast of South Vietnam during the battles at Phuoc Long. Instead the fleet sailed to Africa while U.S. officials hurried to deny that any U.S. military activity was aimed at Vietnam and issued a statement on March 7 saying only that the president was concerned and "watching the situation closely." Four days later the U.S. issued its official response to the Phuoc Long offensive: a note of protest sent to the secretary-general of the United Nations. The document charged North Vietnam with "flagrant violation" of the cease-fire agreements. Produced by the State Department, the protest detailed a long list of transgressions including the NVA build-up of men and supplies and the improvements of their logistics system of roads.

Reasons for such a mild response abounded. At the time the Communists took Phuoc Long in January, President Ford had been in office only five months. The loss of a strategically unimportant handful of outposts in South Vietnam could easily be ignored when weighed against crises elsewhere in Southeast Asia, the Middle East, or for that matter, up the street on Capitol Hill.

Initially fears of further Vietnam crises had been allayed at an emergency meeting on January 7 of the Washington Special Action Group, the administration's crisis management team, called by Secretary of State Henry Kissinger. There CIA Director William Colby minimized the threats to South Vietnam by quoting a report that ruled out the possibility of a Communist offensive in 1975 even though there might be heavy fighting. Accurate as it was about the NVA's initial intentions, what the estimate could not report was that these goals were rapidly being outdated by new Politburo decisions.

Perhaps with this assurance in mind, Ford and Kissinger allowed continuing problems in the Middle East to overshadow events in Southeast Asia. During the winter of 1974–75, "negotiations between Israel and Egypt about the return of the Sinai had reached a dangerous stalemate," the president recalled. To grapple with the problem, Kissinger, the key figure in any decision concerning U.S. action abroad, was preparing for another round of shuttle diplomacy that would keep him in the Middle East for most of February and March.

Domestically, Ford's administration was already being blamed for inaction on unemployment, a rising national debt, and the severe energy crisis still affecting the nation in the aftermath of the 1973 oil embargo by the Organization of Petroleum Exporting Countries. And the president himself was preoccupied with selecting a new cabinet and dealing with a CIA wire-tapping scandal.

But even if attention had been riveted on Indochina, Congress had already blocked most of the president's options through the passage of the Indochina Prohibition of 1973 and the War Powers Act in November of 1974. Ford later contended that the legislation "severely limited [the president's] ability to enforce the peace agreement." The War Powers Act required the president to report to Congress within forty-eight hours after he ordered troops into action abroad or increased the number of foreign-based troops equipped for combat. The act also empowered Congress to revoke any such presidential order without the threat of a White House veto. Realizing he retained only a limited amount of leverage on Congress, Ford refused to test his remaining war-making powers in a hurried military reaction. He was certainly not going to spend political capital before he knew more about the actual situation in South Vietnam. "Everyone knew the problems . . . were serious," he wrote in his memoirs, "but no one seemed to know just how critical they were." But probably the most important factor in his reluctance to act militarily was knowledge that "the situation in neighboring Cambodia was even worse. The Khmer Rouge had encircled the capital of Phnom Penh and were preparing for the kill." Until that crisis was resolved, Ford "was not about to take a major military action such as renewed bombings."

The fight for aid

The president's other option, then, was to request more aid for South Vietnam. Though he did not yet know the Russians had decided to quadruple military aid to North Vietnam, Ford was quickly being disabused of any similar inclination of Congress toward South Vietnam or Cambodia. In Ford's opinion, the Foreign Assistance Act of 1974 cut economic and military aid to South Vietnam and Cambodia "to levels that endangered their ability to survive as free nations." In addition to imposing a $1 billion ceiling for total military aid to South Vietnam in fiscal year 1975, the act limited assistance to Cambodia to $227 million. Further, it prohibited the president from transferring military aid from one country to another. But despite his promise of continued support to Thieu in 1974, Ford decided to swallow the restrictions, take what Congress offered, and continue the fight for more aid through subsequent requests. So the president signed the bill.

On January 8, almost before Ford's ink dried, the White House announced it would seek additional military aid for Cambodia, Laos, and South Vietnam to fund them through the end of the fiscal year in June: $300 million for Vietnam and $222 million for Cambodia. Charging that the "other side has chosen to violate most of the major provisions of this [Paris] accord," Ford insisted that U.S. unwillingness to provide sufficient assistance would seriously affect America's credibility as an ally throughout the world. In a press conference on January 28, Secretary of State Kissinger joined Ford's offensive. There he said that "it was the belief of those who signed" the Paris accords, "encouraged by the U.S.," that the agreement was only to remove American forces and not to end the support of South Vietnam. The president continued the attack on February 26 when he rhetorically asked a group of journalists, "Are we to deliberately abandon a small country in the midst of its life-and-death struggle?"

The appeals were not well received. To the majority of Americans, the president's request to come to the aid of Vietnam revived painful memories of the nation's step-by-step embroilment in the early 1960s. Peaceful demonstrators holding lighted candles marched past the White House to protest the president's aid request, while mail, overwhelmingly against the proposal, stacked up in Congressional offices. Describing the administration's measures as "face-saving," some congressmen even questioned the president's sincerity. They cited the failure to lobby key congressmen for their support as evidence that Ford himself did not really believe he could achieve passage of a supplemental aid bill.

There was, however, another explanation for Ford's behavior. His request came just as the House was completing reorganization of the new 94th Congress. Seventy-five freshman Democrats had been elected to the House the previous November. A series of reforms they undertook were to shatter the established patterns of organization and seniority. As a result, the small group of predominantly southern members who had dominated the key Congressional committees and could be counted on to "deliver" votes when compromises with the executive were needed had virtually disappeared from power. Executive consultation with Congress thus became far less likely to result in an acceptable deal.

The administration could only hope that legislators harbored doubt about how their constituents would feel later should a successful NVA offensive take place. If the lawmakers did not already sense that Ford was playing on this fear, they were alerted to it when Senator Edward Kennedy made a string of stinging accusations before the Senate on January 31. The administration was using "threats and scare tactics," he said, to substantiate its aid request. "Once again we are hearing the same old arguments and the same old controversies over the same old war. The lingering and bloody conflict deserves more of our diplomacy, and not more of our ammunition."

In early February, Ford told *Chicago Tribune* reporters he was prepared to stop large-scale military and financial aid to South Vietnam within three years if Congress would agree to appropriate sufficient funds during that period. The president, invoking Ambassador Martin's assurances that with adequate dollars South Vietnam would survive, cited annual figures of $1.3 billion to Vietnam and $497 million to Cambodia in military aid.

Congressional reaction was swift. Within twenty-four hours, eighty-two of the bipartisan Members of Congress for Peace Through Law wrote that they saw no "humanitarian or national interest" to justify continued aid. Senate Majority Leader Mike Mansfield announced that he was "sick and tired of pictures of Indochinese men, women, and children being slaughtered by American guns with American ammunition in countries in which we have no vital interests."

Nor was Ford's cause helped by the fact that the governments of Lon Nol in Cambodia and Thieu in Vietnam were invariably depicted by the press as venal, corrupt, and incapable of functioning at even the barest level of efficiency. Unconvinced of the value of supplemental military aid and weary of the human costs of war, foreign affairs committees in both the Senate and House determined to rein in U.S. policy by exercising their power over the purse. Senator Hubert Humphrey stated unequivocally on "Face the Nation" that "additional military aid will merely prolong the agony" and predicted that his Subcommittee on Foreign Aid would vote funds only for food and other humanitarian assistance.

Crisis in Cambodia

While the aid debate continued to fill the air of Washington, the climate of crisis in Indochina intensified. Ford's decision not to use the limited United States forces in Southeast Asia to intervene at Phuoc Long now seemed justified because Cambodia finally appeared to be nearing collapse and the forces would be needed to extricate Americans from the capital of Phnom Penh.

That Cambodia, which could never match South Vietnam's strategic interest to the U.S., should demand such attention was much the result of the American ambassador to Phnom Penh, John Gunther Dean. Responsible for negotiating the Laotian cease-fire, he had provided a hard-nosed assessment of events that convinced the State Department and President Ford of his good judgment. Now Dean pursued relentlessly a goal of publicizing the facts about deteriorating conditions in Cambodia. His accurate, heartfelt reporting ensured that events in Cambodia overshadowed those in South Vietnam. This intense concentration on Cambodia prevailed even though there was little hope for a reversal of the government's decline.

Ambassador Dean had arrived in 1974 hoping for "some kind of nonmilitary solution" in Cambodia. After surveying the military situation sufficiently to recognize impending defeat, he suggested immediate negotiations with the Khmer Rouge leader Khieu Samphan. The state of the army dictated that Cambodia find a "compromise settlement" quickly even if it entailed forming a government without Lon Nol. Ambassador Graham Martin thought that Cambodia was draining away resources from Saigon, where U.S. interests really lay. Martin had long advocated returning to power the deposed Cambodian leader, Prince Norodom Sihanouk, from his exile in China and urged that this be arranged through the Chinese. However, Martin was told by the U.S. envoy to Peking, David Bruce, that Kissinger waited for the Chinese to bring up the matter, which they never did.

But Martin's and Dean's views meant nothing without the agreement of their boss, Henry Kissinger. He flatly rejected their ideas. "I knew that Cambodia was doomed," Kissinger wrote in his memoirs. But he also believed that the Khmer Rouge would violate any agreement they did not block. "Those who sought to end the war by throttling Lon Nol," the secretary of state explained, "thought nothing could be worse than a continuation of the war" and as a result would allow a Communist takeover. But as to Sihanouk's ability to influence the Khmer Rouge after such a takeover, Kissinger quoted as the authority on the subject the former Cambodian chief of state himself: "When I shall no longer be useful to them [the Khmer Rouge] they'll spit me out like a cherry pit." Journalist Arnold Isaacs gave a different interpretation in his book, *Without Honor*. He contended that Kissinger saw the resignation of Marshal Nol as a "bargaining chip" to be traded only if the Communists were prepared to make "significant concessions." The whole issue was probably moot, however, because Lon Nol's forces were reeling at every blow, so there seemed little reason for the Khmer Rouge to talk.

Under heavy pressure from the Communists, Lon Nol's *Forces Armées Nationales Khmères* (FANK) was "very much embattled"; it had survived until 1975 only because U.S. B-52 strikes, monsoons, and a temporary shutdown of North Vietnamese aid to the Communist insurgents had halted previous rebel offensives short of victory. Commanded by Lieutenant General Sosthene Fernandez, a Cambodian-Filipino, FANK was racked by "lack of resupply, inefficiency, misunderstandings and discontent provoked by the conduct of certain senior officers," according to its last chief of staff, Lieutenant General Sak Sutsakhan. There were few field rations issued except dry rice. An absence of pay allotments for wives and children meant that in order not to starve dependents followed FANK even into combat. These problems were compounded by disagreement between civil and military authorities. Although the government could still field a few crack brigades, it was primarily American-supplied artillery that gave FANK the firepower to ward off Khmer Rouge blows. According to an official American military assessment early in 1975, FANK still existed only because "they have outgunned" the Communists. "War weariness [was] setting in and it was impossible," Dean felt in spring 1975, "to turn this around very drastically."

A second front

By contrast the Khmer Rouge, North Vietnamese trained and Chinese equipped, had become a fanatically motivated 60,000- to 85,000-man army during its five-year history. By early 1975 the Khmer Rouge held 80 percent of Cambodian territory and was methodically squeezing the government into refugee-packed enclaves. They had also cut off all ground routes to the capital.

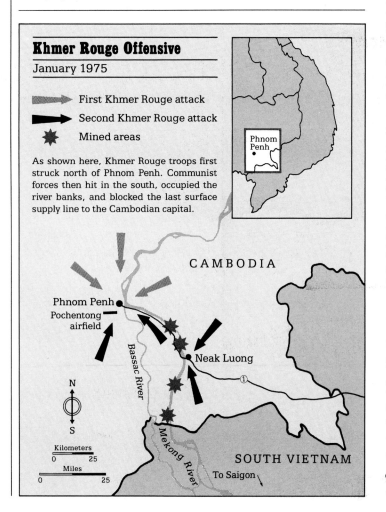

Khmer Rouge Offensive

January 1975

First Khmer Rouge attack

Second Khmer Rouge attack

Mined areas

As shown here, Khmer Rouge troops first struck north of Phnom Penh. Communist forces then hit in the south, occupied the river banks, and blocked the last surface supply line to the Cambodian capital.

Phnom Penh

CAMBODIA

Phnom Penh
Pochentong airfield

Bassac River

Neak Luong

N

S

1

Kilometers
0   25
Miles
0   25

Mekong River

SOUTH VIETNAM

To Saigon

Khmer Rouge commanders, including Defense Minister Son Sen (center) plot their strategy to take Phnom Penh.

Because FANK was weak and the Communists were strong, the U.S.-initiated offers for negotiation were quickly and unequivocally rejected by the Khmer Rouge. On New Year's Day the Khmer Rouge lashed out at FANK positions around Phnom Penh, catching the government forces by surprise and throwing them into confusion. During the first day, the attackers broke through the FANK lines east of Phnom Penh and captured a portion of the bank of the Mekong River opposite the capital city. Even though the battle lines quickly stabilized, from then on the capital came under bombardment from 107MM rockets.

The attacks also heightened the refugee problem as civilians fled to the city from the fighting and Khmer Rouge terror. "Reports of insurgents murdering civilians have been coming in from all fronts," reported *New York Times* writer Sydney Schanberg on January 4. In one incident within twenty-five kilometers of Phnom Penh, the residents of Ang Snuol returned after a Khmer Rouge attack to find their homes burned and forty townspeople bayoneted to death. Avowedly basing their revolution on radical principles, the Khmer Rouge declared their enmity for all but the peasant class. Evidence confirmed that the insurgents were murdering captured soldiers, civil servants, teachers, and anyone else who, for any number of reasons, might be considered counterrevolutionary.

The most damaging blow to the government was yet to come. With FANK forces tied down north of the capital, the Khmer Rouge struck in the south. By January 11 they were blockading a seventy-five-kilometer section of the Mekong River stretching from twenty-five kilometers outside Phnom Penh to the border with South Vietnam. In so doing they surrounded the key garrison town of Neak Luong, halfway between the capital and the border, and besieged its population of 250,000 soldiers, dependents, residents, and refugees. The next day a government convoy of four ships trying to reach the isolated post from Phnom Penh was heavily attacked and turned back. Sydney Schanberg reported that "every 15 minutes or so a shell screams down and explodes and another half-dozen people are killed or wounded. It goes on day and night."

In addition to their positions on the riverbanks, the Khmer Rouge occupied several midchannel islands in the Mekong. From entrenched positions at these critical sites, they launched antishipping mines and poured out fire that sank more than a dozen vessels trying to run the gauntlet to Phnom Penh in January. In one month there were more sinkings than in all of 1974. The last convoy reached the

capital on January 30. This interdiction of supplies created dreadful conditions for the 2.7 million noncombatants who, displaced by the war, crowded themselves into the constricting government positions.

Air links to Phnom Penh had previously been established by the U.S. Air Force, whose pilots flew rice and ammunition from U Tapao, Thailand, to supplement the river traffic. The airlift was stopped, however, when Congress objected to direct U.S. involvement. To replace the uniformed air force pilots who had conducted the airlift, the U.S. contracted with five independent airline companies to fly in the supplies. One of the private airlines, Bird Air, simply recruited pilots for whom the air force supplied C-130 transport planes, fuel, maintenance, and cargo. As the blockade of Phnom Penh continued, flights increased to one every half-hour and brought in 700 tons of cargo daily. Most of the flights headed for Phnom Penh; others airdropped supplies to outposts like Neak Luong.

The Flynt delegation

Even though the airlifted supplies stayed ahead of the needs of the government forces, the multimillion-dollar operation quickly ate up the U.S. funds allocated for Cambodia. Unless the president could win Congressional support for a $222 million supplemental aid package to Cambodia, the airlift would stop by mid-April. Very quickly after that the government army would run out of artillery ammunition. Administration officials continued to press Congress for more money, arguing that if Lon Nol were to be defeated, at least he should have the choice of deciding when to quit. On February 3 the president met with Congressional leaders and suggested that a delegation travel to South Vietnam and Cambodia for an on-the-spot appraisal of the countries' needs for additional military aid. By the end of the month, Congress agreed but chose a delegation not entirely meeting Ford's expectations. Smaller than the twenty-odd membership that the president had suggested, the group was led by Congressman John Flynt of Georgia and included several relatively junior legislators. Making the trip were Senator Dewey Bartlett of Oklahoma and Representatives Paul McCloskey of California, Millicent Fenwick of New Jersey, William Chappell of Florida, Donald Fraser of Minnesota, John Murtha of Pennsylvania, and Bella Abzug of New York. Still, the excursion gave the administration an opportunity to influence Congress, and in Saigon the job of doing the persuading was to be borne by possibly the staunchest supporter of aid, Graham Martin.

Martin had been flabbergasted when the Senate and House had cut to $700 million an original allocation of $1

In early 1975 as the Khmer Rouge close in, American-piloted aircraft drop supplies to the besieged Cambodian town, Neak Luong, on the Mekong River.

Members of the Flynt delegation in Southeast Asia. Top and right. Bella Abzug and Paul McCloskey interview villagers in Cambodia. Above. Millicent Fenwick lights up during her confrontation with PRG representatives over Americans still missing in action.

billion for military aid to South Vietnam. Even before the severe 1975 budget cuts, the option given to the U.S. by the Paris agreement of replacing equipment lost in combat was never completely fulfilled because of limited funds. As Martin watched U.S. financial support slip away, he recognized the threat to the very existence of South Vietnam. The government had to support an army of slightly under 1 million part- and full-time soldiers, which cost far more than the nation's economy could ever generate. To give the GVN even a chance to survive, Martin argued, the U.S. could not end or even reduce aid without giving the South Vietnamese ample warning. He was determined to make the Congressional delegation aware of these realities while they were within his purview.

At first it appeared that Martin would meet with little success. The Congressional visitors arrived on February 26 "suspicious" of Martin, "hostile" to his staff, and "determined to rely as little as possible" on them for advice, as embassy-based CIA analyst Frank Snepp wrote later. Nor were they happy with what they found while investigating the issues of jailed journalists, political prisoners, and civil unrest. Embassy and GVN denials of these problems seemed only to make the delegation members more distrustful. McCloskey said that the arrest of South Vietnamese reporters "goes against the grain of everything Americans believe in." At a dinner with Thieu they so pummeled the president with undiplomatic questions that Ambassador Martin later apologized for them.

The trip worked decidedly against Ford's and Martin's interests until just before the delegation left Saigon. Then the North Vietnamese themselves managed to turn the tide of support. The delegation met with North Vietnamese and PRG representatives to the Joint Military Team quartered at Camp Davis on Tan Son Nhut Air Base. In front of seventy-six journalists they had invited, the Communists refused to discuss America's missing in action and the repatriation of forty-one bodies of U.S. servicemen. After a heated exchange with Representative Flynt, the senior PRG representative, Major General Hoang Anh Tuan, declared the meeting closed. The sharp exchange appears to have swayed several of the undecided to support additional aid. This inclination was reinforced by a quick side trip to Phnom Penh. There, after a tour of a huge center for starving, sick refugees, Millicent Fenwick commented, "I can't believe this. I've never seen anything like it."

Members of the Flynt delegation returned to Capitol Hill on March 2 deeply disturbed by what they had seen. All but Bella Abzug advocated some military and humanitarian aid, reflecting their sense that the United States still bore considerable responsibility for the people of those countries. They also recommended that Kissinger use his influence immediately to encourage Russia and China to reduce their aid to the DRV and pressure North Vietnam to slow the pace of the fighting. The testimony clearly weighed upon the conscience of Congress but did not provoke immediate passage of an aid bill.

The slow pace of the democratic process in Washington, however, was to prove drastically out of synchronization with the rapid escalation of the war in Vietnam. If the delegation members had looked closely at the fact sheets handed to them by DAO representatives as they left Vietnam, they may well have suspected that time was running out for the bill to be of use either materially or morally. The DAO's intelligence pointed out that North Vietnam had increased its strategic reserve from two divisions to seven. This meant that more than 70,000 additional soldiers could be deployed immediately to South Vietnam, where 200,000 combat soldiers and 100,000 support troops were already in place. Those divisions could be moved, for instance, from North Vietnam to the plateau that held Ban Me Thuot and Pleiku within fifteen days. Once in South Vietnam, the infantry units would be supported by 600-700 tanks, twice as many as possessed by the ARVN; 400 heavy artillery pieces; 200 large-caliber antiaircraft guns; and "many" of the deadly SA-7 missiles.

As Colonel William Le Gro, the DAO intelligence chief, later wrote, the NVA had "never in the history of the war been in such a favorable logistical condition," and it still retained its traditional advantage of stealth and surprise. Simply, the Communists could match many times over the strength of the ARVN troops and firepower at any given time and place. The DAO paper also noted ominously that the NVA was increasingly active, infiltrating men and supplies into the South at the highest rate since 1972. The DAO report predicted there would soon be major combat in the northern half of South Vietnam: "The campaign is expected to assume country-wide proportions and a number of indicators point to the introduction of strategic reserve divisions from NVN [North Vietnam]." The DAO report reflected the degree to which circumstances had changed just since the CIA's January intelligence estimate.

Among members of the South Vietnamese high command there was confusion about the actual significance of the Congressional visit and the status of the supplemental aid. "The impression left behind by the departing visitors was one of pessimism and premonition," remembered General Cao Van Vien. "The atmosphere was charged with rumors and speculation, all detrimental to the national cause." Thieu was deeply affected by his encounter with the visitors, whose behavior, Vien observed, generated in the president for the first time the idea that hopes for further American aid might prove fruitless. Yet America's most powerful officials, Ford and Kissinger, supported the requests for supplemental aid to a country for which more than 50,000 Americans had died. How could more aid not be approved? Whatever the merits of the various arguments, there was scant time left to debate. And whether the South Vietnamese were prepared or not, they were on their own, with no extra aid and no thundering fleets of B-52 bombers.

Strangulation of Phnom Penh

In mid-January 1975, Khmer Rouge insurgents began a daily rocket barrage of Phnom Penh. While some fell harmlessly in empty fields, others landed in crowded streets and markets where they killed, on average, a dozen or more people a day.

The 107MM rockets the Khmer Rouge used were weapons of terror. The crude Chinese-made rounds exploded into thousands of jagged two-inch fragments, which could not penetrate anything more solid than a thatch hut. Consequently, they were ineffective against dug-in troops or military targets. But fired into Phnom Penh from positions as close as five kilometers away from the center of the city, they were terrifyingly effective against civilians going about their daily chores. One morning in March, a rocket slammed into a fruit market killing seven people; four hours later another landed in a crowded street in front of the Monerom Hotel, killing eleven people instantly, wounding a dozen more.

Despite the horror that such rockets produced, many residents of Phnom Penh steadfastly refused to alter their lives. The wealthy still lounged about the cafés and dined at the Venise Restaurant. The average citizen, crushed by poverty and hunger, seemed to have more pressing concerns. "I am not afraid," said a disabled government soldier selling parking tokens outside the central market. "With my physical condition and the hardships of my family, I don't think about the rockets."

In the heart of Phnom Penh, panic-stricken civilians run for cover from a Khmer Rouge rocket attack on February 25, 1975.

A futile defense

Phnom Penh's defense perimeter carved out a rough arc swinging from north of the city to the west and then around to the southwest. Government forces struck north but ultimately failed to break through the surrounding Communist insurgents. One key to the weakened government resistance was a shortage of manpower. Most of the battalions in the shrinking Phnom Penh defense lines were fighting with less than 100 men, although their paper strength indicated 300. To compound this deficiency, FANK soldiers suffered great hardship. "I tell you frankly," said a government general, "our army is the poorest in the world—poorly fed, poorly clothed, poorly paid."

Above. In March, government paratroopers defend Prek Phnou, a crucial link in the capital's deteriorating defense perimeter.

Right. Cambodian government troops inspect the bodies of seventy-eight Khmer Rouge soldiers killed in a major Communist offensive near a strategic village in Kompong Seila Province, 128 kilometers north of Phnom Penh.

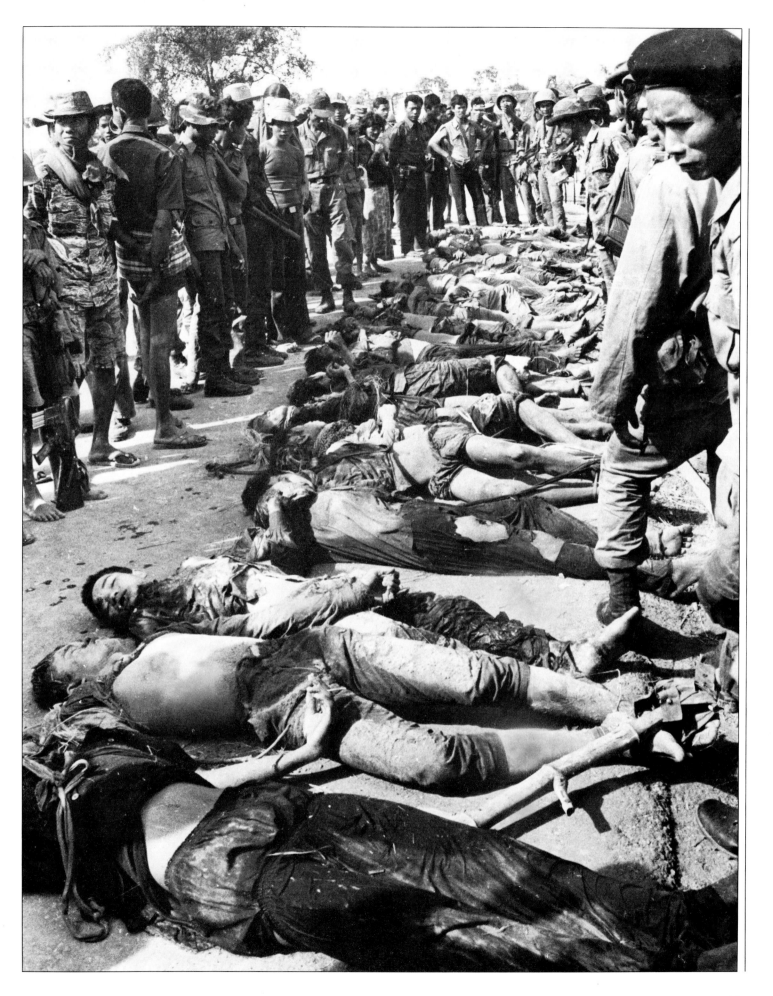

The Mekong River blockade

All ground routes leading into the capital were completely cut off by late 1973, so the Mekong River attained great importance as the principal supply line into the city. In 1973 and 1974 barges and tugs passing through Communist-held territory suffered only minor losses as they brought in some 60,000 tons of civilian and military provisions each month. But in the first days of the 1975 dry season offensive, supply craft from South Vietnam were forced to run a gauntlet of fire along the Mekong's narrowed channel. More than a dozen freighters, tankers, and barges were sunk in January alone, easily surpassing the number lost in all of 1974.

Unless crucial checkpoints were retaken, convoys would no longer be able to pass through to the besieged capital. With this in mind, government forces launched a clearing operation in February. Unfortunately, since a number of units had been recently shifted north of Phnom Penh to counter renewed insurgent pressure, the Mekong forces were critically under strength. The troops suffered high casualties in repeated assaults on Communist riverbank positions. Several boats were sunk as they tried to reach those stranded on the beachheads. On January 23, the last ship reached Phnom Penh. The government's life line—the Mekong—was now cut.

Right. On the Mekong, Associated Press correspondent Matt Franjola helps row a wounded officer of the Cambodian paratroopers down river to the closest medical center near Barong Khnorkar in January.

Opposite above. FANK soldiers attack from foxholes as Khmer Rouge troops close in on Phnom Penh.

Opposite below. A government tanker burns on the Mekong near Neak Luong following a Khmer Rouge attack.

The civilian's plight

After five years of internecine warfare between government forces and the Khmer Rouge, Cambodia had become a nation where civilian suffering was the rule rather than the exception. Children starved to death in the capital. Desperately ill refugees lined up at "free" clinics only to discover that vast shortages of medicine compelled doctors to charge for essential drugs. The government's response to the plight of Cambodian war victims was grievously inadequate, undermined by the decay of the Republic's economy and political institutions. USAID and various international agencies, including CARE and the Red Cross, attempted to alleviate these conditions by expanding relief programs in 1975. But by then, the extraordinary scope of the problems overwhelmed even their best efforts.

Left. *A father cradles his badly wounded child, hit by shrapnel during a rocket attack on downtown Phnom Penh, March 24.*

Below. *A Cambodian child shows the ravages of malnutrition. According to statistics of the Cambodian National Nutrition Service, an average two-year-old in January 1975 weighed nearly one-third less than a two-year-old before the war.*

Campaign 275

In the weeks following the battles for Phuoc Long, an uneasy lull settled over South Vietnam. Still, few observers deluded themselves into believing the North Vietnamese had given up the offensive. Heavy traffic, spotted by U.S. satellites and high-altitude reconnaissance flights, flowed down NVA supply roads and obviously portended trouble. Near the battlefields, however, NVA forces had taken great pains to conceal their movements. As a result, the timing, strength, and direction of their offensive remained a mystery to South Vietnamese and U.S. intelligence.

By early March the scrub land south of the DMZ and the jungles of the central highlands concealed at least ten Communist divisions and several independent regiments. With all their tanks and artillery, they were maneuvering into position for Campaign 275, the offensive to seize the central highlands. Senior General Van Tien Dung set up his headquarters in a grove of trees about thirty kilometers east of Ban Me Thuot, the

capital of Darlac Province and the main target of the campaign. To win this prize Dung prepared to field "5.5 soldiers to the enemy's 1," 20 percent more tanks, and more than double the artillery.

Dung takes command

The army led by Dung was vastly improved over that of 1968 or even 1972. The units moved to the front by trucks carrying plenty of prepared rations and, in some cases, heavy guns and shells made by North Vietnam's own nascent armaments industry. The trucks moved "bumper to bumper in a long, endless line," Dung recalled, "like a great waterfall rushing out to the front." To speed movement of this growing NVA force, a new local road network linked the Ho Chi Minh Trail and the Truong Son logistics corridor to the Communist assembly areas around Ban Me Thuot. The new roads made it possible to concentrate quickly against weak spots in the ARVN defense. The NVA troops assembled about thirty kilometers from their target to avoid detection. From there they could move along the new roads into assault positions close to the enemy within hours.

Through a spider web of telephone lines radiating from his command post, Dung maneuvered his massing army in complete radio silence in order to foil the South Vietnamese and American electronic eavesdroppers who constantly sifted the airways for signs of Communist intent. Avoiding wireless chatter, units in transit moved from one untapped telephone station to another, checking at each point for new orders. By contrast, the South Vietnamese military often communicated with uncoded messages, enabling the NVA's experienced and surprisingly sophisticated radio intercept units to learn from RVNAF air and ground radio transmissions their enemy's every move.

Dung's plan to attack Ban Me Thuot had taken shape during his trip from Hanoi in early February. He applied an old and simple formula, one that had served him well. As a brigade commander in 1952, Dung had led an attack against French Union forces at Phat Diem in North Vietnam. In order to avoid strong enemy defenses on the perimeter of town, his troops crept around the strong points, moved into the urban center, destroyed the headquarters and communications center, and only then turned to strike the surrounding outposts from the rear. The tactic was named "the blossoming lotus" since the attack began in the center of the enemy, then spread outwards "like a flower bud slowly opening its petals." Now, in 1975, the lotus was being cultivated to blossom on a spectacular scale.

Preceding page. *Torn between relief at escape and grief for those left behind in the central highlands, a weeping mother clutches her child as a helicopter bears her away from the battle, March 22.*

Some of the Communists' decisive advantages came from the South Vietnamese and the Americans themselves. The U.S. had imbued ARVN with the tactical concept that superior mobility would allow them to counter any Communist attack. Many senior officers had failed to grapple with the fact that this concept had been made unworkable by growing shortages of air transport, strategic reserve units, and massed firepower, all of which had been caused by the cutbacks in U.S. aid. To strengthen the South Vietnamese forces in one place now meant weakening them in another.

The senior commander of these closely watched ARVN II Corps troops guarding the misty highlands was a frail, sickly major general, Pham Van Phu. He was imposed on the corps by the anticorruption shakeup that had swept aside many able commanders, including his predecessor General Toan. Toan had listened to the advice of his intelligence officers and, if in doubt about the dispositions of the enemy or his own troops, went to the battlefield to see the situation for himself. Phu, however, was a commander of different ilk.

The new II Corps commander brought with him a number of personal problems. As a young French colonial officer, Phu had been captured at Dien Bien Phu. He vowed after that to die rather than face imprisonment again. While in prison he developed tuberculosis, which in 1972 forced him to retire for a year. He was later relegated to a training post until his appointment to MR 2 in November 1974. Although rated an excellent division commander, Phu had no experience with larger units. Now Phu's poor health, inexperience, and possibly his fear of capture, kept him from emulating Toan's faith in intelligence, knowledge of his own troops' capabilities, and insight into North Vietnamese intentions.

General Phu had, in fact, heard from his own intelligence and that of the JGS that some sort of dry season Communist offensive was building. New northern units were arriving, and these troops appeared to be moving around in the central highlands. As Phu's chief of staff, Colonel Le Khac Ly, recalled, however, intelligence reports listed Ban Me Thuot as only one of several possible enemy targets. But since there were not troops enough to guard all the threatened towns, Phu dismissed the intelligence warning.

Reasoning that no one was clear about the enemy's objectives, Phu decided to continue fulfilling the goals given him by President Thieu to defend the main cities of the highlands, Pleiku and Kontum, and to keep Route 19 from Pleiku to the coast open until evidence or events necessitated a change of tactics. In early March a visiting military liaison officer from the U.S. Embassy discussed with Phu reports that the NVA 316th Division was in Cambodia just southwest of Ban Me Thuot. Phu listened and was obviously worried, but he "seemed so possessed with the mission of keeping Route 19 open" that he ignored the opportunity—or need—to reinforce other targets. He was "much more concerned about reports of NVA units in the vicinity of Pleiku." Rather than thin out his troops any further, Phu chose to rely on the mobility offered by the road system and his fleet of CH–47 Chinook helicopters, little realizing that VNAF maintenance operated far less efficiently than under the U.S. system that had been in place when he last commanded in the field. Because of a lack of trained technicians and replacement parts, the stress of combat operations would make it difficult, if not impossible, to keep the aircraft flying for long.

A ruse

For all his limitations Phu almost made the right decision. In response to a suggestion from the JGS in early March, following new intelligence reports of NVA units converging on the Darlac capital city, the general ordered two regiments of the 23d Division in Pleiku to move to Ban Me Thuot, where only two battalions defended the division headquarters, supply depots, and military dependents. But that fortuitous order was quickly rescinded when it was reported that the Communist 320th NVA Division broke radio silence and its headquarters radio was again transmitting from its old position west of Pleiku. To the ARVN general it seemed clear that the 320th could not be closing in on Ban Me Thuot if its headquarters was operating 150 kilometers to the north. If intelligence was wrong about the 320th, and if the 316th was still sitting in Cambodia, that left only the 10th unaccounted for. Even if the 10th was in position to attack the two ARVN battalions and the 23d Division headquarters troops dug in at Ban Me Thuot, surely it could be held until reinforcements could be rushed by convoy or helicopter from Pleiku. Meanwhile, the ARVN regiments could stay in their strongholds around Pleiku, Kontum, and along Route 19, their life line to the coast. Phu believed that an attack on Ban Me Thuot would only be a diversion for the main assault planned for those traditional targets in the northern highlands. Phu told his chief of staff that the terrain around the two big cities was perfect for the enemy to deploy his superior tank force.

It must have afforded Phu some satisfaction that the initial attacks came precisely where he had predicted (see map, page 50). On March 1 the 968th NVA Division struck the government outposts west of Pleiku in what seemed to be an opening thrust toward the province capital. Three days later two big Communist units north of Route 19 blew up several bridges and laid siege to firebases along the road while rockets fell on the runways of Pleiku's air base. Now certain that the enemy's target was Pleiku, Phu pulled more troops into the city's defenses and formed a task force of the 4th Ranger Group and 2d Armored Cavalry to move east clearing Route 19. Meanwhile, elements of two Ranger groups were sent on sweeps around Kon-

tum to locate the missing NVA divisions. Ban Me Thuot remained quiet. The only discomforting news was that Route 21, the link between Ban Me Thuot and the coast and the only major road to the highlands other than Route 19, had also been attacked, two bridges blown up, and an outpost overrun.

In the course of one day's fighting the NVA had isolated the central highlands, but these roads had been closed and reopened before. Phu appeared to retain control of the situation and was in no great trouble. Convoys of troops could still shuttle between Pleiku and Ban Me Thuot on Highway 14 to meet any new enemy threat.

Or so the general thought. Only when it was too late did Phu realize that the enemy's radio signals were a trap and he had snatched the bait. On March 8 the situation began to slip out of South Vietnamese control when the 9th Regiment of the 320th NVA Division, hidden only five kilometers east of Route 14, moved forward and severed the road, completely isolating Ban Me Thuot. The next day elements of the 10th NVA Division captured the ARVN Cambodian border outposts at Duc Lap and Dak Song before noon and with this blow took control of the final stretch of road completing the Truong Son logistics corridor in South Vietnam.

By midday on March 9 enemy units were identified all around Ban Me Thuot. The NVA's plans were now frighteningly clear: As JGS intelligence had predicted, Darlac's capital was the main target. Phu began desperately moving troops south, flying the 21st Ranger Group to Buon Ho, the first town south of the NVA's roadblock on Route 14. Then the general called the JGS for help, but again, as at Phuoc Long two months before, there were no reinforcements to send. What few reserves remained were needed in Military Region 3 to guard Saigon. Phu was on his own.

Attack on Ban Me Thuot

On March 10, in the early morning jungle darkness along the back roads southeast of Ban Me Thuot, NVA tank engines rumbled into motion, coughing up clouds of diesel smoke. Russian–built T54s and armored personnel carriers tore forward through their screen of partly sawed through trees and raced for the Krong River, about halfway to Ban Me Thuot. At the river, the armored columns—joined along the way by trucks and artillery—rendezvoused with ferry boats and scores of rafts that had been assembled in Cambodia and moved up the river into South Vietnam. As daylight neared they joined the NVA 316th Division and regiments of the 10th not engaged at Duc Lap. The soldiers could hear the shelling of ARVN positions that had been going on since the Communists began moving at 2:00 A.M. The 316th and 10th constituted the southern half of a pincer: From the north the 320th Division, minus the regiment blocking Route 14, also closed on Ban Me Thuot.

Barrages from long-range artillery screened the movement of the 25th Independent Regiment, as well as a force of sappers mounted on tanks, that quickly struck at the government command and communications centers. Divided into three assault groups, one unit captured the main supply depot and a second overran a small airfield for light aircraft. But the third NVA attack unit soon stalled in a bloody battle with a battalion of the ARVN 53d Regiment for control of the main airfield on the east side of town. Despite this one failure, the other parts of the "lotus" began to "blossom." Communist forces surrounded the sector headquarters, from where the GVN Territorial Forces were controlled, and the ARVN 23d Division headquarters, which housed the city's main communications.

By midmorning ARVN forces were fighting back savagely after shaking off the initial shock; government artillery was taking a heavy toll of the attacking tanks. But the close fighting illustrated another chronic weakness in the South Vietnamese military—the lack of coordination between the units in contact with the enemy and the artillery

and fighter-bombers supporting them. An artillery shell intended for the NVA tanks pushing into the government positions instead smashed the sector headquarters, shattering all control over the Popular and Regional Forces that made up the bulk of the Ban Me Thuot garrison. The survivors of the attack, fighting from bunker to bunker, retreated to the 23d Division command post at the airfield. By nightfall, the NVA controlled most of the center of the city, while government forces held positions on the perimeter to the east, west, and south. Those on the perimeter, in turn, were being attacked by the fast advancing Communist pincers.

As darkness fell over the battlefield the NVA continued the advance, bringing up flame throwers to support their tank and infantry attack. The South Vietnamese fought back with light antitank weapons and wire-guided missiles but were steadily pushed back to the airport. To blunt an NVA probe the 23d's deputy commander, Colonel Vu The Quang, requested close air support from a flight of A-37 attack aircraft that had just arrived over the city. As the aircraft roared in to attack, the air force repeated the morning's artillery error by unloading bombs on the division's tactical operations center and its collection of long-range radios. From that moment, all direct communications were lost between II Corps headquarters in Pleiku and the embattled garrison. With no information from the battlefield, desperately needed air support quickly dropped from 200 to 60 sorties per day. This took considerable pressure off the advancing Communists. By noon of March 11, the attackers had taken the remaining bunkers of the 23d Division command post and captured many senior officers, including the province chief and Col. Quang, who told his captors, "After the Phuoc Long battle we estimated that . . . you would not yet strike large towns. When Ban Me Thuot was attacked, we still thought it was a diversion."

General Phu, from Pleiku, announced on March 12 that all organized resistance inside Ban Me Thuot had ceased. This was not, however, the end of the battle. The remnants of two ARVN battalions fought on in the ruins of the city's outlying airfield, and the South Vietnamese still controlled Phuoc An airfield about thirty kilometers east of the city, a site close enough to fly in reinforcements for a counterattack to retake Ban Me Thuot.

Counterattack

The 21st Ranger Group, which moved to Buon Ho on Route 14 before the battle began, arrived at Phuoc An first and was to be followed by the remaining two regiments of the 23d Division, although Phu was unconvinced the available II Corps forces could retake the city. The general confided in his chief of staff, Col. Le Khac Ly, that he was sending the troops only at President Thieu's orders. But once again an internal weakness of the American-de-

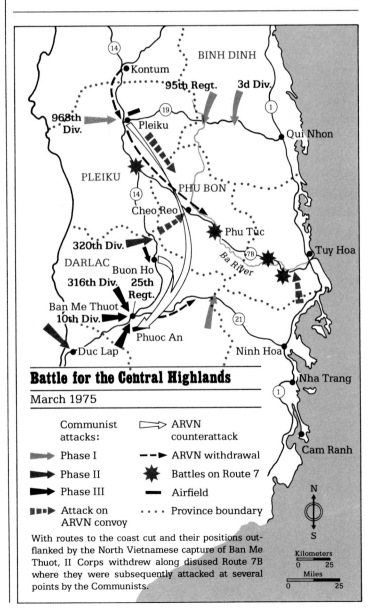

Battle for the Central Highlands

March 1975

Communist attacks:

➤ Phase I
➤ Phase II
➤ Phase III
■■▶ Attack on ARVN convoy

⇨ ARVN counterattack
- - ▶ ARVN withdrawal
✦ Battles on Route 7
— Airfield
· · · · Province boundary

With routes to the coast cut and their positions outflanked by the North Vietnamese capture of Ban Me Thuot, II Corps withdrew along disused Route 7B where they were subsequently attacked at several points by the Communists.

The battle still in doubt, ARVN soldiers attack to relieve Ban Me Thuot's besieged garrison on March 10.

signed South Vietnamese military ensured failure on the battlefield. The much planned on aerial mobility disappeared within three days of operations. Between the initial attacks on the airfield, ground fire, and maintenance problems, the number of air worthy troop–carrying CH–47s dwindled from a dozen to one. By the time the airlift sputtered to a halt on March 14, the task force assembled at Phuoc An consisted of the 45th Regiment, only one battalion of the 44th, and a single battalion of the 21st Ranger Group.

In reality even this modest grouping was a paper force. When the men of the 23d Division jumped from the helicopters, the first thing many of them saw were members of their families in the stream of refugees fleeing Ban Me Thuot along embattled Route 21 toward the coast and safety at Nha Trang. Within hours an epidemic of desertion stripped the task force of much of its fighting ability as soldiers sought to find and evacuate their families.

The orders for the soldiers were to march west on Highway 21, link up with the survivors holding out at the Ban Me Thuot airfield, and retake the city. The orders ignored the fact that because of poor planning, the infantry had arrived without artillery or armor support. Dutifully the remaining ARVN soldiers pushed off on March 15 but within a few kilometers bumped into the NVA 10th Division. The South Vietnamese advance stalled and by the next day

turned into a retreat as the task force survivors followed the column of refugees east. That day, as the ARVN retreated, the remaining holdouts in Ban Me Thuot were killed or captured and Phuoc An, the last air bridgehead from which to launch a counterattack, also fell. The battle for the Darlac Province capital was over.

There were few survivors of Ban Me Thuot to reach government positions on the coast and tell the story of what had happened. Most were strung out in small groups along Route 21, dodging the NVA patrols and roadblocks. Two who made it out were Ly Thi Van and her sister, both living on army widows' pensions in Ban Me Thuot when the Communist attack began.

"We picked up everything and ran," she told a reporter. "We closed our eyes. We did not want to open them. Everywhere there were bodies; there were shells flying all over." The two widows and their brood of children dodged down alleyways and made it out of the city into a rubber plantation where they hid with hundreds of other refugees. They were desperate to escape because, like many others in the town, they were related to ARVN soldiers and refugees from North Vietnam. They were sure the NVA would kill them. From the plantation they walked east until they found space aboard a jammed bus headed for Phuoc An, thirty kilometers east of Ban Me Thuot. Several kilometers later they were halted by a Communist roadblock on Route 21.

"There were three VC on the road and many hidden in the jungle," Ly Thi Van recalled. "All of a sudden we heard planes overhead. One VC in the jungle yelled, 'Open fire.' There were explosions all around, the bus exploded. People began firing at us." Only two of her five children lived through the attack. Three days later she made it to Phuoc An on foot. There she met an old friend of her husband's, a helicopter pilot who flew her, the sister, and the two surviving children to the relative safety of Nha Trang.

After the fall of Ban Me Thuot, South Vietnam's strategic situation was desperate. There remained no organized ARVN forces between the Communist troops at Ban Me Thuot and the South China Sea. The NVA was very close to cutting South Vietnam in two, and the remaining government forces in the central highlands were isolated in Kontum and Pleiku. The only other sizable II Corps force was the 22d ARVN Division, which was already engaged with the NVA in Binh Dinh Province near the coast, far to the north. Nor were there any Saigon based reserves left to throw into the fight to stop the NVA if they decided to march to the sea.

New plans for the North

But, the South Vietnamese soon learned, General Dung had other plans. Among the Communist senior officers following the course of the battle, a mild case of euphoria was taking hold; the limitations contemplated for the 1975 offensive began to look distinctly conservative. General Dung advised Hanoi that he planned to turn his tanks north, capture Pleiku, and surround Kontum. Meanwhile, in Hanoi, Le Duan pressed the General Staff to exploit the NVA's series of successes. It was two months before the monsoon season, when the thrust of the offensive would have to switch from the battlefield to the negotiating table. Both Dung and Le Duan, like COSVN's General Tra in December, were chafing under North Vietnam's restrictive rules of warfare that demanded such careful scrutiny of each investment of manpower and machinery. Both men pondered ways to take aggressive advantage of the foothold they had established in the highlands. The opportunity was beguiling: ARVN had offered less resistance than imagined; GVN reaction remained weak; the U.S. had offered only a paper protest; and the situation promised even greater gains.

A Communist photograph shows well-equipped North Vietnamese Army regular troops supporting the advance of a Soviet-built T54 tank during the pivotal battle for the city of Ban Me Thuot in early March.

On the South Vietnamese side, the mood was one of gloom edged with panic. For the first time the South Vietnamese high command entertained serious doubts about continued U.S. military aid. What is more, the loss of two entire provinces made a mockery of Thieu's declared intent to defend every foot of South Vietnam. These circumstances required Thieu to abandon his heretofore inflexible Four No's, and not even the staunchest anti-Communist among his army supporters could criticize a change in strategy based on the new realities. Thieu also hoped that the emergency might stifle his political opponents and unite the country in common cause. The dis-

aster in II Corps even gave Thieu a glimmer of hope that the U.S. might renew its support to avoid appearing as a feckless ally.

On the night of March 10-11, after communications with Ban Me Thuot had been lost, President Thieu weighed the realities of his nation's situation and finally accepted the necessity of a new strategy. As the man who, in Vien's words, "made all the decisions as to how the war should be conducted," Thieu concluded that to consolidate his dwindling army, air force, and supplies he must now start trading land for time.

Next morning Thieu called for the prime minister, Tran Thien Khiem, his assistant for security affairs, Lieutenant General Dang Van Quang, and the chairman of the JGS, General Vien. "Given our present strength and capabilities," he told them, "we certainly cannot hold and defend all the territory we want." Then on a small-scale map the president outlined the areas he wanted the army to fight for. The lines encompassed all of Military Regions 3 and 4, where most of South Vietnam's resources and population were centered; the area south of, and including, Ban Me Thuot in MR 2 and its potentially oil-rich coastal area; and tentatively the coastal area of MR 1 "up to Hue or Danang," Vien recollected in his memoirs. If these cities

could not be held, Thieu went on, "then we could redeploy farther south to Chu Lai or even Tuy Hoa."

It took the others only moments to realize the ramifications of the plan. Pleiku and Kontum were to be abandoned. Thieu erased any doubts of his meaning by ordering all the military resources of II Corps to be used to retake Ban Me Thuot. There was no objection from the three officers.

Truncation

The president now had to announce the new strategy to his corps commanders. He arranged to meet General Phu at Cam Ranh, the big American-built seaport, on March 14. Atop a sand hill, in a house built for Lyndon Johnson's visit to Vietnam in 1966, Thieu and his confidants from Saigon met with a demoralized II Corps commander. Phu began with a profoundly pessimistic briefing on the situation in the highlands: All the major roads were cut, Ban Me Thuot had fallen, and Pleiku, already under siege, would probably not be able to hold out for more than a month. Thieu asked, "Can Ban Me Thuot be retaken?" Phu parried the question by asking for more reinforcements, but General Vien reminded Thieu of what he already knew: There were no reserves left. The president stood beside a map of South Vietnam and explained the new strategy, outlining with gestures the areas General Phu was to hold. It was now II Corps's task to redeploy its remaining forces. This meant abandoning Pleiku and Kontum in order "to reoccupy Ban Me Thuot at all costs" so Vien remembered Thieu's words.

Thieu then asked for a plan for abandoning the northern half of the highlands while retaking the Darlac capital. Vien took his turn at the map, pointing out that the main road from Pleiku to the coast, Route 19, remained blocked, and even if II Corps's remaining division, the 22d, attacked to clear it of NVA troops from the eastern end, it would be a desperate, perhaps impossible, task for ARVN to break out to the coast. There remained only one other route to retreat from the highlands: Interprovincial Route 7B, a long-disused logging road that dipped and curved and bumped for about 200 kilometers from just outside Pleiku southeast to the coastal town of Tuy Hoa.

General Phu did not object to using Route 7B and believed that surprise could be achieved because Phu Bon Province, through which the track twisted, "was forgotten by the enemy and friendly too." With careful planning it could work. It was preferable to the certain decimation that awaited along the other occupied routes. Phu reckoned no one would anticipate a corps-sized force with all its equipment and vehicles attempting such a daring exit from the highlands. With any luck the force would be gone before the NVA spotted the move and reacted.

There were, of course, factors militating against a clean getaway. No one knew exactly how badly the disused

road had deteriorated except that a major bridge across the Ba River had been destroyed and the final thirty kilometers outside Tuy Hoa had been extensively mined by South Koreans earlier in the war. Yet, if the JGS provided sufficient river-crossing equipment, Phu believed he could extricate the II Corps forces from the highlands while Regional Forces screened the movement at Pleiku and along the route. Everyone then promptly forgot about or ignored the thousands of Territorial soldiers. They, in fact, were not told of the evacuation. It has never been explained how the RFs and PFs were to protect an operation they knew nothing about.

When General Phu reached Pleiku he took little time to plan the withdrawal. Thinking only of speed, the general called his staff together and told them that in two days, on March 16, they would leave the highlands. On each of four days a convoy of about 250 vehicles would leave the city and drive down Route 7B to Tuy Hoa. The 20th Combat Engineer Group would lead the first convoy to build fords, repair roads, and replace bridges. The II Corps commander estimated that the repairs along the entire length of the road would take no more than two days. Artillery, medical units, staff, and remnants of the 23d Division, protected by the tanks of the 21st Armored Battalion, would be sandwiched in the middle. Brigadier General Pham Duy Tat's Ranger groups would march as a rear guard. Units were to receive their orders to depart only one hour in advance.

Since the military had only two days to begin the move, the air force units would have to concentrate on evacuating aircraft, personnel, and dependents instead of flying close air support for the land convoy. Among the first tasks of the air division was the evacuation on March 15 of General Phu and the bulk of the II Corps staff, who moved to Nha Trang on the coast. As he was leaving Phu told Col. Le Khac Ly, his chief of staff who was to travel with the convoy, "We will plan to retake Ban Me Thuot from there."

When Ly asked about arrangements for evacuating the Territorial Forces at Pleiku, he was told by Phu, "Forget about them. If you tell them about [the evacuation], you can't control it and you cannot get down to Tuy Hoa because there would be panic."

In command of the column withdrawing from Pleiku was General Tat, commander of the II Corps Rangers, who had just been promoted. Col. Ly assumed a subordinate role as head of the corps staff and logistical units. In a curious move that muddied responsibility for direction of the column, Phu also appointed Brigadier General Tran Van Cam, his assistant for operations, to "oversee" the evacuation. No one, including Cam, knew what this meant. Cam, irked at having to share command with Tat, flew to Tuy Hoa soon after Phu left for Nha Trang. With the key commanders and staff members gone, Ly turned to Tat for direction only to be told the general was busy pulling in the Rangers from Kontum and preparing his six groups for the march. Col. Ly was ordered to plan the withdrawal. The chief of staff did as he was told; the Popular and Regional Forces were not notified of the evacuation and thus formed no screen for the evacuating forces.

The rumor of withdrawal seeped down the chain of command, and as it did many leaders simply packed up and began their own evacuations. The province chief of Kontum discovered what was happening when a nearby Ranger force pulled out. He scrambled into a jeep and joined the tail end of the column only to be killed in an ambush before he reached Pleiku. Such gaps in command and communication as these also helped destroy any likelihood that the Territorial Forces could be employed to keep the NVA at bay.

Within the limits of his orders Col. Ly did what he could to pass the word of withdrawal. He called Americans working for the DAO, CIA, and other organizations in Pleiku. "At first they didn't believe me," Ly said. "But I said go, don't ask." By 10:00 A.M. on the fifteenth the message that the ARVN was withdrawing had been flashed to Saigon by the Americans. At noon the embassy ordered all U.S. citizens out of the highlands. Air America, the CIA's contract airline, began a helicopter shuttle between town and the airfield where C-47 and C-46 transport aircraft flew round robin hops to Nha Trang. Within four-and-a-half hours 450 American and Vietnamese employees of the various U.S. agencies were alerted, assembled, and evacuated from Pleiku.

Although the embassy in Saigon and officials in Wash-

The Convoy of Tears. Rags tied around their faces to ward off the choking red dust, motorcyclists roar past some of the thousands of South Vietnamese civilians evacuating the central highlands along with the military in March 1975.

ington were taken by surprise, South Vietnamese officials had dropped a number of hints to Americans that an evacuation was contemplated. On the eleventh, Thieu sent his economic minister to ask American economics counselor Dan Ellerman whether the U.S. ambassador was "an advocate of a truncated South Vietnam?" In Ambassador Martin's absence Ellerman and the acting chargé, Wolfgang Lehmann, answered that it was the Vietnamese who had to decide whether to abandon any part of their nation.

When word of the withdrawal was passed to Washington on the sixteenth, NSC deputy Brent Scowcroft contacted Graham Martin at his family home in North Carolina where the ambassador to South Vietnam was recovering from a severe infection caused by abscessed teeth. The ambassador said he had been told before leaving Saigon that II Corps headquarters was to transfer to the coast, but knew nothing more than that.

Word of the loss of Ban Me Thuot reached Secretary of State Kissinger during a flight between Middle Eastern capitals. In the absence of alarums from Ambassador Martin, Kissinger decided there was no real crisis. He told staff members that it was probably Thieu's first move to consolidate his forces and prepare a stronger defensive line.

The convoy of tears

Not until two days later did the Americans learn of the reasoning behind the withdrawal. On the night of March 17, at a dinner for a few senior Americans and South Vietnamese at the home of Saigon's CIA chief, Thomas Polgar, General Quang, Thieu's security adviser, took a page from history to explain Thieu's decision. Just as the Russians had destroyed Napoleon's armies in 1812 by trading land for time, so the South Vietnamese would defeat the NVA. "Perhaps the monsoons will do for us," he said, "what the winter did for the Russians."

In the central highlands the civilians were not waiting for explanations. They acted on empirical evidence. When the NVA shelled Kontum, the road to Pleiku filled with private citizens escaping the shelling. As ARVN units began leaving their positions in Pleiku and the transport aircraft swarmed in and out of the airport around the clock, they knew it was time to follow the army.

On Sunday night a column of trucks in the advance guard moved out of Pleiku bumper to bumper with their lights on. Reporter Nguyen Tu thought it "looked like a column of traffic returning home for the weekend." Behind, loud explosions marked the destruction of ammunition dumps, and the sky glowed with the flames of burning fuel supplies.

As the convoys headed south kicking up clouds of red

NVA shells crash into Route 7B as refugees from the highlands fighting race toward the coast.

dust, unbroken lines of civilians on foot paralleled the path of the army on each side of the road. A Catholic nun remembered "babies and children were put into oxcarts and pulled. Everyone was in a panic. People were trying to hire vehicles at any price." For three days, March 16, 17, and 18, the evacuation went as planned. Lines of trucks moved smoothly out of Pleiku, and in between military columns hundreds of civilian vehicles joined the exodus. Thus began what would become known as the "convoy of tears."

Halfway to the coast the column was stalled as the II Corps engineers tried to complete a pontoon bridge across the Ea Pa River a few kilometers southeast of Cheo Reo (or Hau Bon), the capital of Phu Bon Province. Phu's predicted two days for repairs on Route 7B stretched to three at the first major bridge alone. By the evening of March 18, vehicles and soldiers from three days' worth of convoys and a mass of refugees were stuck along the road and clustered around Phu Bon's capital city. The thin resources of the highlands town could not meet the needs of the civilians, many of whom had left their homes with only what they could carry. Propelled by panic and the enemy threat, suffering from hunger, thirst, and occasional bands of leaderless Territorial troops, the crowd pressed mindlessly forward. Critically for the military, the mass of people and machines made it impossible to set up a military defense. As had happened when the Germans closed in on Paris in 1940, the city's population fled, blocking all roads and making it impossible for the military to move to protect them from the enemy. The situation threatened to slip into chaos. Organizing hands were needed. But General Tat was still in Pleiku preoccupied with his Rangers and the rear-guard convoy, while Colonel Ly, stuck in the traffic jam, was forced to leave his vehicle and walk to the command post at Cheo Reo.

When the ARVN began its move down Route 7B, Communist General Dung had been fooled as Phu planned. Before the start of Campaign 275, the general had repeatedly quizzed the commander of the 320th Division about possible routes the ARVN might use. After repeated assurances that the old logging trail was virtually impassable, Dung dismissed it as a viable escape or reinforcement route for the government troops. However, after receiving Western news reports of civilians leaving Pleiku, intercepts of VNAF radio traffic discussing flights to Nha Trang, and finally a message from Hanoi on March 16 that ARVN II Corps headquarters had moved to the coast, he began to reconsider his foes' possible alternative escape routes. At 4:00 P.M. on the same day that Hanoi's wire arrived, an NVA reconnaissance team reported a long convoy of vehicles headed south from Pleiku toward Ban Me Thuot. The sighting put the Communist leader in a dilemma. Was the ARVN counterattacking or escaping? Should he dig his troops in to repel an assault or have them drop their packs and follow in pursuit? Soon the gen-

eral's intelligence gave him his answer. The South Vietnamese were blowing up their ammunition dumps, many fires were raging in Pleiku, and the convoys were turning off the main highway onto Route 7B, leading into Phu Bon Province.

The Communist headquarters staff went to work frantically poring over maps of the central highlands with flashlights and magnifying glasses in search of a way to bottle up their enemy. As his staff calculated distances and marching times for the NVA units nearest Route 7B, General Dung turned his wrath on the 320th Division commander, General Kim Tuan, who for weeks had soothed the commander's concerns about the road. Dung told Tuan that the time for excuses or any discussion was long past. The fact that his 9th Regiment was still blocking Route 14 between Pleiku and Ban Me Thuot, and not yet pursuing the enemy, was something verging on criminal. "At this time if you waver just a bit, are just a little bit negligent, hesitate just a bit, are just a bit late, you have botched the job," Dung seethed over the telephone. "If the enemy escapes . . . you will have to bear responsibility."

As he put down the telephone, the general sensed the startling significance of what was happening. If Thieu had ordered the whole of II Corps out of the central highlands, the withdrawal was not simply a tactical maneuver but a move of deep strategic significance. "For the first time in the Indochina War, within the bounds of a campaign, an enemy army corps with modern equipment had had to abandon an important strategic area," the general later wrote of his revelation. "It would cause a military and political chain reaction that would reach even to America."

Here before Dung was the opportunity to catch and destroy a major South Vietnamese command. He could not resist it. Putting aside Hanoi's mandate for military conservatism, the general ordered the 320th Division with its artillery and armor to drive northeast from its positions along Highway 14 and strike into the flank of the ARVN column on Route 7B. The division's task was to slow the South Vietnamese while the 968th Division advanced through the remaining forces around Pleiku and struck the rear of the column. Dung's final orders were for the B-1 Front forces along the coast to cut Route 7B in advance of the retreating South Vietnamese as they moved toward their refuge at Tuy Hoa.

Disaster

The South Vietnamese prayed for a few more days of grace from enemy attack, but just at darkness on the eighteenth the first Communist shells exploded among the densely packed highland evacuees. Their escape route

At Phu Bon on March 22, after North Vietnamese Army forces split the refugee column, a family prepares to board a helicopter that will fly them to the coast.

was no longer a secret and the enemy was upon them.

The lead units of the NVA 320th caught up with the II Corps column at Cheo Reo on the night of March 18. That same day other Communist units began hitting the 6th Ranger Group at the tail end of the column around the town of Thanh An at the crossroads of Routes 14 and 7B. ARVN Col. Ly's long walk through the crowd had finally brought him to the command post at Cheo Reo in time to help wheel the 23d Ranger Group into position to hold the NVA ground attack at Ban Bleik Pass just west of the capital city. Meanwhile, NVA shells blasted the convoy, which still stretched from Cheo Reo to within a few kilometers of Pleiku. The next morning bodies of dead and wounded soldiers and civilians lay unattended in the streets of Cheo Reo alongside hundreds of destroyed, damaged, or abandoned vehicles. A VNAF helicopter pilot reported, "When I flew low, I could see bodies scattered alongside the road—burning with the trucks."

Although the Communist forces had captured the city's airfield, the 23d Rangers still held the pass, and the crucial bridge southeast of town had at last been completed. This offered a respite and Col. Ly and his battalion commanders got the convoy moving again, along with all that could still be driven of some 2,000 vehicles jammed along the road. But no sooner had the column begun moving than Phu ordered Ly to fly out of Cheo Reo by helicopter. With Gen. Tat still directing the rear guard, this left no one who could control the withdrawal. From the nineteenth, what leadership there was came from individual battalion and group commanders who led whatever nearby troops would still obey orders.

Helicopters, braving the NVA ground fire, began swooping in to pick up wounded soldiers and civilians from the stricken rear of the column. When the refugees reached the landing strip in Tuy Hoa, they told tales of unrelenting horror. "They hit us with everything," said Ranger Private Nguyen Van Sau, wounded at Cheo Reo. He described a deadly shower of heavy artillery shells, mortar rounds, and rockets flying from the jungles into the stream of refugees. "People were lying all over the road as we tried to fight our way out. Soldiers died and the people died with them."

The push on the nineteenth took the head of the ARVN column to the Con River, only about forty kilometers from the coast. But farther back in the column, halfway between Cheo Reo and the Con, the NVA struck into the flank of the column again, this time at the town of Phu Tuc. One VNAF air strike called in to halt the enemy advance instead bombed men of the 7th Ranger Group, wiping out most of a battalion. Still the weakened 7th continued to fight and kept the road open.

The convoy flowed through Cheo Reo until March 21 when the NVA cracked the defenses of the 23d Rangers and pushed past them to capture the province capital and finally cut the road. Many of the 160,000 civilians in the convoy were now isolated along with the 8th and 25th Ranger Groups and the survivors of the 23d. On orders from Phu, Gen. Tat, still at the rear of the column, told the trapped elements to abandon all heavy weapons and war materiel and try to escape from Phu Bon Province as best they could. Thousands took to the jungles. Soldiers, with families clinging to their sides, were pursued and attacked repeatedly. A few managed to flag down helicopters that flew them to safety, but most had little chance to avoid starvation or capture.

The lucky ones, young mothers "smeared with blood," old men and women "swathed in muddy bandages," and weeping, barefoot soldiers, tumbled out of the helicopters before reporters gathered at the landing pad in Tuy Hoa. "We were on a truck," said a woman from Pleiku holding a child with leg wounds. The North Vietnamese Army "came from the jungle and told everyone to stop moving. We were on a slope. We kept moving. They just began firing on all of us."

The helicopters started carrying American field rations, rice, and dried milk because many in the column were beginning to starve. An army sergeant, Nguyen Dan of the 22d Division, said they left Pleiku with three days' worth of food, but by March 21, children were dying of hunger. "There is nothing to eat," said Vo Van Cuu, a civil servant, and "nothing to drink." A priest, the Reverend Nguyen Huu Nghi, observed people so weak and exhausted they could "barely climb onto helicopters."

As the fighting raged around the rear of the column that day, the lead ARVN units stood at the last physical obstacle, the broad Ba River, only twenty kilometers from Tuy Hoa and safety. The pontoon bridge promised by General Vien had arrived in Tuy Hoa on schedule, but to the ARVN's dismay, the Communist forces had already set up roadblocks between the river crossing and Tuy Hoa. The bridge could not be trucked to the river crossing site. The South Vietnamese were forced to transport the bridge, piece by piece, with four big CH–47 helicopters borrowed from IV Corps.

On March 22, a full week after the "convoy of tears" left Pleiku, the bridge across the Ba was at last in place. The first rush across the river was so great that an overloaded pontoon capsized, tossing men and vehicles into the water, but by the end of the day traffic was again moving across the Ba. Then even the weather joined the Communists in making the final leg of the refugees' journey to Tuy Hoa a passage of agony.

The sunshine and heat that parched the evacuees now gave way to cold and rain. Not only did this torture the weak and ill, but the bad weather also stopped air operations, a necessary support for ground attacks. An air

Just a few kilometers ahead of the NVA, highlands refugees cross the newly completed bridge over the Ba River, the convoy's last hurdle before reaching the coast at Tuy Hoa.

force grounded by bad weather meant the infantry would have to dig out NVA soldiers one by one from their entrenchments along the road. The South Vietnamese could not pause until the weather cleared because the NVA had again caught up with the rear of the column. From March 22 on, the 6th Ranger Group was locked in a brutal rearguard fight with the pursuing North Vietnamese. The Rangers assembled a force of tanks and artillery pieces and defended the road where it wound through a narrow valley northwest of the bridge over the Ba. They bought more time for refugees and troops to make it across the river ahead of the NVA.

In the meantime the lead elements of the convoy, now on the south bank of the Ba, had to begin breaking through the roadblocks. Desperately, survivors of the 7th Ranger Group, which had suffered heavy casualties only days before from a misplaced bombing attack, assembled more than a dozen M113 armored personnel carriers from the convoy. Using them as light tanks the Rangers began systematically charging the roadblocks, smashing them one at a time until, on March 25, the last NVA position was destroyed and the Rangers linked up with soldiers from a Territorial Force that had been fighting east from the town of Tuy Hoa.

The column that limped into the coastal city was heartbreakingly small. Approximately 60,000 civilian refugees had completed the trip, perhaps a third of the number that started. The military statistics were even more jolting. About one-quarter of 20,000 logistics and support troops completed the withdrawal. Of 7,000 men of the six Ranger groups, only 900 made it to II Corps headquarters at Nha Trang to take up defensive positions around the city. "Seventy-five percent of II Corps combat strength, to include the 23rd Infantry Division as well as Ranger, armor, artillery, engineer, and signal units, had been tragically expended [between March 10 and 25]," the chairman of the JGS noted grimly. As for the operation to counterattack and reoccupy Ban Me Thuot, there were simply no II Corps troops to attempt it.

Phu's gamble to take Route 7B could have worked if the

A soldier finds his four children at Tuy Hoa after the column reached the coast on March 25.

bridges had been built in time, and for that General Vien faults the II Corps commander himself. Vien believed Phu should have delayed the evacuation to give the engineers a head start on construction. He also thought the delay would have allowed for some rudimentary planning, especially for the control of civilians. To a U.S. general who knew the senior Vietnamese officers well, the problem lay not in Phu's plans but with Phu himself, for losing Ban Me Thuot in the first place. A more aggressive corps commander might have avoided the need for such a withdrawal. "A strong commander like Toan [the previous II Corps commander]," declared the American liaison officer, "counter-attacking toward Ban Me Thuot, employing all available forces plus all available air [power] probably would have been capable of containing the North Vietnamese in the highlands and staving off defeat for another year."

But by March 25, 1975, second-guessing or recriminations could do no good. The "self-inflicted defeat," as Vien described the withdrawal from the highlands, was complete and had created a psychological and political nightmare for Thieu, for the armed forces, and for the people of the Republic of South Vietnam. A rumor began to sweep the country and even circulated among the ranks of high military and government officials: President Thieu and the Americans, in a secret codicil to the Paris peace agreements, had made a deal to give up large parts of the northern half of South Vietnam to the Communists. Why else would a Vietnamese army that had fought without breaking for nearly twenty years suddenly run from the central highlands and abandon Pleiku and Kontum without a fight?

The morale-shattering loss of four provinces in three months and the RVNAF's extensive and vain sacrifice to recapture Ban Me Thuot left little confidence among the South Vietnamese that the Thieu government could protect them. Who else, though, could lead? Thieu's opposition was disorganized and ineffectual, and the Americans continued to maintain their distance. It was Thieu who had to find some way to rekindle the country's will to resist. Before he could move in this direction, more bad news came from I Corps in the northern provinces.

This crippled ARVN veteran has led a group of refugees on the 125-kilometer flight from Ban Me Thuot to Nha Trang.

A Glimpse of Apocalypse

"We've been betrayed," ARVN Brigadier General Nguyen Van Diem bitterly told the senior officers gathered at 1st Division headquarters the morning of March 25. "We have to abandon Hue." Orders had arrived from the high command in Da Nang directing Diem to save the men by giving up, without a battle, the city in which their families lived. As artillery fire muttered in the background, the division commander declared, "It is now *sauve qui peut* [every man for himself]."

The message instructed the soldiers to make for the shore of the South China Sea and from there to follow the beach south. The South Vietnamese navy would pick up the sick and exhausted while the able-bodied continued the march to a rallying point on the south side of the Hai Van Pass on the outskirts of Da Nang. General Diem closed the briefing by telling the officers to keep radio silence and wishing them luck. A successful withdrawal is the most difficult of all battlefield ma-

neuvers, but with that cursory order and no detailed planning—which in March had become the trademark of ARVN operations—the retreat from northern Military Region 1 began.

Just a month before, the defenses of MR 1 had been the nation's strongest. The battlewise I Corps commander, Lieutenant General Ngo Quang Truong, had worked hard at refitting and reinforcing his troops after the bloody fighting of summer and fall 1974. In fact, the I Corps troops remained the best in the nation.

Stationed in MR 1 were the Marine Corps and Airborne Divisions, both of which consisted of elite volunteers and carried proud traditions and strong combat records. Inspectors invariably rated the 1st as the best among the regular divisions. The 3d, after being overrun by greatly superior forces in 1972, now operated at full strength under an aggressive new commander, Major General Nguyen Duy Hinh. The 2d Division suffered from poor leadership and heavy combat losses but was supported by two Ranger groups.

Through the early months of the year the officers and men of I Corps carried out General Truong's defensive plans with precision: The Marines defended Quang Tri; the 1st occupied the critical ridge line west and south of Hue; the Airborne protected the Hai Van Pass and the outposts west of Da Nang; Hinh's 3d covered the southern approaches to Da Nang; and the southernmost units, including the 2d, were in place around Chu Lai.

Truong was confident his five divisions could stop any NVA attack in the DMZ area. Even if the Communists sent down the strategic reserve divisions being readied in North Vietnam, ARVN could further strengthen its defenses by concentrating its forces along the seacoast. Truong's subordinates carried contingency plans for a withdrawal into three defensive hedgehogs around Da Nang, Hue, and Chu Lai. In these redoubts I Corps could hold out until reinforced or withdrawn by sea.

Thieu's surprise

At the start of the Communist offensive Truong's faith in his troops' readiness seemed fully justified. On March 8 and 9 Airborne and Regional Forces fought back an NVA attack east of Route 1 in Quang Tri Province while the Marines shattered another tank-supported Communist force west of Hue. A few days later the 1st and 2d Divisions fought off heavy assaults aimed at cutting the vital Route 1 and inflicted heavy Communist losses.

But on March 10 all Truong's careful plans foundered when the attacks on Ban Me Thuot and west of Saigon convinced President Thieu that Saigon was the main Communist target. Giving in to the JGS suggestions that he build a reserve force around the capital for defense of the South Vietnamese heartland, Thieu cabled Truong to ready his elite Airborne troops to leave MR 1 in three weeks. Two days later the president demanded the Airborne be sent to Saigon immediately. When Truong tried to convince the JGS chairman, General Vien, to intervene he learned the president's decision was irrevocable. Later, Vien assured him, the Airborne would be replaced with a new brigade of Marines being formed at the time.

Still dissatisfied, Truong flew to Saigon the next day, March 13, to meet with the president and argue his case personally. At the meeting with Truong and Thieu were General Vien, General Quang, and a newcomer, General Toan, who had bounced back from banishment to a training post to become the new III Corps commander. Truong briefed the group on the difficulties presented by taking the Airborne from MR 1's defenses. Removal of the Airborne would probably lead to the loss of Quang Tri Province and could also endanger Hue.

The president did not directly offer a solution to the general's problem. Instead, Thieu launched into an explanation of his truncation plan. To Truong's surprise Thieu now declared himself willing to abandon northern South Vietnam. Pointing out that military aid was decreasing and U.S. military intervention seemed unlikely, the president told his generals that increasing enemy pressure forced him to redeploy the nation's forces to protect the heartland, Saigon and the Mekong Delta, and to rebuild a strategic reserve. The resulting losses in MR 1 and 2, he assured Truong, were preferable to a coalition government with the Communists.

In the end, General Truong could not sway Thieu, although he was given four more days to adjust his defenses before the Airborne Division had to begin moving to Saigon. Equally important, the commander in chief agreed that Da Nang would have to be defended but the rest of Military Region 1 might be considered expendable in the crisis. They withheld from Truong for the time being the unhappy news that withdrawal of the Airborne Division presaged that of the Marine Division. Thieu and Vien had already made the decision, but Truong was allowed to redesign his defenses believing he would command four divisions in MR 1.

A misunderstanding

Truong returned to Da Nang furious at having his defenses sabotaged. Meeting with his staff, the general first railed against Thieu's decision and threatened to resign but soon turned to sorting out just how much of MR 1 a

South Vietnamese troops fight to hold positions near the Cambodian border west of Saigon on March 12 as Communist pressure increases around the capital.

ARVN I Corps commander Lt. Gen. Ngo Quang Truong.

shrunken I Corps could defend. Truong might have questioned the president's decision, but he would not disobey. Because of Thieu's ambiguity and vacillation in dealing with truncation and the reshuffling of troops, however, Truong misunderstood the president's intent. The general told his chief of staff, Colonel Hoang Manh Dang, that he had been ordered "to give up most of I Corps," keeping only Da Nang, its seaport, and the immediate surrounding area. Truong ordered that the troops be redeployed immediately. The strong 1st, 3d, and Marine Divisions were to fan out in an arc around the port city, while the weaker 2d Division would be held in reserve.

As a first step Truong replaced most of the Marine units in Quang Tri Province, the northernmost of his positions, with Territorial Forces. During the next several days following the March 13 meeting, these Regional Forces served to screen and delay enemy discovery of the ARVN pullback. All three brigades of the Marine Division took new positions. The 369th Marine Brigade dug in along the Bo River just outside the northern city limits of Hue, the 258th Marine Brigade relieved the Airborne brigade north of the Hai Van Pass, and the 147th Marine Brigade took over the paratroopers' bunkers west of Da Nang. Two 1,200-man Ranger groups plugged the largest holes in the thinned northern MR 1 defenses. General Truong also ordered the heavy 175MM guns, big M48 tanks of the 20th Tank Regiment, ammunition, and stores in the Hue area evacuated south to Da Nang.

When the troops began moving from one part of MR 1 to another, a problem crystallized that had troubled Truong since his return to the northern provinces in 1972, that is the emotional attachment between the civilians and nearby military units. The regular ARVN divisions stayed in one area with their families nearby. This was a boost to morale in more peaceful times but major enemy attacks could put the dependents in peril. In such circumstances soldiers often deserted to see to their families. For that reason Truong especially valued his Marines and Airborne troops because their families lived in Saigon and they had few ties in MR 1. However, a dependency formed anyway. The population took comfort from the elite units' presence. When these troops moved in mid-March, it frightened the people of Quang Tri and Hue.

As truckloads of troops ground through the towns, many Catholics remembered they left North Vietnam in 1954 to escape the Communist occupation. Others recalled the horror of Tet 1968 when after the NVA occupation of Hue more than 2,800 of their neighbors were found buried in mass graves, many of them bound before execution. Also, some people believed that instead of settling for a coalition with the Communists, Thieu would offer them a slice of South Vietnam. They did not want to be caught on the Communist side of a new partition.

Consequently, civilians began leaving Quang Tri and Hue for Da Nang. In some cases government officials encouraged the exodus. On March 15, as the 369th Marine Brigade pulled out of Quang Tri, Lieutenant Colonel Do Ky, the province chief, suggested to government civil servants and regional military personnel that they evacuate their dependents. At first only a thin stream of the well-to-do and the families of senior officials headed south, but soon the few became a throng as insecurity among the influential sparked panic among the poor. By March 18, Route 1 north of the Hai Van Pass was flooded with civilians, and the population of Da Nang had doubled to almost a million.

Prime Minister Tran Thien Khiem flew to Da Nang that day at the pleading of General Truong, who realized a solution to the refugee problem was beyond the means of I Corps and local government agencies. Only Saigon possessed the resources to provide relief. After surveying the clogged roads and listening to province chiefs and mayors, Khiem promised that a commission would be sent to Da Nang to take charge of the refugees and allow the army to concentrate on fighting the war. He also promised to send commercial ships to evacuate military dependents and civilians. But Khiem brought some bad news as well; he told Truong the promised fourth Marine brigade was to stay in Saigon. There would be no reinforcements for beleaguered I Corps.

Shortly after the prime minister left for Saigon, Truong received a summons from the president. Dutifully, on March 19, the general went south to attend yet another palace meeting. As usual Truong opened with a briefing on the situation in I Corps during which he outlined anticipated routes of withdrawal into Da Nang.

But to Truong's amazement, President Thieu rejected the plan. Truong, it became apparent, had misinterpreted the president's orders. Although Thieu had assured Truong at the March 11 meeting that Hue was less important than Da Nang, the president had not agreed to its evacuation. Truong could, if necessary, give up Chu Lai but not Hue. Thieu demanded that the evacuation of Hue be stopped and ordered that a taped speech be broadcast on the twentieth announcing his decision to defend Hue at all costs. Two reasons have been put forth to explain Thieu's decision. General Vien later wrote that the president, realizing that his order to leave the central highlands had caused a military disaster, could not bring himself to allow another major withdrawal. Some Americans thought differently. Through information gathered by a CIA listening device in the cabinet meeting room and other informed reports on Thieu's activities, embassy officials knew that the president had been visited by Bui Diem, the former ambassador to the U.S., and Tran Van Don, deputy prime minister and a former general. The pair advised Thieu either to resign or do something to give new heart to the nation. A gallant defense of the old imperial capital might provide the spark.

While surprised by Thieu's decision, Truong was not too discomfited. The roads in northern MR 1 were so choked with refugees that quick overland withdrawal was impossible, and there were so few ships available that evacuation of his forces by sea was also unrealistic. So he thought it best to "stay in Hue and fight."

Truong asked about rumors that the president planned to move the Marine Division to Saigon. Thieu assured the general of I Corps's continued control of the division, but Prime Minister Khiem told Truong privately that there were indeed plans to move the Marines south.

The defense of Hue

A dispirited General Truong flew back to Da Nang on the afternoon of March 19 to find a dangerous situation growing worse. Long-range NVA artillery pounded the I Corps forward headquarters near Hue and a tank-led Communist force, finally realizing the Regional Forces offered only a screen, brushed aside the RFs at Quang Tri and pushed ahead to the ARVN's next defensive line along the My Chanh River, halfway to Hue. From these river positions ARVN had stopped the 1972 Communist invasion. Meanwhile, south of Hue, lead elements of the 324B and 325C NVA Divisions attacked the 1st ARVN Division and the 15th Ranger Group, which were strung out in positions paralleling nearby Route 1. The highway, even under NVA shelling, continued to be jammed with motorcycles, buses, autos, transferring troops, and a mass of foot traffic.

On the morning of March 20 General Truong flew to the

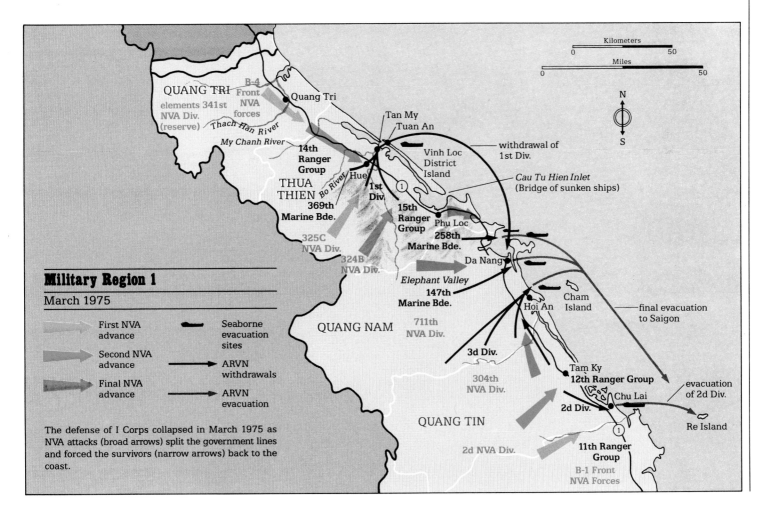

Military Region 1

March 1975

First NVA advance
Second NVA advance
Final NVA advance

Seaborne evacuation sites
ARVN withdrawals
ARVN evacuation

The defense of I Corps collapsed in March 1975 as NVA attacks (broad arrows) split the government lines and forced the survivors (narrow arrows) back to the coast.

Marine command post just south of the My Chanh line and there told a gathering of northern I Corps commanders of Thieu's order to hold Hue. The officers were gratified to have at last a firm directive and they occupied their well-prepared entrenchments with confidence. At 1:30 P.M. Thieu's recorded voice announced over the radio that Hue would be held "at all costs."

It was a startled general, therefore, who returned to his headquarters in the late afternoon to find an order rescinding the order to hold Hue. A secret flash message from Saigon stated that the JGS possessed the means to supply only one enclave in MR 1 and that meant to Truong that he must choose. Truong's interpretation was that Thieu was dictating a withdrawal to Da Nang, the president's choice as the most important city in the north. However, the JGS officer who drafted the message for Thieu meant it only to grant the discretion to pull back to Da Nang should the situation demand. General Vien afterward agreed the language was ambiguous, as many of the president's commands had become. Once again, though, Truong believed his orders were to withdraw to Da Nang; certainly the ARVN defenders were not to fight to the death for Hue.

On March 20, the same day that Thieu complicated the task of his general, Hanoi clarified the objectives of theirs. The NVA General Staff ordered the B-4 Front forces and the 2d Army Corps to redouble their efforts and go all out to cut Route 1 and isolate Hue. The edict resulted from information their spy on Thieu's staff had passed to the Communists regarding the GVN's truncation plans. Hanoi's leaders realized they must attack quickly to prevent ARVN from making an orderly withdrawal into well-defended coastal enclaves or sailing off to Saigon.

In response to the new orders, the NVA's 324B and 325C Divisions put their full weight against the 15th Rangers and 1st Division south of Hue. ARVN defenses stiffened and held through the morning of March 22, but at about two that afternoon the remnants of the 15th pulled out of their fighting positions near Phu Loc and withdrew north through the rear of the 1st Division. The left flank of the 1st tried desperately to establish a new line along the Troui River twenty kilometers south of Hue and failed, but that night after brutal hand-to-hand fighting near Phu Bai airfield, they succeeded in temporarily halting the NVA advance. However, the NVA attack had severed Route 1.

By the twenty-third Hue was cut off from Da Nang except by sea. The city came under Communist artillery fire as the surviving Rangers and the 1st Division conducted a fighting withdrawal toward the city from the south. To the north, the Rangers along the My Chanh River gave way, but the 3,000-man Marine brigade reestablished a line about eight kilometers outside Hue along the Bo River. That evening I Corps headquarters advised the senior American in MR 1, Consul-General Al Francis, that the NVA had again outflanked the 1st Division, and the ARVN troops would be unable to prevent an enemy breakthrough. By day's end the few Americans in Hue went by helicopter to Da Nang.

Disaster in I Corps

At 6:00 P.M. on March 24, believing himself under orders to abandon Hue and to save as many men as possible, Truong ordered his staff to evacuate all troops defending the walled city. The Marines and other troops west and north of Hue were to pull back through the port town of Tan My, ten kilometers to the northeast, to the ocean village of Thuan An for evacuation by ship. Their withdrawal was to be covered by the 1st Division which, in turn, was to march to the coast. There Vinh Loc District Island stretched thirty kilometers south directly toward Da Nang. Reached by ferry or small boat the island seemed to provide a sandy route that skirted the NVA positions on the mainland. The single obstacle to a clean getaway was Cau Tu Hien Inlet. However, the mouth of the huge lagoon at the south end of Vinh Loc Island was to be bridged by navy and ARVN engineers. Once on the south side of the inlet the retreating ARVN could pick up Route 1 and cross the Hai Van Pass into Da Nang.

The Marines moved through Thuan An in good order on March 25 although they lost valuable time clearing civilians from the docks and beaches where military equipment and troops were to be loaded. By the time the leading elements of the 1st Division pulled out behind the Marines—following General Diem's pessimistic "sauve qui peut" speech to his officers—tens of thousands of armed stragglers and civilians clogged the road to the coast. The division found itself trapped by the congestion. Unable to maneuver and no doubt influenced by the edict of "every man for himself," soldiers left their units to find their families. The entire division soon dissolved into the crowd. Behind them the first NVA troops reached the eastern gate of Hue's citadel and raised their flag.

By afternoon large groups of withdrawing soldiers and refugees had already reached the northern side of the Cau Tu Hien Inlet. The NVA, with their own troops now entering Hue, switched their artillery fire to the crowded roads and assembly areas of the South Vietnamese, inflicting heavy casualties and feeding panic among those waiting for the evacuation ships to appear.

The officer in charge of the seaborne evacuation, Commodore Ho Van Ky Thoai, had received orders only the night before. No plans existed to bring out the more than 50,000 people awaiting evacuation, but he was determined to do what he could with the perhaps 100 light junks, river craft, and barges available in Da Nang.

A family of four lies dead on Route 1 near the Hai Van Pass on March 21, killed in a stampede during the rush from Hue to Da Nang.

To bridge the Cau Tu Hien Inlet, he ordered a flotilla of small boats sunk to form a causeway across which the troops could walk. Strong currents frustrated the early efforts to bridge the lagoon mouth. Meanwhile crowds of soldiers gathered on the tidal flats. Finally, unnerved by NVA shelling and frantic at the slow pace of the engineers, a group of armed men captured the flotilla commander. With a gun at his head the navy officer ordered the small fleet to sail the renegade soldiers to Da Nang, thereby eliminating any possibility that a causeway could be completed for use by the tens of thousands behind them. Some men tried to make their way across the sandbars to the other side on foot, but the incoming tide trapped and drowned many. A sea lift remained the only means of saving the Hue force.

The navy managed to pull about 7,700 people off Vinh Loc Island, but a lethal combination of low tides, rough seas, and increasingly accurate NVA artillery fire soon prevented the ships from reaching the shore. Most of one regiment of the 1st Division was picked up as was a single boatload of Marines, about 600 men. But soon two large landing craft were swamped in the heavy surf and a third sunk by a direct hit. After that, said navy Captain Nguyen Xuan Son, no one got onboard "except a few who succeeded in paddling out" past the breakers to the ships offshore. Bodies of many who attempted the swim bobbed in the surf. Navy officers placed some of the blame on landing craft manned by army transportation troops who arrived late and, unable to handle their ships in the rough water, refused to attempt landings.

Some of the survivors reached Da Nang with a poignant story of what took place as the NVA closed in on those left at the beach. Five battalion commanders assigned to the Marine brigade gathered in the waning hours of the evacuation and walked apart from the frantic crowds. Each spoke farewells, stepped away, and shot himself. It represented in miniature the story of the fight for northern I Corps. Moved about by quickly changing and often conflicting orders, pulled from strong positions, often without a fight, and finally told to retreat, a brave but confused and leaderless army died in the midst of chaos, anarchy, and, at the last, headlong flight.

Worse, Hue represented only half of the disaster that faced General Truong. When the NVA attacked north of Da Nang, they also launched an infantry regiment and armored column south of the city and captured Tam Ky, severing Route 1 about halfway to Chu Lai, the headquarters of the 2d ARVN Division. As Truong prepared a new defensive plan for southern MR 1, a delegation of officers from the JGS arrived to give Thieu's order that the Marine Division be released immediately for the defense of Saigon in MR 3.

A North Vietnamese photograph shows Communist troops charging into the old imperial capital at Hue on March 26.

Truong could not believe the order. Defend Da Nang without the Marines? Impossible, he said. The JGS representatives did not relent. Instead, they recommended evacuating the 2d Division from Chu Lai to replace the Marines at Da Nang. Truong reluctantly agreed. He arranged for LSTs (landing ships tank) sailing from Saigon to pick up the 2d Division. Once again a lack of planning cost a heavy price in ARVN lives. Territorial Forces and outlying 2d Division troops were forced into hasty withdrawals along unprotected routes to meet the evacuation deadline. In the process they were ambushed repeatedly by the 2d NVA Division before reaching the landing site at Chu Lai. On the night of March 25 some 7,000 troops, about two-thirds of the division, and 3,000 civilians were pulled out of the city and sent to Re Island, fifty kilometers offshore. The division had lost so much equipment and cohesion during its evacuation that it would need reorganization before being inserted into the battle for Da Nang.

Impasse in Washington

In Washington on the night of March 25, as Hue and the central highlands fell, staff aides for Secretary of State Henry Kissinger scrambled to finish briefings for their boss who had returned from the Middle East only the day before. The cable traffic from Saigon had suddenly taken on an alarming tone, indicating that the military situation in South Vietnam was shifting rapidly. The secretary's staff now rushed to prepare him for a session at the White House to determine strategy for Indochina.

The meeting, attended by the president, Kissinger, Ambassador Martin, army Chief of Staff General Frederick Weyand, and NSC Staff Deputy Brent Scowcroft, opened with a discussion of the latest reports from Saigon, which had lost their previously optimistic tone. One CIA assessment suggested that "in the face of recent supply losses and continuing NVA pressure on all fronts, government forces are not likely to regain the initiative or recoup their strength in the near future. . . ." Not everyone at the White House that day was convinced the situation was so dire. Ambassador Martin advised "a degree of skepticism" in considering the alarmist reports. He affirmed his determination to check personally the reports' accuracy when he returned to South Vietnam.

The group soon turned to debating just what the U.S. government could do within the legislative limits of the War Powers Act and the Cambodian bombing restrictions. They decided that it would be difficult if not impossible to use American forces even for the rescue of the South Vietnamese army. But the government could employ civilian aircraft and ships under contract to move Vietnamese forces and equipment from endangered areas. The group agreed to commit U.S. ships to the extent they could pick up refugees outside Vietnam's international boundary three miles out to sea.

The discussion moved to the question of direct aid for replacement of arms and munitions lost in the northern military regions. The Pentagon already had a request in hand from Defense Attaché Major General Homer Smith asking that arms and supplies previously ordered be sent as quickly as possible. Sketchy initial reports indicated that South Vietnam could survive, but much depended on the rehabilitation of battered I and II Corps troops and their ability to hold on to their coastal enclaves. Perhaps, the group concurred, if Congress became convinced that South Vietnam was in serious danger, their intransigence to granting new aid might weaken.

But it appeared that neither the White House nor Congress was disposed to compromise on the question of military aid. The administration continued to blame Congressional reductions for military setbacks in South Vietnam. On March 20, Defense Secretary James R. Schlesinger had said that if Congress had been "less niggardly" with aid, "the position of South Vietnam would be far better today" since the RVNAF would not have been forced to withdraw from the central highlands. Nor would the North Vietnamese have been able to take advantage of ARVN's defensive move to launch "a major offensive." "The outcome is far more devastating," Schlesinger argued, because of the "weakened position" of South Vietnam.

Few congressmen appear to have been moved by the administration's argument. The day Schlesinger made his remarks, Republican Senator Charles McC. Mathias, Jr., of Maryland and Democratic Senator Adlai E. Stevenson 3d of Illinois introduced legislation to terminate all military aid to South Vietnam on June 30, a proposal they expected would provide the focal point for Senate opposition to increased aid.

Congressional leaders, caught between the administration's requests and the opposition of their colleagues, used the Easter recess that began March 25 to put off considering the administration's request for $300 million in additional military aid. Since Congress did not reconvene until April 7, there was no chance that an emergency aid supplement for South Vietnam or Cambodia would be acted upon before mid–April.

The siege of Da Nang

As Washington's indecision continued, the resolve of the Communist General Staff and Central Military Committee had grown with each day. Reading the messages from their battlefield commanders and reports from the spy in Thieu's staff, they developed an accurate assessment of their own army's successes and the enemy's growing disarray. The vision of victories greater than ever before began to color the rhetoric of even staid senior army officials. Orders from Hanoi called for big wins in the Da Nang battle to "create conditions for a strategic victory later." To lend strength to these edicts the Politburo named a local commander for the forces attacking ARVN's I Corps, Major General Le Trong Tan.

The appointment produced tremors in the COSVN command. It meant that once more General Tra's design for the quick isolation of Saigon was to be pushed aside in favor of a plan engineered by the northerners. As originally outlined in the Politburo's two-year plan, Dung was to turn south and support Tra's offensive against the nation's capital after conquest of the central highlands. But with Pleiku, Kontum, Hue, and Chu Lai under Communist control, the temptation to finish the GVN in the north was too great. The NVA high command anticipated the imminent fall of Da Nang and doubted the possibilities of either U.S. intervention or a successful South Vietnamese counterattack. But the presence of the RVNAF troops in Da Nang still made the cautious General Staff anxious, so they decided to eliminate any U.S. or South Vietnamese temptation to use Da Nang as the springboard for a riposte by taking the city immediately. It may have been that Tra's argument for a direct assault on Saigon was still too radical for the NVA's senior command. Or perhaps they still believed they would yet have to negotiate a settlement with the GVN. Whatever the reasoning, "After heated discussions," Dung said, "we agreed that the best direction was to the east."

Early in the morning of March 26, General Dung read the awaited message from Hanoi for the Communist troops surrounding Da Nang: "most rapidly, most daringly, most unexpectedly" attack. The General Staff had given orders opening the new Communist offensive, effective immediately.

Even as General Tan sped from North Vietnam over the roads of the Truong Son Corridor to join his command, the siege of Da Nang began with an artillery barrage. Three columns of Communist infantry, each supported by artillery and tank regiments, moved against Truong's thinned forces. The B-4 forces pressed southward along Route 1 toward the Hai Van Pass. The 324B and 325C Divisions advanced from the east through Elephant Valley. The 711th and 304th Divisions made up the attack force from the south along with independent regiments of the B-1 Front.

That same morning in Da Nang, MR 1 Consul General Al Francis, appointed by Ambassador Martin the previous fall, was busy updating the plan to move Americans and their South Vietnamese employees and informants from the city before it fell. The consul general worked under a handicap, having been out of the country a month for treatment of a serious thyroid condition. Still in a weakened state, he tried to deal with a crisis that had appeared within a matter of days. No official word came from the South Vietnamese about abandoning Da Nang, but the signs were unmistakable. At I Corps headquarters James Schofield, a DAO intelligence officer initially assigned to Hue, discovered the atmosphere "extremely pessimistic and confused. None of the I Corps staff officers felt that Danang could be held." Their primary concern was securing seats for their dependents on Air America flights.

Since Martin was in Washington, Francis relied on his own judgment. He decided to get the Americans out of Da Nang: consulate dependents immediately, contract employees and families next, and, finally, any other Americans. Only the essential members of the consular staff would remain. "My decision to press forward [with the evacuation] was cinched by the realization the Communists were using the refugees as a shield. They were hoping to bulldoze thousands of them in on us, and thus demoralize and cripple the army as they had at Hue."

To avoid creating panic Francis tried to continue an appearance of business as usual. But by the morning of the twenty-sixth he had discussed an evacuation with General Homer Smith of the DAO in Saigon, who sent a small fleet of five tugs, six barges, and three cargo vessels to Da Nang. The ships were to pull out critical military stores and heavy equipment, even personnel if necessary.

Not everyone in Saigon agreed with Francis's view of the situation in Da Nang. Wolfgang Lehmann, Ambassador Martin's deputy in Saigon, called to protest the tenor of the consul general's messages, but Francis held to his assessment. "I'm the man on the spot," he told Lehmann, "and I say time is running out."

The air attaché to Saigon, Colonel Gavin McCurdy, flew to Da Nang that Wednesday morning to make his own survey of MR 1. A look at the crowds of refugees and a short discussion with Francis convinced him of the need for a rapid evacuation. By afternoon the colonel was back in Saigon trying to impress on the U.S. Mission and the 7th Air Force Command in Thailand just how desperate the situation in Da Nang was. But McCurdy's calls and requests were futile. The U.S. Special Advisory Group in Thailand, which controlled most of the aviation forces left in Southeast Asia, could not supply even a single helicopter. All air force and navy aircraft were on alert waiting for "Eagle Pull," the anticipated evacuation of Phnom Penh. Plans for Eagle Pull had been made without foreseeing a simultaneous catastrophe in South Vietnam.

Because of Ambassador John Gunther Dean's graphic portrayal of the tragedy in Cambodia, said a CIA analyst, "even the most apocalyptic reporting from Saigon paled by comparison." Dean had made his case so effectively that each morning Assistant Secretary of State Philip Habib opened his East Asia staff meetings with a briefing on Cambodia. The news from Saigon rated only second, even third place. As a result, attention remained focused on one disaster while another of even greater proportions took shape.

The now palpable tension was felt by another DAO representative when he arrived in Da Nang on the twenty-sixth. E. G. Hey, a civilian employee of the army transportation section, was assigned to supervise loading

Life Behind Communist Lines

While the combat soldiers of the NVA drove south in spring 1975, behind them political cadres and occupation troops began the consolidation of power in the conquered areas. The troops from the North were greeted with enthusiastic welcomes, the PRG announced. And, indeed, in each town that became part of the "liberated zone" of South Vietnam in March and April of 1975, the attitude of many Vietnamese was, if not one of enthusiasm, at least one of relief. A businessman from Da Nang told a *Washington Post* reporter that despite widespread anxiety about what the revolution would bring, "at the moment ... [people] are just glad to be out of the war."

One of the most reassuring aspects for the "liberated" populations in those first days was the stern official standard of conduct imposed on all Communist troops. They were under orders not to take even a "needle or thread" from the people. These rules, codified into a ten-point poster, were prominently displayed as soon as troops entered a town. For the most part, the rules appeared to have been scrupulously observed.

Although many towns seemed surprisingly unaltered as they resumed their routines—the buses ran, the electricity worked—there were signs of change. Communist slogans were posted where GVN slogans had been, and "revolutionary" films showed where American movies had played. Countless NLF flags flew and the troops addressed officials as "brother" or "sister." North Vietnamese technicians who had been rushed to the South could be seen organizing shipments of captured arms to the front. Other North Vietnamese had been sent to begin planning the economic, medical, and educational aspects of postwar reconstruction. Students who had joined the revolution wore red arm bands or, if they had been given permission to carry weapons, white arm bands. Hanoi time replaced Saigon time (an hour's difference), just as the DRV *dong* replaced the *piaster*. American-style flowered shirts and flared slacks became less common and more traditional attire reappeared.

For the moment, the concrete ways in which life was affected by the occupation were limited for most to enforced attendance at nightly meetings where instruction in "revolutionary" thought began at the hands of seasoned cadres. For some the Communist presence meant the security of knowing there would be no more harassment by the GVN police; for others, it meant fear of an unknown future at the hands of the new authorities.

To govern the new territories, the Communists hastened to set up makeshift administrative institutions in the towns and villages. Ban Me Thuot was placed under the jurisdiction of an NVA colonel of montagnard origin, according to *Le Monde*. In Da Nang, a nine-member "committee of military control" headed by a member of the NLF Central Committee was said to be in charge. Local Communist-approved governments began to function most quickly in areas that had the most deeply entrenched guerrilla infrastructures. But Vietnamese who left Communist-controlled Da Nang told Fox Butterfield of the *New York Times* that while "local people long associated with the Vietcong have been appointed to new jobs in the Communist civil administration ... the troops in charge are North Vietnamese."

The official position of the Communists remained that they were fighting for observance of the Paris agreement. Therefore the principles of coalition government would be applied in the "liberated" areas. This posture was reflected in the attendance of a non-Communist leader of the Buddhist Forces for National Reconciliation at a meeting of Hue's revolutionary committee.

Since much of the public relations work of the new leadership involved efforts to allay the population's misgivings about Communist rule, some attention was given to the question of religion. *Time* magazine reported that "Hanoi ordered its ... troops to revere temples, pagodas, and churches." On the eve of the Communist entry into a town, guerrillas would tell its inhabitants to hang Buddhist flags if they did not have NLF flags.

Perhaps most anxious were those who had held positions in the South Vietnamese military, administration, or police forces. While reprisals against some senior officials and soldiers occurred, there were few reports of official executions. Deaths among GVN officials in reeducation camps and new economic zones would be high in years to come, but in March and April 1975 the Communists still paid lip service to the Paris agreement. Unsure just how far the offensive would take them, the Communists needed to retain the option to negotiate. Any talks would have been practically impossible to pursue if there had been a repeat of the Communist massacre of GVN officials that occurred at Hue during the Tet offensive of 1968.

If summary treatment of ex-GVN officials was the exception in early 1975, what then was the rule? For some, the prospect of reeducation, or *hoc tap*, loomed. In various towns, certain people were designated for this process, but nobody really knew what it would mean. Many ARVN officers were held in custody. For most soldiers and officials, however, all that was demanded at this point was that they register with the authorities and list all their past political activities and affiliations. For low-level officials, continuity was the norm and many stayed at their posts. The Communists allowed teachers to return to their classrooms although they were to be retrained for a new curriculum and new teaching methods. Meanwhile, some captured ARVN soldiers were impressed into service as drivers and technicians for the last phase of the offensive.

All of these first steps of the Communists in their new domains, happening even before the end of the war, were only the beginning of what would be an immense administrative task. From clearing mines to resettling refugees in their villages, from restoring order to the economy to introducing huge populations to "revolutionary" thought, the tasks the Communists had waited to begin for thirty agonizing years of war were under way.

of heavy equipment and stores on the fleet of boats and barges General Smith had sent north. When checking in at the consulate that afternoon, Hey was surprised to find tense staff members burning and shredding documents—surprised because Da Nang was not supposed to be in any immediate danger. But Hey had a job to do, and after a few words with the staff he went back to the business of preparing military supplies for movement to Saigon. A bit later, while surveying the city docks and deep-water piers, Hey saw the survivors of Hue arriving at the waterfront but noticed no attempt to receive and organize the soldiers. They simply slipped into the crowds of refugees gathering around the harbor.

Originally there had been a plan to deal with the crowds of refugees and the confusion they caused. ARVN troops had set up roadblocks at the edge of Da Nang in mid-March to keep them on the outskirts of the city. When the Communist shelling began, however, General Truong could not leave the civilians under the merciless enemy fire and they were allowed into the city. Regardless of his decision, the refugees would interfere with his troops' defenses. Outside ARVN's lines they blocked the army's fields of fire; behind the lines they jammed communication and resupply roads and overwhelmed the city's military and civilian police.

As of yet, however, the refugees had not disturbed operations at Da Nang's main airport. Throughout the morning of the twenty-sixth, flights moved smoothly with Air Vietnam, World Airways, Air America, and Vietnamese Air Force aircraft shuttling in and out. Even with the expanded volume of traffic, however, demand outstripped supply as senior Vietnamese officials and their families, Americans, and citizens of other countries awaited space on outgoing aircraft. Only in the late evening did some scuffling occur as VNAF personnel and their dependents shoved onto a flight scheduled for U.S. consular personnel.

Since no attempt had been made to organize the 1st Division survivors from Hue and the 2d Division remained on Re Island, Truong was feeling the shortage of combat troops. Intact units left to I Corps were the 3d Division, two brigades of Marines, and a number of Territorial units of only marginal value against the tank-supported NVA regulars. Only the Vietnamese Air Force attack squadrons, available to fly close support missions from the city's two airfields, ameliorated Truong's difficult position. Yet the VNAF could never match the 300 sorties a day the U.S. flew in the defense of I Corps during the Easter offensive of 1972. Nor could they deliver anywhere near the bomb tonnage dropped by the Americans.

For some South Vietnamese soldiers the status of their air force was now irrelevant. Late that night, as Staff Sergeant Walter Sparks, the NCO in charge of Da Nang's six-man U.S. Marine detachment, stood talking to a South Vietnamese guard in front of the consulate, more evacuees from Hue landed at the nearby docks. Near-naked Viet-namese soldiers carrying rifles ran past, weeping and crying out to those they met. The guard himself burst into tears and repeated their hysterical litany to the American. "They were 1st Division," he was told, "the South Vietnamese were not helping them, the Americans were not helping them, and their country was lost."

We will be in tomorrow

From the consulate, Sparks watched the change in the city. Overnight on March 26-27, crowds of Vietnamese had set up camp in the streets and occupied every available inch of ground in the downtown area. Armed soldiers, obviously no longer under control, wandered aimlessly.

After twenty-four hours of fighting his way through the refugee-jammed streets between loading sites, Hey, the DAO logistician, finally realized how inappropriate were his efforts. People were now the prize to be salvaged from Da Nang, not guns or trucks. He once again made his way to the consulate and there recommended to Francis that it was time for a change in shipping priorities. He pointed out that the backlog of passengers at the airport was continuing to grow. The tugs and barges assigned to move military supplies would soon be the only way to transport large numbers of military men and civilians from Da Nang, including the remaining Americans. Francis quickly approved the idea of shipping people, and Hey began making arrangements using a landing craft as his personal water taxi to avoid the blocked streets.

The Americans assigned to the consulate staff stayed put until Thursday afternoon, March 27, but with the ominous word from the Air America dispatcher that the airport was periodically closed by a sea of people on the runways, Francis could avoid a decision on the evacuation of the American staff no longer. After heated debates with some who argued that a pullout of the official U.S. presence would only worsen the situation, Francis at 5:30 P.M. ordered the remaining fifty-odd Americans to leave Da Nang. The message was passed to assemble either at the consulate, the Alamo apartment complex, or Francis's home, all within a half-mile of the city docks.

At Da Nang's main airfield the situation had slipped beyond control. At dawn on the twenty-seventh the refugees crowding the terminal and parking ramp areas had appeared sleepy and tranquil. However, the loading of a World Airways flight at 9:00 A.M. turned into a free-for-all. Panicked crowds mobbed every subsequent aircraft landing at Da Nang.

Officials eased the problem temporarily by ordering arriving aircraft to stop in remote sections of the huge airfield. Selected passengers would then be driven to the aircraft. Smaller Air America C-46s and C-47s were diverted to the Marble Mountain airfield west of Da Nang where the military still controlled access to the field. Helicopters shuttled passengers there from landing pads near the consulate downtown and the main airport.

By evening, chaos ruled Da Nang airport. At 8:00 P.M. Consul General Francis halted all U.S.-controlled flights except for those out of Marble Mountain. Americans at the airport who missed getting out were moved downtown to the Alamo apartments. Behind them at the airfield "the runways were littered with rubber sandals, fragments of silk clothing and bamboo hats, broken toys, electric fans and the other flotsam left by fleeing people," wrote *New York Times* reporter Malcolm Browne. "Children here and there wept bitterly, hugging puppies and kittens."

That night, as Sgt. Sparks moved among the three assembly points, he could hear firing all around the outskirts of the city. To the north, the sounds of heavy artillery boomed from the Hai Van Pass. At one point, his reveries were broken by a jeep with a loudspeaker blaring in Vietnamese. His heart sank when the message was translated. "Be calm, don't panic, raise your Buddhist flags; we [the NVA] will be in tomorrow to restore order." "Oh my Lord," Sparks thought, "they are already here."

Horror at the docks

Shortly before midnight at the city docks, Hey had seen the first load of South Vietnamese navy and army personnel and their dependents pulled away from the docks for transfer to the ships newly arrived from Saigon and anchored offshore. At 1:30 A.M. on March 28 he was aboard the tug *Shibaura* still directing the movement of barges when the captain of the boat received a message from Francis to pick up the consulate staff in two hours. Hey had to scramble to locate two empty barges for the assignment.

On shore, consulate staff members bribed the ARVN colonel in charge of dock security to make sure the mass of Vietnamese was kept out of the dock area when the barges arrived. However, the Americans assembled at the Alamo and Francis's house still had to travel the half-mile to the docks without being seen. Attracting attention could mean a stampede for the barges or even an attack from the panic-stricken Vietnamese.

Garbage trucks saved the situation. Vietnamese consulate employees rode on the outside while the Americans hid in the center of the truck beds. The convoy, with Sparks in the last truck, nosed slowly through the sleepy early morning crowds in the streets, the drivers ignoring threats from leaderless soldiers, until they reached the safety of the cordoned-off dock. The garbage truck ruse had worked. When the trucks arrived at the dock, the tug boat crew watched in wonderment as Honda motorcycles, large boxes, and suitcases belonging to the Vietnamese employees appeared on the barges within minutes. Just as promptly the crewmen tossed the baggage into the water to make room for the crowd waiting to board.

The ARVN colonel's security troops had held the crowds back for hours, but a rush of refugees through the dock gates at 5:30 A.M. overwhelmed them. Hey, realizing they had to get out now or be shoved off the barges, began to knock people aside to cast off the lines holding the barge to the dock. But as quickly as one was freed, the Vietnamese tied it back again while others began inching hand over hand along the rope to the two barges. Aware of the futility of the task, Hey signaled the captain of the tug to use full power to break away from the pier. It took several tries to break free. Each time the tug pulled forward the lines to the dock pulled taut, breaking the grip of those clinging to the ropes and pitching them into the water. Then the lines recoiled, snapping the barges back into the dock, crushing those in the water.

Sparks, who had seen men die before, described the scene as the most tragic he had ever witnessed. But he also saw bravery and courage: "Vietnamese mothers saved their children by throwing them [from the dock] to British girls, Aussies, everybody [on the barges] grabbing babies" and trying to keep the elderly and infirm aboard from falling or being pushed into the water by other panic-stricken refugees.

Finally the lines gave way and the horror ended. The Americans left Da Nang ten years and twenty days after the U.S. Marines had first landed there. The barges slipped down the Da Nang channel toward deep water leaving behind the smoke of the burning city and the pounding of the NVA artillery. Sparks noticed that after the tragedy on the docks it was suddenly very calm and beautiful; the sun was rising and a haze clung to the sides of Monkey Mountain, which loomed over the harbor. "People were quiet on the barge," he realized. "I could just look back over the years. I thought, 'God, what a waste.'" As the shock wore off, those on board noticed they were surrounded by hundreds of fishing vessels and small Vietnamese naval craft aswarm with people making for deep water and the rescue fleet. Occasionally they heard the popping of gunfire as desperate refugees tried to take over less-crowded craft and those aboard the threatened boats fought back with equal desperation.

At midmorning on the twenty-eighth, the tug and barges steered alongside the cargo ship *Pioneer Contender* and tied up. At first only medical personnel were allowed on board to set up a hospital area while Americans and other foreign nationals formed a security force for controlling the loading of the Vietnamese onto the cargo ship. At noon the refugees began transferring to the *Pioneer Contender*. After three hours the crowd on the barges was little diminished. As quickly as anyone left the barge, small boats pulled up and more Vietnamese climbed on board. Crewmen shot at the small boats to run them off but it did no good. Finally, realizing the ship, already carrying more than its limit of 6,000 people, was going to be severely overloaded, the captain gave orders for the *Pioneer Contender* to steam away from the crowd of small boats.

The *Pioneer Contender* finished loading at 6:00 P.M. when the last of 12,000 refugees came on board. As crewmen boarded the barge to cut it loose, they found the bodies of 30 people. Most of the victims were the very young and the very old who had died in the crush and the trauma of the day's trip. Sgt. Sparks, though, discovered that not everyone was dead. Using a flashlight the marine spotted an old man lying in the refuse of the barge deck, and when Sparks picked up the frail figure, the old man screamed; his leg was broken. Sparks made another discovery; close by, petrified with fear, but alive, sat the old man's wife. At 7:00 P.M., this final aged couple on board, the *Pioneer Contender* sailed for Cam Ranh Bay.

The evacuation of I Corps

About the time that the consulate staff had sailed around Monkey Mountain, General Truong, the I Corps commander, met with his subordinates and ordered his lines pulled back toward Da Nang so that the remaining ARVN artillery could be centralized and thereby offer more con-

centrated fire support. The move was also dictated by an increasingly acute shortage of combat troops to defend the perimeter. The Territorial troops were slipping away from their positions to find relatives and search for a ride south.

At noon, however, Truong's latest defensive plans took a body blow. A message from the JGS advised that NVA forces would launch an all-out assault during the night. All helicopters and jets were therefore to be evacuated from Da Nang immediately to save them from destruction.

Realizing that no part of his command was out of range of the enemy artillery and that there was no more air force to strike at the enemy heavy guns, Truong at last admitted to himself the futility of any further defense of Da Nang. The general radioed Saigon recommending to President Thieu that Da Nang be evacuated immediately to save the remaining I Corps forces for the defense of Saigon. But the nation's leader once again suffered from indecision. "He did not tell General Truong whether to withdraw or to hold and fight," General Vien later said. Thieu asked how many people could be taken out but issued no orders.

A few of the South Vietnamese infantrymen who escaped Hue from the beach aboard a raft scramble onto a navy ship.

Within minutes of the inconclusive conversation, communications between I Corps and Saigon were destroyed by gunfire. NVA artillery spotters who had already infiltrated the city were improving the bombardment's accuracy.

The destruction of communications relieved Truong of the burden of waiting for a presidential decision on withdrawal. The general sent for his naval commander, Commodore Ho Van Ky Thoai, to plan the evacuation of Da Nang. As it evolved, the scheme called for each of the infantry units to move toward one of three embarkation points to be picked up by available ships: the 258th Marine Brigade at the foot of Hai Van Pass, the 147th Marine Brigade at the beach near Marble Mountain, and the 3d Division at the Hoi An Estuary about twenty-five kilometers south of Da Nang.

Yet while Truong could still direct his army, he could not control the civilians. By the time of his meeting with Thoai, the city's population had swollen to 2 million. The streets were so jammed it proved impossible to transport 340 wounded soldiers from the hospital to the airport. Every public building, all the public roads, and the harbor had been taken over by refugees. "The chaos and disorder were indescribable," said Lieutenant General Le Nguyen Khang, a JGS representative in the city. "Hunger, looting, and crimes were widespread." The Saigon government, which only days before assured Truong it would deal with the refugee problem, did nothing and remained, as the general noted, "silent on the problem."

For Consul General Al Francis, who had elected to stay behind, labors this Friday centered around the makeshift airlift operations he managed to continue from the Marble Mountain airstrip. Late in the afternoon, he recognized a group of South Vietnamese refugees that had been mistakenly consigned to an isolated section of the field and forgotten. As he directed them toward an awaiting Air America C-47, Francis noticed an ARVN artillery battery with its howitzer barrels pointed down the runway. Negotiating desperately, Francis promised to evacuate some of the officers, troops, and their families in exchange for not interfering with the flight. As the aircraft taxied for a takeoff, however, scores of soldiers ran after it, grasping at the wings and tail to prevent its flight. Francis ran after them yelling and throwing punches at those he could reach. The diversion worked but the disgruntled soldiers turned on the American and beat him savagely. He survived only by playing dead. Two British charity workers who saw the beating helped him away. That flight proved to be the last authorized out of Da Nang.

That evening, battered and sore, Francis and his British companions left the airfield and walked to General Truong's nearby headquarters. They found him almost alone, destroying the last of his files and battle maps. The four men soon climbed into the remaining undamaged helicopter and flew to the Vietnamese naval headquarters near the base of Monkey Mountain. It was a short-lived refuge. At midnight heavy NVA artillery began pounding the navy buildings and hit barges filled with refugees at the nearby docks. Dodging explosions, the American consul general and the two Englishmen ran for a nearby beach, swam through the surf, and were picked up beyond the breakers by a small South Vietnamese navy patrol boat.

Shortly after midnight on the morning of March 29, Truong, who had remained at naval headquarters, ordered Major General Nguyen Duy Hinh, commander of the ARVN 3d Division, to establish a beachhead north of Hoi An with his three regiments so that naval vessels could pick up the troops. For Hinh, who over three years had molded the 3d into a confident, formidable fighting force, the defense of Da Nang was already a morale disaster. For a week his men, ordered from position to position, had never been allowed to make a stand against the Communists. Their major combat came while withdrawing through positions southwest of Da Nang supposedly held by Territorial troops. As the Regional units dissolved, NVA sapper units infiltrated to set up ambushes and roadblocks. When the 3d Division pulled back, they were forced to clear Route 1 and recapture Hoi An from the NVA advance units.

Now, Hinh wondered, just how well had I Corps provided for his men's evacuation? The orders provided directions that in case too few ships reached the pickup point, the division must move to Cham Island, twenty kilometers offshore, "by its own means." Confiscated civilian fishing boats would be the only alternative for the escape to Cham Island. The men in the ranks must have shared Hinh's thoughts, for when the division moved out at 1:30 A.M., many of the 12,000 troops broke ranks and drifted away to search for relatives and their own way south.

The men of the 3d were not alone in searching for a way out. Just as the division pulled out for the beach at Hoi An, the last of the senior officers left I Corps headquarters in Da Nang. Commodore Thoai, who planned the evacuation, and Major General Bui The Lan, commander of the Marine Corps Division, had already sent their staffs out to the rescue fleet by small boat when small-arms fire near the headquarters convinced them it was time to leave. Thoai went from room to room and found only a single navy lieutenant still burning classified documents. When Thoai and Lan walked outside, they realized General Truong had taken the last flying helicopter to naval headquarters. Other copters sitting on the strip were damaged and useless.

Taking a boat from the nearby beach appeared to be the next option for escape. The pair walked past the main gate where lay four NVA sappers killed by security guards. For a while they waited for a boat, but each time one approached it drew fire from the frustrated crowd on the shore. Thoai and Lan then decided to find a less crowded beach along the base of Monkey Mountain.

About 4:00 A.M., after hours of wandering lost in the jungle, they discovered a rocky shore on the north side of the mountain from which they hailed a passing naval boat and swam out to be rescued. Thoai and Lan soon transferred to the flagship of the South Vietnamese fleet from which the commodore continued to oversee the increasingly chaotic pullout.

After daybreak, General Truong decided that he too had done everything possible on shore and the time had come to attempt his own evacuation. The I Corps commander left the naval headquarters, waded into the surf, and with the help of an aide made it to the safety of a patrol boat. He soon joined Thoai and Lan on the flagship.

In the early Saturday morning fog that had set in along the coast, the junks and small boats commanded by the South Vietnamese navy moved into the assembly areas to

As the great exodus took place from the beaches of Da Nang, another act of high drama played itself out at the city's airport. Early that morning of the twenty-ninth, World Airways President Edward J. Daly had decided on one last flamboyant attempt to save people in the surrounding city. The U.S. Embassy had expressly requested that any more flights be canceled because of the disorder at the Da Nang airport. But Daly persisted. Using two Boeing 727s he had contracted to haul cargo for the U.S. government, Daly and his crews took off from Saigon and flew north to the surrounded city. While one aircraft circled, the other with Daly aboard landed at an apparently peaceful airfield. The touchdown of the aircraft, however, set a mass of people in motion. The mob came at the aircraft "roaring across the tarmac on motorbikes, jeeps, scooters—and on foot," remembered United Press Inter-

pick up the Marines and soldiers of I Corps. As at Hue, the ships could not beach because of low tides. The troops were forced to wade and swim to the awaiting vessels. The two brigades of the Marine Corps Division made it from the beaches in good numbers. Despite the loss of the third marine brigade at Hue, the attrition of a week of rear-guard actions, and the corrosive effects of the hysteria that ravaged Da Nang, 6,000 Marines boarded the ships.

The 3d Division fared much worse. Eventually 5,000 men assembled on the Hoi An beach and at noon 1,000 of them were taken off, but the next boats did not arrive for six hours. By the time four naval vessels approached the beach the soldiers were enraged and self-destructive. They fired on the craft, according to General Hinh's account, and drove them off. Commodore Thoai noted that realistically, even if the ships had beached, very little space was left on board. The remaining troops of the 3d Division were left behind on the beach with the option of either finding a boat for themselves or awaiting capture.

The last flight from Da Nang, March 29. Four men survived the World Airways 727 flight to Saigon by hiding inside the wheel wells. The legs of one who did not survive dangle from a landing-gear door.

national reporter Paul Vogle, a passenger on the flight.

Daly and the reporter positioned themselves at the bottom of the passenger ramp to face the crowd, but at the forefront raced the tough volunteers of the 1st Division's *Hac Bao* (Black Panther) strike company. They had made it through the debacle at Hue and were now determined to survive the evacuation of Da Nang. Before Daly and Vogle managed to fight their way back on board and signal the crew to take off, 270 Vietnamese had jammed themselves into the cabin. Except for two women and a baby all were soldiers.

"As we started rolling insanity gripped those who had lost their chance," Vogle wrote. "Government troops opened fire at us. Somebody lobbed a hand grenade toward the wing. The explosion jammed the extended flaps." Noticing that army trucks had blocked the main runways, the pilot gunned the aircraft into the air from the short taxi strip. As the 727 took off, observers in the other aircraft could see people hanging from its undercarriage and wheel wells. Because the aircraft wheels were not retracted during the flight, several of them survived the trip and miraculously walked away from the aircraft after landing in Saigon.

It is lost

General Tan's North Vietnamese regulars entered Da Nang Easter morning, March 30, but stayed in the outskirts far from the anarchy that gripped the city docks. By slowing their advance, they gave the madness that gripped the populace a chance to burn itself out. It also allowed the last Americans to escape. It is probable that the Communists did not want to have to deal with the capture of large numbers of foreign nationals and the resulting political complications. Why should they risk giving the U.S. a reason to intervene by stopping the evacuation of Americans and their South Vietnamese associates? Perhaps the NVA also sought to avoid unnecessary casualties when I Corps was rapidly disintegrating by itself. Whatever their motivation, the Communists held back and allowed the frenzied evacuation to continue as an international flotilla of Japanese, Vietnamese, Chinese, and American ships gathered to pick up thousands who found some way to reach the deep-water anchorage off Da Nang.

On board the flagship of the South Vietnamese evacuation fleet, the powerful naval radios once again put General Truong within reach of President Thieu's messages from Saigon. Thieu apparently had no idea of Da Nang's fall since Truong's decision to evacuate came only after communications at I Corps had been destroyed. As navy Captain Nguyen Xuan Son and other senior South Vietnamese officers watched the final agony of those abandoned and bombarded on the beaches of Da Nang, he noted that Truong began "receiving messages from the president ordering that we hold Danang at all costs." One of the staff speculated that "either Saigon was completely in

the dark or the message was just for the historical record." Before nightfall, however, Saigon had accepted the truth; Deputy Premier Phan Quang Dan called for a meeting of newsmen in the capital to say the battle for Military Region 1 was over. "It is lost," he said. "The Communists have taken Danang."

Just a few miles out to sea from the lost city, E. G. Hey was back, this time aboard the *Pioneer Commander*. He had returned after seeing ashore the first loads of refugees at Cam Ranh Bay, the huge American-built base selected as the collection point for many of the evacuees from the north. On Hey's first trip the Vietnamese of Da Nang had been panicky, but on this Easter Day their mood had degenerated into a murderous frenzy. As a barge jammed with refugees pulled alongside to unload, the American was staggered by the sight of perhaps 8,000 on board—twice the previous load. So great was the crush that several people fell overboard and drowned as the two vessels moved together. Soldiers made up about half of the barge population, but few retained any discipline. When the lad-

der lowered from the *Pioneer Commander*, shooting broke out as the troops intimidated and ran over the civilians in a rush to be the first aboard. Attempts to control the soldiers were futile.

By 5:30 P.M. the loading was complete. As Hey looked toward Da Nang he realized no more small boats were leaving the inner harbor and the gunfire had ceased. Flying an Air America helicopter from ship to ship, the DAO representative met with the senior Americans scattered throughout the small fleet. Anticipating that the advancing Communists might use the weapons discarded on the beach to shell the rescue vessels, they agreed that it was time to get out.

When Hey returned to the *Pioneer Commander* he was stopped by a delegation of English-speaking refugees who warned that Communist sappers were on board. The American immediately ordered guards into place to protect the engine room and navigation areas, but the warning was apparently only another manifestation of the hysteria that ruled the crowds on board.

Shortly before midnight Hey, on the boat deck amidships, glanced toward the stern of the ship and found himself witnessing an execution. A Vietnamese man, brought to the ship's rail by soldiers, was stripped, searched, and finally executed with a handgun; then the ghastly tableau was repeated with a second victim. Horrified, Hey ran to a group of English-speaking officers on the main deck who informed him the troops were executing those who had no identification cards as Communist infiltrators. When quizzed as to the likelihood of the allegations, the officers speculated that perhaps some were Communists, but others were simply robbed and then killed to eliminate them as witnesses. "Fearing for our own safety," Hey later wrote, "we did not attempt to interfere." Finally the hellish night came to an end and the ships again unloaded at Cam Ranh; left behind on the *Pioneer Commander* were twenty-five bodies.

As the ships unloaded on Monday, March 31, the last vessels floating off Da Nang, those of the Vietnamese navy, received orders to depart. As they sailed, abandoned were scores of tanks and artillery pieces, hundreds of tons of ammunition, 180 aircraft, and perhaps 70,000 regular and Territorial troops among whom the NVA already moved, sorting out the South Vietnamese marked for execution or imprisonment as well as those the NVA could use to drive the captured trucks and tanks as the Communist juggernaut turned south.

The evacuation of Da Nang capped a disaster greater than the flight from the central highlands. Of the government's four infantry divisions, four Ranger groups, armored brigade, air division, and thousands of Territorial, support, and staff troops, around 16,000 men were pulled out. Of the 2 million civilians who packed Da Nang at the end of March, only slightly more than 50,000 were evacuated in the sea lift.

However in Washington on that Monday, Defense Secretary Schlesinger, known for his lack of self-delusion, still saw hope for South Vietnam. "There would be major actions" in the next month or two, he said, but if the military can hold "there is no reason to despair."

South Vietnamese troops are sorted out by their Communist captors after the fall of Da Nang.

83

Evacuation Without End

During March of 1975, South Vietnam collapsed so rapidly that civilians fleeing before the Communists had no sooner been settled in one city than they had to be transported via sea lift to new refuges farther south. For many the journey began in the imperial city of Hue, taken by the NVA on March 25. From the port of Tan My just a few kilometers east, Vietnamese navy vessels that had been ordered to remove troops and materiel began loading distraught civilians trapped by the Communist blockade of Highway 1. The ships headed for Da Nang, eighty kilometers to the south. In the past, American bombers and long convoys loaded with fresh troops and supplies had sallied north from Da Nang to thwart the Communist advances in 1965, 1968, and 1972, but not this time. As Hue emptied out, the five provinces defended by I Corps troops began to fall to the Communists in rapid succession.

As NVA forces close in on Hue in March 1975, a South Vietnamese naval vessel steams to Da Nang with a cargo of civilians and soldiers.

At Da Nang

Refugees from Hue began arriving at Da Nang on March 23. Over a decade before, U.S. Marines had first waded ashore on a beach near the city. Now Da Nang was swollen with terrified families, lost children, and dying hopes. Hundreds of thousands crowded into the city from the surrounding provinces, and soldiers from shattered units wandered the streets aimlessly, no longer concerned with defending their homeland. Remarked one 1st Division major who had fled Hue on a sampan: "I don't even know where my wife and children are. Why should I care about my division command?"

Above. *A landing craft arrives in Da Nang with refugees from Hue on March 24.*

Left. *A South Vietnamese marine comforts his wife aboard a ship near Da Nang.*

Right. *Human "cargo" is unloaded at Da Nang, March 24.*

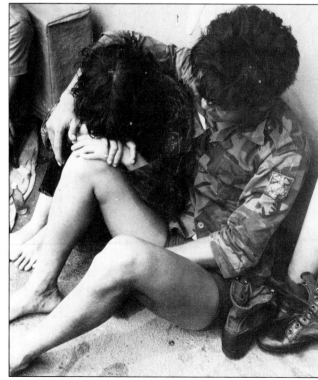

Da Nang proved no safer than Hue, as South Vietnamese troops were ordered to abandon the city in late March. Here, leaving their military equipment on the beach, ARVN soldiers paddle out through the surf on inflated inner tubes in a desperate effort to reach waiting landing craft on March 31, 1975. Eventually 1,000 men of the 3d Infantry Division and two brigades of marines boarded the last boats from Da Nang.

No safe haven

On the thirtieth, Communist troops entered Da Nang virtually unchallenged as the South Vietnamese troops pulled out. Civilians again boarded evacuation ships—freighters and LSTs with inadequate toilet facilities, no food, and little water—and endured yet another journey, this one to the southern sanctuaries of Cam Ranh Bay, Vung Tau, and Phu Quoc Island. Among the 90,000 refugees, approximately 16,000 were I Corps soldiers evacuated from the beaches at Da Nang, the ragged remainder of a force that had once been nearly ten times that size.

Above. *On April 6 a Vietnamese child, one of the thousands fleeing the Communist advance, is lowered onto the LST Booheung Pioneer.* Right. *Refugees in a tub float ashore at Vung Tau.*

"You Must Win"

On March 31, as regular soldiers of the North Vietnamese 2d Army Corps swept through the streets of Da Nang attempting to restore order, a "flash telegram" from Hanoi arrived at General Dung's headquarters in the central highlands. Signed by Le Duan, first secretary of the Lao Dong (Workers') party, the communiqué brought final confirmation of a "historic decision" reached by the North Vietnamese Politburo six days before. Emboldened by the unanticipated swiftness of ARVN's collapse in the highlands and Military Region 1, but also aware that less than two months remained before the onset of the summer monsoons, the North Vietnamese leadership had resolved to seize the "once-in-a-thousand years" opportunity that lay before them and "liberate Saigon before the rainy season." The two-year plan outlined the preceding fall had been abandoned. The "reunification of the Fatherland" was to be accomplished in 1975—not through negotiation, but by force of arms.

Although Dung, as a member of the Politburo, had endorsed that decision, as the field commander for all North Vietnamese forces in the South he discerned "two major, nearly contradictory characteristics" in Hanoi's new plan. On the one hand, there was "the need to prepare a strong, multifaced force" capable of coordinating attacks on a scale unprecedented for the Vietnamese Communists. This, Dung calculated, would require "a relatively long period of time to achieve good results" since the South Vietnamese, with their forces now concentrated into a much smaller area, could be expected to fight more tenaciously than they had in the earlier stages of the current campaign. On the other hand, there was "the extreme urgency of the new strategic opportunity," an urgency emphatically underscored by the latest missive from Hanoi. The "final decisive battle for our army and people," it declared, must be carried out "at the earliest time—best of all in April. It must not be postponed."

In accordance with long-standing revolutionary military doctrine, which called for the patient, methodical preparation of the battlefield prior to launching an attack, Dung had requested the support of two additional divisions from North Vietnam as well as permission to consolidate the conquest of Military Region 2 before turning south. The Politburo promptly acceded to the first request, dispatching the 338th and 312th Divisions of the 1st Army Corps from Ninh Binh Province on March 25. But after initially granting Dung "a few days" to carry through his blitzkrieg to the coast, his comrades in Hanoi decided they would delay no longer. At last embracing the plan that General Tra had advocated from the outset, the Politburo ordered Dung on March 31 to commit all available units and resources under his command to the southern front. Dung himself was to proceed at once to the regional military base camp near Loc Ninh where he would be joined by COSVN Chairman Pham Hung and 4th Army Corps Commander General Tran Van Tra. All three were to await the arrival of "Brother Sau," the code name for no less prominent an emissary than Le Duc Tho, who would apprise them in person and in detail of the Politburo's plans.

The first days of April thus brought a sudden and ominous shift in the disposition of North Vietnamese forces, as unit commanders moved to comply with the new campaign slogan: "Lightning speed, daring, surprise, certain victory." Leading the way were three of the four divisions that had participated in the highlands campaign, now organized into the 3d Army Corps. The 316th Division was the first to set out, advancing along Route 14 toward Saigon from the northwest. The 320th Division, after seizing Tuy Hoa on April 1, was ordered to turn back and retrace its march along Route 7B and then move in from the north.

In the meantime the 10th Division would proceed with its scheduled attacks on Nha Trang and Cam Ranh, then swing westward along Interprovincial Route 2 to Route 20, closing in on the capital from the northeast. Behind these units the 968th and 3d Divisions, followed by the three divisions of the 2d Army Corps, would push down coastal Route 1 and eventually take positions on the eastern front. Further reinforcements were to be provided by the reserve divisions of the 1st Army Corps, which had already completed the first leg of a high-speed motorized advance that would carry them more than 1,700 kilometers in less than a month.

To expedite the movement of men and supplies, "all military zones, all local areas, and all levels of government" were ordered to give first priority to the needs of the southern battlefront. In Hanoi the printing presses of the General Staff map service began stamping out thousands of maps of the Saigon-Gia Dinh area, while in some of the "liberated" provinces of the South, captured ARVN soldiers were impressed into service as drivers and repairmen. By the middle of the first week of April long convoys of trucks, armored personnel carriers, tanks, and artillery pieces were running bumper to bumper, day and night, along the major thoroughfares of the coast and the highlands, snaking their way southward toward Saigon. Helicopters, transport planes, and even some passenger planes were also mobilized to convey troops and munitions in and out of the captured airfields at Da Nang, Phu Bai, and Kontum, while heavier equipment and thousands of tons of rations were moved by sea to Da Nang and Qui Nhon.

Sensing that they were about to participate in the "final decisive battle" of the Vietnam War, the NVA troops enjoyed especially high morale. "The number of our soldiers who sacrificed their lives or were wounded was very small, compared to the victories we had gained," General Dung explained, "and we had expended little in weapons and munitions." The South Vietnamese, on the other hand, were "confused and vacillating," while "the United States appeared completely impotent." Such was Dung's assessment of the strategic situation on the eve of the campaign to "liberate" Saigon as he left the highlands for his rendezvous at Loc Ninh with "Brother Sau."

The Weyand mission

The North Vietnamese were not the only ones reconsidering their options in late March and early April. Stunned by the rapid loss of the northern provinces, hamstrung by the constraints of the War Powers Act, and still unable to gain Congressional approval of its $300 million supplemental aid bill, the Ford administration undertook its own reappraisal of South Vietnam's dwindling capabilities. As Congress adjourned for its Easter recess and he prepared to take a golfing vacation at Palm Springs, President Ford

---

Preceding page. Bo doi of the NVA 2d Army Corps roll into Da Nang on March 31.

dispatched Army Chief of Staff and former COMUSMACV General Frederick C. Weyand to Vietnam to examine the situation firsthand and recommend alternative courses of action.

Accompanied by Ambassador Martin, who had returned to the U.S. several weeks before to lobby Congress for additional aid, Weyand arrived in Saigon on March 27 and immediately began interviewing high-ranking American and South Vietnamese officials about the overall balance of military forces. What he learned was hardly encouraging. According to CIA estimates, 150,000 South Vietnamese troops and militia in the northern half of the country had been dispersed, abandoned, or annihilated. Of the ground combat forces deployed in MR 1, three Ranger groups, the entire 1st Division, two-thirds of the 2d and 3d Divisions, and one-third of the Marine Division had ceased to exist. In MR 2, the bulk of the 23d Division and five Ranger groups had been decimated, along with two of the four regiments that made up the 22d Division. Twelve provinces and almost $1 billion worth of equipment, including some 400 planes and helicopters, had fallen under Communist control. Moreover, the entire GVN intelligence apparatus in the north had been obliterated, making it nearly impossible to monitor the movement of North Vietnamese forces.

The defense of what remained of South Vietnam thus rested with the various ground and air units organic to Military Regions 3 and 4, the three Airborne brigades previously withdrawn from MR 1, and whatever forces might be reconstituted from the 40,000 regular and irregular troops extracted from the northern provinces. The three divisions assigned to MR 3, however, were already locked in heavy combat north of the capital, while the three divisions in MR 4 were fully committed to the defense of Route 4, the vital artery linking Saigon to the rice-rich delta. With one Airborne brigade similarly tied down by enemy forces northwest of Nha Trang, the need for additional mobile reserves was acute.

Yet as Weyand soon discovered, the South Vietnamese Joint General Staff had done virtually nothing prior to his arrival to reorganize and reequip the troops that had straggled back to the south. No one, in fact, seemed to know just which units had survived, where they were located, or what equipment they needed in order to become combat-ready. At the insistence of the DAO, the RVNAF Central Logistics Command finally came forth with a reconstitution plan on March 27. But this initial scheme was quickly rejected by the Americans as unrealistic, if not wholly preposterous. Not only did it assume Congressional approval of a huge supplemental aid appropriation, but it included no timetable for the activation of new units prior to June 15 or any concept of how these units might be deployed.

When further efforts to goad the JGS into action failed, Major General Homer Smith, the U.S. Defense Attaché,

decided to take matters into his own hands. Actively assuming an advisory role for the first time since the signing of the Paris agreement, he ordered the Operations and Plans Division of the DAO to draft its own blueprint with the nominal assistance of a few South Vietnamese logisticians and training commanders. Based upon a "building block concept of battalion-sized units," the American proposal called for the gradual reconstitution of ARVN's forces in four phases. First, and most important, materiel already in Vietnam or on its way from the U.S. was to be used to reequip eighteen infantry battalions and three artillery batteries, the first to be deployed on April 12 and the last no later than April 19. In the subsequent three phases, four fresh infantry divisions, four Ranger divisions, and twenty-seven RF regiments were to be formed between May 20 and September 30, pending the successful defense of MR 3 and 4 and an influx of additional aid from the United States.

Although the South Vietnamese military command formally approved the DAO plan on April 1, in practice they ignored one of its central provisions. Rather than integrating newly formed battalions into existing combat divisions, as the Americans had strongly recommended, the JGS decided to resurrect in full several of the regiments and brigades that had been shattered in the north. Understaffed and in some cases severely understrength, these independent units were then hastily redeployed to the battlefield, where some—like the reconstituted 4th Infantry Regiment of the 2d ARVN Division—had the unfortunate distinction of being defeated a second time by the NVA.

The ineffectiveness of the JGS in the face of the mounting Communist threat found its analogue, and to a large extent its source, in the curious silence that emanated from the presidential palace in late March. Ever since his public avowal to defend the city of Hue "to the last," President Thieu had become more isolated and detached than ever. In response to popular calls for his resignation and widespread rumors of an impending coup, he continued his crackdown on the press, arrested a few alleged "plotters," and promised to form a new "fighting cabinet." But he made no effort to rally the nation behind him or to provide any real leadership to the government and armed forces. Within the GVN bureaucracy, one American journalist reported, "officials either stopped working altogether or kept mindlessly issuing routine instructions that could not be carried out," such as the reprimands sent to civil servants who had abandoned their posts in territories now occupied by Communist forces. "The President had all the power in his hands and could easily impose his policy," recalled Bui Diem, former South Vietnamese ambassador to the U.S., "but somehow there was no sense of purpose or direction among the high officials of the government" or "strangely enough . . . any sense of urgency about the situation." Instead Thieu clung to the hope that somehow, in some way, the Americans would come to his rescue.

In a series of meetings with General Weyand, the South Vietnamese president repeatedly stressed the need for additional American support. Eschewing any personal responsibility for the calamity that had befallen his country and accusing the United States of preparing to "sell out" the South Vietnamese, Thieu at one point brandished President Nixon's letter of November 1972 promising "swift and severe retaliatory action" if the North Vietnamese violated the terms of the Paris agreement. When told by Weyand that any direct reintervention was highly unlikely, he continued to press for a massive commitment of new equipment and supplies. To drive the point home, he broke his self-imposed silence and went on national television to explain that the fall of the north was the result of "weak American assistance." Dozens of banners posted around Saigon proclaimed the same message in English: "THE PEOPLE AND ARMY OF SOUTH VIETNAM ARE NOT LACKING IN COMBAT SPIRIT, BUT ONLY NEED THE MEANS FOR COMBAT."

President Thieu was not alone in his contention that supplemental aid held the key to South Vietnam's survival. Ambassador Martin and General Weyand also believed that a "lack of bullets and fuel" was the single most important cause of ARVN's collapse in the north and therefore that a fresh infusion of "basic military necessities" might well reverse their fortunes on the battlefield. Although Martin was privately doubtful that an "adequate" level of aid would be approved by Congress, both men publicly maintained that a reaffirmation of U.S. support would have an immediate impact on the South Vietnamese armed forces. Not only would it provide a desperately needed boost in morale to ARVN's beleaguered troops, but it would also furnish the means for rebuilding the reserve units required to shore up Saigon's vastly shortened defense line. If the RVNAF could only hold off the NVA until the arrival of the monsoons—roughly six weeks away— Martin and Weyand reasoned there was a chance that an independent, albeit truncated, South Vietnam might still be salvaged from the wreckage of the current military campaign.

Other American officials were not so optimistic. In fact, on two separate occasions DAO intelligence chief Colonel William Le Gro flatly told General Weyand that it was "already too late" for aid alone to make a difference. In Le Gro's view, the only way to stop the NVA juggernaut was to send in U.S. warplanes, and even then there could be no guarantee of success. Not only were the North Vietnamese in the process of heavily reinforcing their ground units in MR 3, but there were reported sightings of cigar-shaped SA-2 antiaircraft missiles moving into Phuoc Long Province northwest of Saigon. Without additional "mate-

SA-2 antiaircraft missiles travel south along Highway 1 near Da Nang in April as the Communists prepare to defend their newly won territory against possible air strikes.

rial and political support" *and* "the application of US strategic airpower," Le Gro predicted in his written summary of March 31, "defeat is all but certain within 90 days." Two days later CIA Director William Colby offered a similarly grim prognosis. "The balance of forces in South Vietnam has now shifted decisively in the Communists' favor," he told members of the Washington Special Action Group. "The process of demoralization and defeatism already under way could prove irreversible and lead quickly to the collapse of the GVN and its will to resist."

The fall of Nha Trang

Colby arrived at that judgment shortly after learning of the abandonment of Nha Trang, coastal capital of Khanh Hoa Province and the northernmost point along ARVN's latest defense line. Triggered by the fall of Qui Nhon the night before, the disintegration of Nha Trang began on the morning of April 1 with the unilateral decision of the local province chief to close down all government offices. Upon learning that the municipal bureaucracy, including the police, had ceased to function, General Phu panicked. Without notifying anyone, he bolted out of his office in the newly established MR 2 headquarters compound, climbed aboard his private helicopter, and screamed at the pilot to "Get Out!" The American contingent in Nha Trang quickly followed. Shortly before noon, as news of Phu's departure flashed across the city and crowds of Vietnamese began to gather outside the front gate of the U.S. consulate, MR 2 Consul General Moncrieff Spear ordered the immediate evacuation of all consulate personnel. Soon Air America Huey helicopters were landing in the consulate parking lot every five minutes, ferrying up to twenty passengers at a time to the main airfield on the edge of town, where they were transferred to transport planes bound for Saigon. In the meantime a number of American officials set out in search of local Vietnamese who had worked for them and to whom they had promised escape.

By midafternoon the entire city had dissolved into chaos. "It was Danang all over again," wrote journalist Arnold Isaacs, "if on a smaller scale." Armed men roamed the streets, exacting money and food at gun point, while other soldiers and refugees swarmed the airfield seeking a way out. At the consulate marine guards used rifle butts and fists to fend off the throngs, now swollen into the thousands, attempting to crash the main gate and scale the cyclone fence surrounding the American compound. Other local residents rushed toward the beach front, where they crammed aboard fishing boats destined for Cam Ranh Bay and other points south.

Although consular officials tried to make sure that all Americans, "third country nationals," and Vietnamese employees of U.S. agencies were evacuated, amid the panic and confusion more than 100 consular employees were left behind. So were several boxes of classified American documents, including those identifying local intelligence operatives. Some Americans stationed in Nha Trang later blamed Consul General Spear for these failings, pointing to the lack of contingency planning that preceded the abrupt U.S. pullout. But there were other factors at work as well. In recent days Spear had been strongly encouraged by embassy officials in Saigon to project an image of confidence in ARVN and avoid any activities that might signal an imminent American withdrawal. That message had been further reinforced by a visit from General Weyand, who used the occasion to assure accompanying U.S. reporters that the South Vietnamese, far from being "demoralized in any sense of the word," were "giving a fine performance." Yet after General Phu abandoned his post and local ARVN troops began rioting, Spear came under equally intense embassy pressure to complete the airlift as soon as possible. When the final order came from ambassadorial special assistant George Jacobson around 5:30 P.M. to "Get the hell out of the city now, you and the rest of the Americans," the emphasis was unmistakable. What was important to the embassy was that the Americans got out, regardless of what happened to Vietnamese who had placed their trust in the United States government.

What made the chaotic evacuation of Nha Trang doubly tragic was that it was unnecessary. Unaware that Hanoi had already committed itself to "total victory," and unable to track the movement of enemy units with any precision, neither the South Vietnamese nor the Americans realized that General Dung had begun to divert his main forces away from the coast toward more vital targets in the south. Although there were reports of some fighting forty-eight kilometers west of the city, on April 1 the Communists posed no direct threat to Nha Trang. "There was no attack on the city," said one of the last ARVN officers to leave. "There was not a Vietcong anywhere to be seen." Not until April 5 did Communist troops actually occupy the abandoned city and declare its "liberation."

In rapid succession and in similar fashion, other major cities in MR 2 also fell to the Communists during the first week of April. Cam Ranh Bay, the former site of the principal American logistics installation in South Vietnam and at the time a relocation center for tens of thousands of civilian refugees and ARVN stragglers, fell without a fight on April 3 as elements of the 10th NVA Division closed in. The following day the citizens of Da Lat invited Communist troops into the mountain resort town to put an end to rampant looting by ARVN soldiers. In addition to ceding large new chunks of territory to the enemy, the South Vietnamese were forced to destroy all the heavy equipment that had been ferried to Cam Ranh from the north and, in Da Lat, to leave behind a small nuclear reactor that had been built by the Americans in the mid-1960s. Shortly be-

On April 1, montagnards stand in Nha Trang's harbor, hoping to board boats to Saigon. Some waited for days in vain.

fore the Communists entered Da Lat, however, a special American team from the U.S. Atomic Energy Commission swept in and extracted the reactor's radioactive rods, thus rendering the facility inoperative.

Thieu under fire

In the South Vietnamese capital, news of the latest territorial losses raised the level of tension to the brink of panic. Every day hundreds of Saigonese converged on the banks to withdraw their money, exacerbating a downward trend that saw the piaster lose 80 percent of its value during the first few days of April. Others, anxious to communicate with relatives in the threatened provinces, crowded into the central post office, where each morning a large blackboard listed the cities for which telegrams were no longer being accepted. "It is like an avalanche," exclaimed one distraught civil servant as yet another provincial capital was chalked up on the board. Rumors—of an imminent coup, of a secret deal between Hanoi and Washington, of American rescue as well as an American pullout—abounded, while protest against the Thieu government steadily mounted.

On April 2, one day after the fall of Nha Trang, the South Vietnamese Senate passed a resolution accusing Thieu of "abuse of power, corruption, and social injustice" and calling for the formation of a new "government of national union." Although in the past the Senate had functioned as little more than a legislative rubber stamp for the president, forty of forty-one senators endorsed the measure, including many long-standing Thieu allies. Two days later the influential archbishop of Saigon, Nguyen Van Binh, issued a demand for Thieu's resignation, saying that "everyone urgently wishes an orderly change." Father Tran Huu Thanh went a step further. At a street rally that same day where more than 100 demonstrators clashed with police, the self-appointed leader of the Anti-Corruption Movement declared that "we are going to push for [Thieu's] ouster in a military coup." More insidiously, former Premier Ky echoed the archbishop's call for the president to step down voluntarily but privately, and unsuccessfully, tried to organize a military overthrow.

President Thieu reacted to the escalating attacks in characteristic fashion. On April 3 he ordered army censors to confiscate all copies of the daily newspaper *Chinh Luan* because of an editorial blaming "dishonest leadership" for the loss of the northern half of the country. He also announced the arrest of another group of "conspirators," including one of Ky's aides and his own former chief political adviser, Nguyen Van Ngan. Another series of directives moved the evening curfew from 10:00 P.M. to 9:00 P.M., tightened restrictions on public gatherings, and authorized local police to "shoot and kill on the spot those violators who try to resist or flee."

The following day, the South Vietnamese president attempted to shore up his crumbling base of support in the legislature by replacing Prime Minister Tran Thien Khiem, whom Thieu suspected of complicity in the most recent coup plot, with National Assembly Speaker Nguyen Ba Can. In a televised speech Thieu told his countrymen that Can had been asked to form a new "government of war and national union" dedicated to the defense of South Vietnam's remaining territory. Tran Van Don, the incumbent deputy prime minister, was later named as the

The pier at Nha Trang is littered with corpses, victims of the crush to escape. In the background a barge loaded with refugees stops for water on its way from Da Nang to Saigon.

new defense minister-designate. Filling the other positions in the Can cabinet proved more difficult, however, since many prominent politicians refused to serve under Thieu unless he agreed to relinquish some of his power. As a result, ten days passed before the new premier presented a full cabinet to the president. During the interim, South Vietnam in its hour of ultimate crisis was, in effect, without a working government.

As Thieu maneuvered to keep his domestic political opponents at bay, he also came under increased pressure from the Americans to do something to stabilize the steadily deteriorating military situation. Aware of the growing popular perception in the U.S. that the South Vietnamese armed forces had lost the will to fight, American officials realized that any hope of additional U.S. support now depended upon a strong show of resistance on the part of ARVN. At a meeting with the South Vietnamese president on April 2, General Weyand suggested that the South Vietnamese draw a new defense line, anchored at Tay Ninh in the west and running through the garrison town of Xuan Loc to Phan Rang on the coast. Although both the Americans and the South Vietnamese still expected the main Communist thrust to come at Tay Ninh, the strategic as well as geographic centerpiece of the proposed plan was Xuan Loc. Situated just north of the intersection of Routes 1 and 2, and just east of the intersection of Routes 1

and 20, the capital of Long Khanh Province controlled the principal eastern gateway to Saigon as well as the most direct route to Bien Hoa Air Base, where 60 percent of ARVN's remaining ammunition was stored. The successful defense of Xuan Loc by the 18th ARVN Division, which had its headquarters inside the town, was thus vital to South Vietnam's survival.

After hearing Weyand out, Thieu promptly accepted the plan and ordered General Toan, the MR 3 commander, to make the necessary preparations. Toan in turn directed his old friend Lt. General Nguyen Vinh Nghi, the former MR 4 commander who had been sacked for corruption the previous fall, to establish a new forward headquarters at Phan Rang with a brigade of the Airborne Division. He also deployed an armored brigade and several Ranger units to reinforce the 18th Division at Xuan Loc. In the meantime President Thieu made another plea to the Americans for B-52 air strikes but was again turned down. Deputy Assistant Secretary of Defense Erich Von Marbod, a member of the Weyand party, nevertheless promised that 15,000-pound "Daisy Cutter" and CBU fuel bombs would be made available to the VNAF for use against enemy troop concentrations.

Prospects for a negotiated settlement

While many American officials in Saigon doubted that the RVNAF would be any more successful in holding the new defense line than they had the old ones, some believed that there was still a possibility that the Communists might agree to a negotiated political settlement. Among those particularly enticed by this prospect was the CIA station chief, Thomas Polgar. Although convinced that the North Vietnamese could not be stopped militarily if they chose to blast their way into Saigon, Polgar also calculated that it was in Hanoi's own best interests to achieve their ends bloodlessly rather than by force. In the first place, he reasoned, a negotiated victory in the form of a Communist-dominated coalition government would be easier for the DRV to justify to its supporters abroad, including the détente-minded Soviets. Moreover, on more practical grounds Polgar doubted that the North Vietnamese had enough trained political cadres to administer the entire South immediately.

At the time a variety of evidence seemed to support such speculation. Hints dropped privately by two members of the Hungarian ICCS delegation that neither Moscow nor Hanoi sought to humiliate the Americans encouraged Polgar's hopes despite contradictory intelligence indicating that the NVA was preparing to "go-for-broke." Yet there were other, more public, signals as well. On March 31 the Provisional Revolutionary Government announced over Liberation Radio that it was prepared to engage in talks with the GVN but only on the condition that the "traitor Thieu" first be removed from power. Two days

later the PRG foreign minister, Madame Nguyen Thi Binh, issued a similar statement in Algiers, reportedly naming General Duong Van Minh as the one man with whom the Communists would be willing to negotiate. Deputy Prime Minister Tran Van Don later disclosed that the same offer was secretly communicated to him when he toured abroad to drum up support for the South Vietnamese cause. Stopping in London on April 1 en route back to Saigon, Don learned that French Prime Minister Jacques Chirac had some "very important information" to convey to him. According to this "most reliable source," as Don put it, Chirac wanted him to know that "the three superpowers have agreed to the reunification of the two Vietnams under Hanoi's control." There was, however, one stipulation: Any political deal with Hanoi would have to be consummated within eight days.

Whether there was any substance to the alleged "eight-day ultimatum," or to any of the other hints at the possibility of negotiated settlement in early April, remains a matter of conjecture. According to one interpretation, all were part of an elaborate ruse orchestrated by Hanoi to undermine Thieu and keep the GVN off balance as its forces moved into position for the final assault on Saigon. But others, including Ambassador Martin, have speculated that the PRG actually wanted a political solution in order to avoid total postwar domination by the North Vietnamese. Similar questions surround the roles played by the Hungarians and the French. As Martin later pointed out to members of the House International Relations Committee, even in retrospect it was difficult to know whether the Hungarians in Saigon were trying to be "helpful" but "operating hopelessly behind the curve of events" or deliberately "trying to provide a deception center" for their allies in Hanoi. While the French were clearly not acting in league with the Communists, it is quite possible that they were being used by them to "disinform" the Americans and the South Vietnamese.

However obscure the motives involved, the effects of the so-called peace gambit were immediate and profound. The PRG demand for Thieu's ouster as a precondition for any talks provided the president's domestic opposition with yet another lever to use against him and, at the same time, led some U.S. officials, notably Polgar, to conclude that Thieu had become a liability. Expressing his conviction that Hanoi would "move to the very brink of military victory . . . and then call for negotiations," Polgar sent a cable to Washington on April 2 suggesting that if Thieu were not removed from power, the GVN would fall within "the next few months." In the meantime the French, working through the agency of their ambassador to South Vietnam, Jean-Marie Merillon, began actively promoting General Minh as Thieu's heir apparent.

Minh's emergence as the leading candidate to replace Thieu was in some respects surprising. A member of the triumvirate that deposed President Diem in 1963 and once a favorite of the Americans, who dubbed him "Big" Minh in recognition of his comparatively tall (five-foot-eleven-inch) stature, he had later been swept aside by younger generals and forced into retirement. In recent years he had taken up a position on the periphery of South Vietnamese political life, espousing a self-styled "neutralism" that allowed him to criticize the Thieu regime without being branded a Communist. But he gained few disciples, and the Americans continued to ignore him. Although generally regarded as an honest and courageous soldier, he had a reputation for crippling indecisiveness and for stating his views in unintelligibly ambiguous terms. "He was," wrote one foreign observer, "the opposite of an intellectual: a man without ideas, without visions." Or as one Vietnamese put it: "His greatest quality is his height."

For all his failings, however, Minh was well positioned to challenge Thieu. What he represented, according to Italian journalist Tiziano Terzani, was "an equivocation, but an equivocation acceptable to everyone." To the Communists, whether they were seriously interested in negotiations or not, Minh's distance from the actual centers of power in Saigon made him especially credible as a figure they might be willing to live with. To the French, he seemed the most convenient vehicle for realizing their plan for a new coalition government ruling over what had formerly been Cochin China. To the Americans, he offered a means of putting additional pressure on Thieu to moderate governmental policies and take stronger military action. And to the so-called Third Force, the disorganized and largely leaderless collection of groups dissatisfied with both Thieu and the Communists, he provided a potential "neutralist" rallying point.

For his part, Minh did all he could to encourage the belief that he was the one man capable of saving South Vietnam. In addition to cultivating the sponsorship of the French, he opened contacts with the head of the National Liberation Front and the president of the PRG, taking advantage of his own brother's status as a high-ranking PRG official to sound out the other side. He also met secretly with Tran Van Don and outgoing Premier Khiem, the two men who had joined him in staging the 1963 coup. Personally convinced that the PRG was more southern than Communist, he tried to persuade his old comrades in arms that its leaders preferred to share power with Saigon "neutralists" in a coalition government rather than accept a unified Vietnam dominated by Hanoi. But before any concrete steps could be taken in that direction, Thieu would have to go.

Thieu, of course, had no intention of going anywhere. As he repeatedly told American officials and publicly vowed to the South Vietnamese people, he would not resign, he would not relinquish any of his power, and he would not even talk to the enemy. When apprised by Don of the ostensible "eight-day ultimatum," Thieu made it clear to his deputy prime minister that he thought the

French were lying. He made no attempt, however, to crush Minh's bid for power, chiefly because he regarded his new rival as a wholly ineffectual pretender: a general without troops and a politician without any popular support. Perhaps more to the point, Thieu knew that Minh could pose no real threat to him unless he gained the backing of the Americans. And at least for the time being, he had no indication that that was going to happen.

Drawing down

Of all Thieu's American supporters, none was more steadfast, or more influential, than Graham Martin. Not only did Martin regard Thieu as the most able leader available, but he was also, he said later, determined that "the U.S. should not repeat the appalling blunder it had made in participating in the violent overthrow of President Diem a decade before." Moreover, he feared that any extra-constitutional change of government might set off the same kind of mass panic that had consumed Da Nang and Nha Trang, precipitating the collapse of the GVN and endangering the lives of the 5,000 to 6,000 Americans still in South Vietnam. Martin therefore worked behind the scenes to forestall any coup attempts, particularly by Ky and his clique, and closely monitored French efforts to work out a negotiated settlement. Although doubtful that a political solution was in the offing, he was intrigued enough by the possibility to allow a door to be cut in the wall separating the adjacent French and American embassies and a bug-proof telephone line installed between his own office and that of Ambassador Merillon.

In the opinion of many other Americans in Saigon, however, Martin's continuing loyalty to Thieu was as misplaced as it was futile. As more than a dozen NVA divisions bore down on the capital and political discontent neared the flash point, they believed that the ambassador's time and efforts would be better spent preparing for a full-scale evacuation. Like every American diplomatic mission around the world, the U.S. Embassy in Saigon had a standing evacuation plan spelling out various options for action in the event of an emergency. Code-named "Talon Vise" (and later "Frequent Wind"), that plan had been updated in late February after the onset of the North Vietnamese offensive. But it was still based on a series of assumptions and contingencies that no longer applied after the fall of Da Nang. It assumed, for instance, that conditions in Saigon would remain relatively peaceful and local authorities cooperative. It addressed only the evacuation of U.S. citizens and "third country nationals," set a limit of 8,000 people, and thus made no allowance for the extraction of Vietnamese nationals. And three of the four options it outlined relied on the use of fixed-wing aircraft and/or naval transport ships to move people out over an extended period of time. Only Option IV, following a "worst case" scenario, envisioned the need for helicopters and a ground security force under hostile conditions. "The embassy's plan," recalled Lieutenant Colonel (then Captain) Stuart Herrington, a U.S. representative to the Joint Military Team, "was an accident waiting to happen—a sure prescription for failure."

"What Captain Herrington did not know," Ambassador Martin later maintained, "was that USSAG [the United States Support Activities Group based in Thailand] … had full detailed plans in case military assets would be needed in any possible future evacuation." Martin noted that he had initially reviewed the plan in the fall of 1973 and knew that "it was being constantly updated." On his return to Saigon with the Weyand party, he designated General Smith, the defense attaché, to integrate the standing embassy plan with the USSAG plan. In addition, the ambassador arranged to borrow Rear Admiral Hugh Benton from CINCPAC to ensure that local planning was fully coordinated with whatever assets the Pacific forces could make available.

On April 1, the day that Benton arrived, General Smith established a Special Planning Group at the Defense Attaché Office to review "all evacuation options" and coordinate preparations for the systematic "drawdown" of DAO personnel. As a first step, he ordered the new team to establish an Evacuation Control Center at the DAO annex adjacent to Tan Son Nhut airfield and to equip it with enough food, water, medicine, and fuel to support 1,500 people for five days. Other officers were assigned a more bitter task: rigging the DAO headquarters compound for demolition should the worst come to pass. "I'll be damned if I'm going to leave it for the bastards," Smith declared.

During the next few days DAO staffers scurried to make the new processing center fully operational on a twenty-four-hour basis. Stacks of C rations were moved in, additional bunkers and latrines built, auxiliary generators put in place, and extra telephone lines installed. As an added precaution, a bulldozer and several other pieces of heavy equipment were brought in to clear landing zones in the event of an emergency evacuation. In the meantime Colonel Le Gro and his intelligence staff drew up preliminary lists of "non-essential" DAO personnel and "sensitive" Vietnamese whose past or present association with the Americans made them likely targets for Communist retribution. Other DAO officials worked in conjunction with representatives from the CIA and USIA to compile a "density plot" of the U.S. population in Saigon. Using a variety of techniques, including the examination of liquor-ration files at the commissary and the membership list of Le Cercle Sportif, the Saigon sports club, within three days the officials succeeded in identifying and locating more than 6,000 American citizens still residing in the South Vietnamese capital.

To begin the process of "thinning out" the DAO community, Smith cabled Admiral Noel Gayler, the commander in chief, Pacific, requesting authorization to accelerate routine personnel cuts slated for June. Gayler promptly agreed. So did Ambassador Martin, who concurred with Smith that the removal of these "non-essentials" could be presented to the South Vietnamese as an economy measure designed to release funds for the GVN's war effort. In granting his approval, however, Martin stipulated that all departures must be strictly voluntary. Not only did he lack the authority to order U.S. citizens out of the country, he pointed out, but he feared that any visible sign of a U.S. pullout might result in a violent backlash against the Americans still in Saigon. To underscore his point, the ambassador released "an unusual public statement," as New York Times correspondent Fox Butterfield described it, affirming that "the embassy has not ordered or suggested the evacuation of its American personnel."

A tangle of South Vietnamese emigration restrictions and U.S. immigration rules further complicated the "drawdown" plan. Many of the "non-essential" Americans slated for evacuation, including several thousand contract workers and army retirees drawing salaries from the DAO, refused to leave unless accompanied by their Vietnamese families, girlfriends, or common-law wives. Yet according to South Vietnamese law, no citizen of the RVN could depart without a passport and an exit visa, documents that typically took six months and hundreds of dollars in bribes to obtain. Moreover, any Vietnamese wishing to enter the U.S., even if directly related to an American citizen, required a special dispensation, usually in the form of a "parole," from the Immigration and Naturalization Service.

"Operation Babylift"

While American officials proceeded with plans to begin moving out their "non-essential" employees, World Airways President Ed Daly was at work on a small-scale evacuation scheme of his own: a proposal to airlift several thousand South Vietnamese children, some of them orphans, to the United States. When Ambassador Martin learned of the plan upon his return from Washington, he was "disturbed." He had "no interest in evacuating hundreds of Vietnamese babies," he recalled, and regarded the entire venture as but another of Daly's "publicity-seeking stunts." Yet since Daly had already gained the endorsement of some of the voluntary agencies in Saigon as well as the attention of the American press, the ambassador believed it would be more damaging to the South Vietnamese cause to cancel the airlift than to let it go on. After arranging for official U.S. transports to be used instead of World Airways planes, he wrote to the GVN's minister for refugee affairs to explain his thinking. Noting that he shared the minister's "revulsion" at the "public relations" aspects of the idea, he also pointed out that if the South Vietnamese government were now to step in and prohibit the flights it would have a profoundly negative

Operation Babylift

At Tan Son Nhut Air Base on April 4, DAO officials loaded a U.S. Air Force C-5A Galaxy, the largest transport plane in existence, with 243 South Vietnamese children and 62 adults. Thirty-seven of the adults were DAO employees, and their exodus as staff members for "Babylift" began the organized attempt to evacuate "non-essential" U.S. government personnel from Vietnam. But shortly after takeoff the plane crashed, killing most of those aboard.

Above. *The wreckage of the "Babylift" plane at Tan Son Nhut.* Left. *Passengers aboard the C-5A before takeoff.*

impact on American public opinion. On the other hand, there was a chance that the spectacle of Vietnamese children escaping to America might generate some sympathy for South Vietnam's plight on Capitol Hill. Even if that did not prove to be the case, there was still something to be gained. As General Smith quickly realized, the outgoing "orphan" flights would provide an opportunity to begin the "drawdown" of "redundant" American personnel from South Vietnam.

From the very outset a swirl of controversy surrounded "Operation Babylift," as a USAID dispatch of April 2 officially labeled the venture. Some observers voiced suspicions of the U.S. ambassador's motives. Others charged that many of the children slated for evacuation were not orphans at all but rather the dependents of well-placed South Vietnamese officials. Still others argued that the operation deflected attention away from the more crucial task of evacuating Americans and "high risk" South Vietnamese. But in the end, most were willing to concede that the plan represented a worthy first step in the right direction. At a time when many Americans, back in the U.S. as well as in Vietnam, felt increasingly helpless about the crisis in South Vietnam, it provided a welcome outlet for humanitarian action, regardless of any other purposes that may have been involved.

Operation Babylift began shortly after four o'clock on Friday afternoon, April 4, when a giant Air Force C-5A Galaxy carrying 243 children and 62 adults, 37 of them female DAO employees who had volunteered to serve as attendants, took off from Tan Son Nhut. A half-hour later it ended in tragedy. The plane was only eighteen miles out of Saigon on its way to the coast when the pilot noticed a blinking red light on his instrument panel, signaling decompression problems. He radioed the control tower at Tan Son Nhut to say that he was returning. But just as he began his descent toward the airfield, the aft pressure door exploded, damaging the aircraft's elevators and causing an immediate loss of pressure in the lower cabin. Many of the passengers who were strapped to their seats died instantly from lack of oxygen; others were sucked out of the aircraft through the open hatchway. Moments later the plane slammed into a rice field near the Saigon River and broke

President Ford in Palm Springs on April 5 with General Weyand and Secretary of State Kissinger.

apart as it skidded over a series of dikes. Some of the passengers who survived the initial crash then drowned as water rushed into the torn wreckage of the plane.

Soon Air America helicopters arrived and began shuttling the survivors and the casualties back to the field hospital at Tan Son Nhut. It was a gruesome scene. Amid the luggage, pieces of clothing, and twisted shards of metal strewn across the field lay bodies so thickly caked with mud it was often difficult to distinguish the living from the dead. In fact, in many cases no definitive determination could be made until the victims reached the hospital. "The nurses would simply pass the children under the shower," recalled one witness, "saying, 'This one's alive, this one's dead.'" Identifying many of the orphans proved even more problematical, since none wore name tags, only wristbands designating the site of their foster homes—"New York," "New Jersey," "Chicago."

All told, over 200 children and all but one of the DAO employees were killed, making it the second worst crash in aviation history up to that time. To some Americans it seemed sadly symbolic of their nation's long and star-crossed involvement in Vietnam—yet another example, to quote *Time* magazine's coverage of the disaster, of the "failure of the American technology and know-how that a decade ago had been billed as the key to the country's salvation." Others saw it as a grim portent of things to come. "If one hastily organized flight could end so disastrously," wrote one CIA official, reflecting on his feelings at the time, "how much more dangerous a massive airlift under full wartime conditions might be." A more cynical view was offered by one Saigon official. "It's good that the American people are taking the children," he told a *New York Times* correspondent. "They are good souvenirs, like the ceramic elephants you like so much. It is too bad that some of them broke today, but don't worry, we have many more."

No one was more anguished by the tragedy than General Smith. Not only did the ill-fated flight mark the first attempt to evacuate DAO personnel, but Smith himself had encouraged those aboard to leave. Nevertheless, the defense attaché did not allow what had happened to divert him from his appointed mission. When the "babylift" resumed the following day, another group of DAO "non-essentials" was sent along. Several hours later they arrived safely at Clark Air Base in the Philippines.

The Weyand report

The crash of the orphan flight was front-page news when General Weyand arrived in Palm Springs, California, on April 5 to report to President Ford on his fact-finding mission to South Vietnam. His return had been eagerly awaited. In the week since Weyand's departure Ford had said almost nothing publicly about the deepening crisis in Southeast Asia, and some of his aides had become concerned about the political impact of nightly newscasts showing the president playing golf while the Vietnamese Republic crumbled. Their sense of embarrassment had been compounded by a strange incident at the Bakersfield, California, airport, when Ford literally ran away from reporters trying to question him about Vietnam. "He ran," one journalist noted sarcastically, "almost as fast as the South Vietnamese army."

Yet from the president's point of view, there were sound reasons for avoiding any confrontation with the issue. There were simply too many different perceptions of the battlefield situation, too many conflicting views of American responsibilities, and too many contingencies to form a basis for action. He therefore delayed, counting on Weyand to guide him.

Lon Nol, president of the Khmer Republic, three weeks before relinquishing his command.

Although Weyand had told newsmen before leaving Saigon that GVN forces "are still strong and still have the spirit and capability to defeat the North Vietnamese," his official report to the president offered a much gloomier appraisal. "The current military situation is critical," he wrote in the preface, "and the probability of the survival of South Vietnam as a truncated nation is marginal at best. The GVN is on the brink of military defeat. . . . Given the speed at which events are moving," he added, for reasons of prudence, the United States should plan now for a mass evacuation of some 6,000 U.S. citizens and tens of thousands of South Vietnamese and Third Country Nationals to whom we have incurred an obligation and owe protection.

Such an operation, Weyand estimated, "would require as a minimum a US task force of a reinforced division sup-ported by tactical air." He suggested that the president obtain from Congress the necessary authority to "use military sanctions against North Vietnam if there is interference with the evacuation."

The general then went on to catalogue the "interlocking web" of problems that had led to this dire state of affairs: "the present size, strength and aggressive activity" of the North Vietnamese Army, which now had "over 200,000 [troops] organized into 173 regiments" operating in the South; "the sheer magnitude of the past three weeks' losses in personnel and equipment" and "the concomitant magnitude of the refugee flow"; a chronic lack of "leadership, direction and guidance" at the highest levels of the GVN; and a "complex of psychological and attitudinal problems" that included a "spreading loss of confidence in the government and a growing "sense of hopelessness and defeatism" within the ranks of ARVN.

For all his pessimism, however, the former COMUSMACV still clung to one slim thread of hope. If the South Vietnamese could somehow "stabilize the military situation," he told the president, there was "a chance" that the Republic of Vietnam might yet be saved. But to achieve such a respite required additional support from the United States: either the use of American military air power or a substantial new commitment of military equipment and supplies. Acknowledging "the significant legal and political implications" of a decision to unleash the B-52s, Weyand recommended that Ford ask Congress for $722 million to fund a major resupply effort to South Vietnam. Not only would such an appropriation allow the RVNAF to replace materiel lost in the great retreat, he argued, but even more crucially it would help to restore the confidence of the average South Vietnamese.

Weyand made no promises that the fulfillment of his recommendations could prevent the NVA from conquering South Vietnam, if that was in fact Hanoi's intention. "In pure capability terms," he conceded, "the North Vietnamese can move and commit existing divisions within SVN faster than the GVN can form new ones." Nor did he believe that President Thieu was capable of providing the kind of leadership that the situation demanded, though he noted that "the odds are mounting" that Thieu "will have to step down." The only certainty Weyand could offer Ford, in fact, was that "the present level of US support guarantees defeat." He therefore urged the president to make a "maximum effort" to obtain Congressional approval of the proposed aid package. "What is at stake in Vietnam now," he concluded, "is America's credibility as an ally."

Within the Ford administration, reactions to the Weyand report were divided. Although everyone agreed that it would be impossible to send in the B-52s, a heated debate erupted over the recommendation for increased aid. On one side stood Henry Kissinger, who strongly endorsed the proposal. Like Weyand, the secretary of state believed that American prestige abroad would suffer if the administration failed to take concrete action in support of South Vietnam. He therefore encouraged Ford to seek the full $722 million as a dramatic sign of U.S. determination to stand by its "moral obligations."

Other members of the administration saw things differently. In the view of Defense Secretary Schlesinger, whom Kissinger had managed to cut out of the decision-making process throughout most of the crisis, $722 million seemed an excessive price to pay for "credibility," especially since South Vietnam's chances for survival were by Weyand's own admission "marginal at best." The need to preserve U.S. prestige abroad would be served just as well, he believed, by the $300 million supplemental-aid proposal already before Congress; anything beyond that seemed wasteful and pointless. Still another point of view was offered by Ford's domestic advisers, led by Robert Hartmann, who wanted the president to disassociate himself from the now-failing policies of his predecessors. Rather than further antagonize Congress with a new aid request nearly two-and-a-half times as large as the one still languishing on Capitol Hill, they advised, Ford should avoid unnecessary recriminations and make a plea for national unity as the basis for future foreign policy decisions.

The siege of Phnom Penh

Before reaching any final decision on the new Vietnam aid proposal, however, administration officials were compelled to confront an even more pressing matter: the imminent collapse of Cambodia. Beginning on April 3, Washington received a series of urgent cables from Ambassador John Gunther Dean in Phnom Penh requesting authorization to evacuate all remaining Americans. Some 30,000 Khmer Rouge troops were rapidly closing in on the Cambodian capital and threatening to shut down Pochentong airport; the situation had become too perilous, in Dean's opinion, to permit further delay.

That news was not unexpected. Ever since Communist forces choked off the Mekong River in late January, forcing Phnom Penh to rely exclusively on the U.S.-sponsored airlift for its food and supplies, many American officials had been convinced that the fall of Cambodia was inevitable.

Despite much brave talk in early February of plans to reopen the river, followed by a few futile counterassaults on key riverbank positions, the ill-equipped, poorly led, and increasingly demoralized Khmer National Armed Forces had been relentlessly driven back. Losses on both sides were enormously high, but they were especially devastating for FANK because the government could not replace them. By the end of March, out of an initial force of 75,000, an estimated 10,000 government soldiers had been killed in action and 20,000 wounded. Another 6,000 to 8,000 deserted, many because they found it impossible to support themselves and their families on their irregularly paid government salary of 12,000 *riels* a month—the equivalent of twenty American cents a day.

As the defense perimeter surrounding Phnom Penh shrank, conditions inside the besieged capital steadily worsened. Swollen by the influx of 1.5 million refugees and terrorized by random 107MM rocket attacks, the once elegant city of 500,000 had been transformed almost beyond recognition. Although foreigners and well-to-do Cambodians, including senior military officers, still frequented the city's fine French restaurants and nightclubs, for most people life had become a nightmare of poverty and hunger, disease and despair. Along tree-lined boulevards children, women, and maimed soldiers huddled in doorways, begging for food or the money to pay for it, while young peasant girls tried to sell their bodies to passersby. Others lay sick and dying, unable to obtain medical treatment for a host of afflictions ranging from chronic malnutrition to tuberculosis. Hospitals became so overcrowded with wounded soldiers and their dependents that only those civilians who could pay were admitted, and even then shortages of medicine, running water, and electrical power made it difficult to provide adequate medical attention.

The unpopular Lon Nol government did little to relieve the distress. Although the daily airlift brought in enough rice to feed the entire population, corrupt officials and war profiteers prevented it from reaching those who needed it most. The government continued to insist, moreover, that only officially registered refugees—about one-third of the total—were eligible for relief. Several international voluntary agencies, including CARE, Catholic Relief Services, the Red Cross, and World Vision, helped to alleviate some of the misery, but they too were bound by the government's registration stricture.

Realizing just how hopeless the situation was, Ambassador Dean pressed Washington throughout February and March to withdraw its support from Lon Nol and seek some form of accommodation with the Khmer Rouge that would bring the killing to a halt. Since he no longer believed that any kind of coalition arrangement was possible, he now advocated what he called a "controlled solution," even if it amounted to no more than a disguised surrender. But Kissinger continued to oppose the idea, for

Cambodia's Anguish

As the Khmer Rouge closed in on Phnom Penh, the capital's siege conditions meant growing misery for all but the elite. The indigenous population and the 1.5 million refugees experienced not only the anguish of hunger and disease but also the terror of rocket attacks. Previously overcrowded hospitals were paralyzed by the huge influx of sick and wounded.

Above. A Cambodian woman at her soldier husband's hospital bed. Right. A boy and his wounded mother.

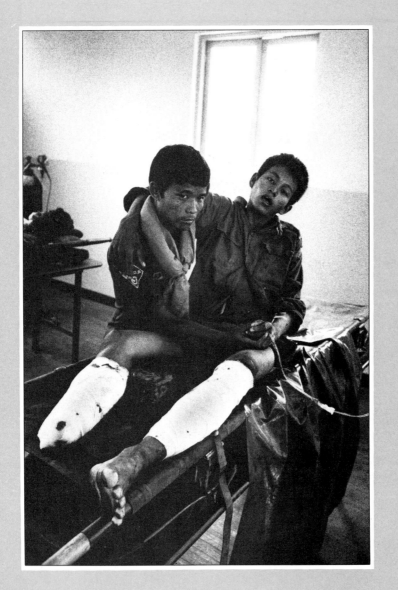

Overcrowding—and sanitary conditions—
became even worse as entire families, the
homeless dependents of patients, moved
into the hospitals. The pictures on these
pages reflect the suffering of Phnom
Penh's people in the days before the
war's end.

*Above. Government soldiers. Right. A
woman hovers over her husband's body.*

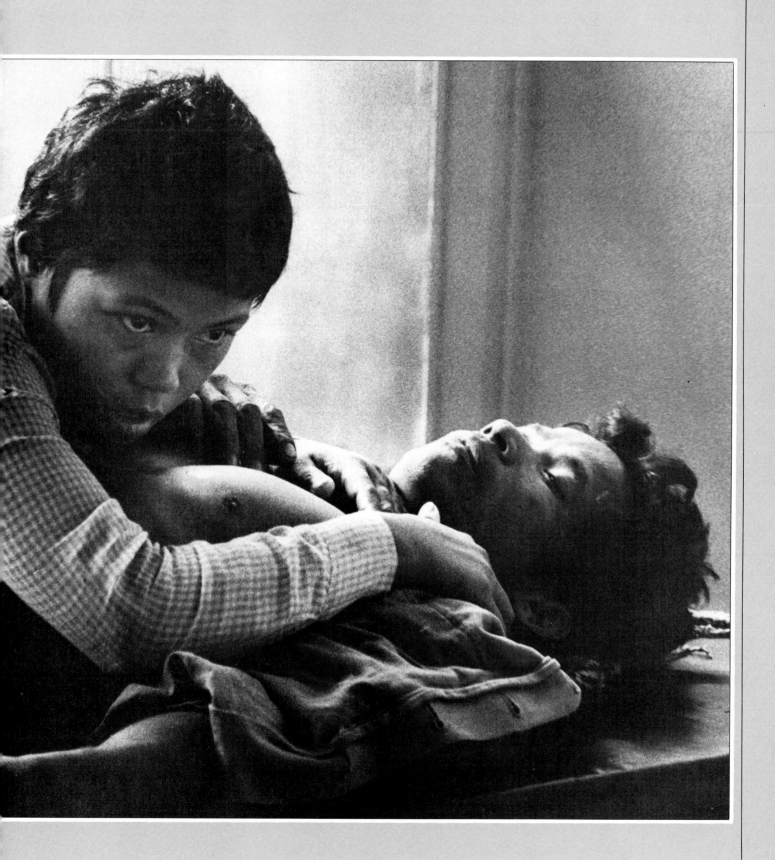

the same reasons he had opposed it in the past. He still maintained that American credibility was at stake, even though the U.S. had no formal commitment to Cambodia, and he still considered Lon Nol to be his major bargaining chip in any negotiations with the Communists. The secretary of state was sufficiently forward looking, however, to allow Dean to begin the "drawdown" of his embassy staff and their dependents on March 18.

Two weeks later, on April 1, the disagreement between Dean and Kissinger became moot when Lon Nol surrendered power at the insistence of more than a dozen generals and ministers of the tottering Khmer Republic. That afternoon the partially paralyzed Cambodian president limped past an honor guard and, without uttering even a word of farewell, boarded an Air Cambodge airliner bound for Djakarta. For face-saving purposes, the government radio station later broadcast an eleven-minute recorded speech in which the marshal insisted that his exile would not be permanent. He would consult with other world leaders about a peaceful solution to the war, he said, and then return "when my health improves or whenever our brothers indicate to me that our national problem requires my presence." Nevertheless, before leaving he insisted that the government provide a half-million dollars to support him and his family while they were abroad. Ambassador Dean later reported that at least $200,000 was actually paid to the Cambodian president.

If there were any thought that Lon Nol's exit might open the way to a peaceful settlement, it was soon dashed. In Peking, Prince Norodom Sihanouk, the man whom Lon Nol had overthrown five years before, immediately denounced the marshal's departure as a "dirty and vulgar trap" planned by the United States. The response of the Khmer Rouge was even more emphatic. As dusk fell on the evening of April 1, Communist forces, in a flaming house-to-house battle, overran Neak Luong, the riverbank garrison town sixty kilometers downstream from Phnom Penh. With the fall of the government's last remaining stronghold along the Mekong, the capital's fate was sealed. Not only were an additional 5,000 Khmer Rouge troops now free to join the siege, but the firepower of those forces had been augmented by the capture of a half-dozen U.S.-supplied 105MM howitzers.

It was in the wake of the fall of Neak Luong that Ambassador Dean decided that the Americans should get out. Initially Washington agreed, and on April 3 fifty members of the embassy staff were flown out through rocket fire from Pochentong airport. The next day, however, the ambassador received a top-secret cable from the State Department asking him to postpone the final evacuation. A telephone call from Secretary of State Kissinger followed. With Lon Nol gone, Kissinger was now pursuing a last-minute political deal with Sihanouk and his Chinese patrons, and he wanted to maintain an American presence as a "stabilizing influence." The evacuation of most embassy personnel could continue, but Dean and fifty members of his staff were to remain as long as there was still a chance that something might be worked out.

"You must win"

The Khmer Rouge, however, had no interest in working anything out. Neither, it seemed, did their North Vietnamese allies. Since the arrival of General Dung and his staff at Loc Ninh on the night of April 3, the Vietnamese Communist high command had intensively deliberated strategy and tactics for the upcoming campaign to "liberate" Saigon. Meeting in a complex of old bamboo huts that served as COSVN's regional headquarters, Dung, Pham Hung, and General Tran Van Tra spent several days studying the topography of the areas surrounding the South Vietnamese capital, calculating the amount of time it would take to move each of their chess pieces into position, assessing the needs of each unit for ammunition, equipment, and supplies. The final result of their endeavors was a plan to assault Saigon from three directions: north, southwest, and east. The main thrust was to come in the east, beginning with a multidivisional attack on the central bulwark of ARVN's defense line, the garrison town of Xuan Loc.

Everyone agreed, General Tra later recalled, that the battle "would be very fierce." The Communists knew that the South Vietnamese had heavily reinforced the units defending the town and that President Thieu had personally ordered his generals to hold the line "at all costs." But they also knew that if they succeeded in capturing Xuan Loc the road to Bien Hoa, and ultimately Saigon, would lie open. "The Saigon quislings and the United States . . . hoped they might be able to hold out there and not lose everything, not collapse completely, not be defeated absolutely," General Dung wrote in his memoirs, but they were only "prolonging their agony." Dung was prepared to use whatever amount of force was necessary to take Xuan Loc. Artillery units would be supplied with extra quantities of shells, tanks equipped with additional fuel and ammunition, and three infantry divisions hurled into the initial battle. If that failed to achieve the objective, other units would later arrive from the coast to complete the task. ARVN might hold out for a time, but eventually Xuan Loc would fall.

On the afternoon of April 7, Dung called together the entire COSVN Central Committee to lay out the operation and gain pro forma endorsement. The meeting had just begun, Dung recalled, when "a motorcycle pulled up in the courtyard carrying a tall, lean man wearing a blue shirt, khaki slacks, and a soldier's hard helmet." "Brother Sau"—Le Duc Tho—had arrived. Slung from Tho's shoulder was "a big black leather satchel" containing the Politburo's latest resolutions.

It was not the first time Tho had been dispatched by

Hanoi to oversee preparations for a major military operation in the South. In 1967, 1971, and 1972 he had visited the COSVN command zone to make sure that field commanders fully understood the Politburo's wishes at the moment of a crucial policy shift. But this occasion was different. In the past he had made the arduous journey on foot over a period of weeks; this time he traveled by plane, car, and motorcycle, completing the trip in ten days. In the past he had always known that there would be other battles to fight after the current offensive was over; now he stood at the threshold of "total military victory." In the past he had come as a former chief political officer in the South and one of the highest-ranking members of the Politburo; now he carried, with more than a little irony, the additional badge of the coauthor of the Paris peace accords.

On April 8 Tho briefed Dung and his colleagues on the instructions he had received from the Politburo. After informing them of world reaction to the offensive and de-

scribing conditions in the North, he announced the establishment of a new special command superseding COSVN to coordinate the campaign against Saigon. General Dung was designated as supreme commander; Pham Hung, the chief political officer; and Generals Tran Van Tra and Le Duc Anh, deputy commanders. In addition, Major General Le Trong Tan, "the conqueror of Danang," was assigned responsibility for leading the pivotal attack on Xuan Loc. Before adjourning the meeting, Tho passed along a note of warning he had received from Tong Duc Ton, the president of the DRV. "You must win," Ton told him on the day of his departure for the southern battlefield. "Otherwise, do not return."

At their headquarters in Loc Ninh, (left to right, seated) Chief of Staff Van Tien Dung, Politburo member Le Duc Tho, and COSVN head Pham Hung plan the final Communist assault against Saigon.

The Noose Tightens

At first it was just a black speck in a cloudless morning sky, a lone Vietnamese Air Force F-5E fighter-bomber streaking high above Saigon shortly before 8:30 A.M. on Tuesday, April 8. Then, just as the aircraft penetrated the prohibited zone surrounding the city's center, it went into a steep dive and dropped two of its four 250-pound bombs as it passed over Independence Palace. One was a dud. The other exploded in the palace courtyard, enveloping the buildings in a cloud of black smoke. Moments later the camouflage-painted jet returned and released its remaining two bombs, again missing the mark but causing some damage to a stairwell inside the palace. After the second pass the pilot headed for the far side of the Saigon River, emptied his 20MM cannon on the Nha Be fuel storage dump, and then flew north toward the Communist-held airfield at Phuoc Long.

As the explosions reverberated through downtown Saigon, early morning traffic snarled to a

halt and pedestrians scrambled for cover. A few nervous soldiers fired their weapons aimlessly into the air. Within minutes fire engines arrived at the palace grounds, accompanied by troops, tanks, and a phalanx of police. Steel and barbwire barricades were hurriedly erected and antiaircraft guns emplaced as a precaution against further attack. At 9:30 A.M. the government radio station announced the imposition of a twenty-four-hour curfew, effective immediately. By noon nearly all shops and businesses were closed and the streets deserted.

Many capital residents initially thought that the bombing signaled a coup attempt, with much of the suspicion focused on Air Vice Marshal Ky and his cronies. Others, believing that the final battle for Saigon had begun, ran through the streets shouting, "The North Vietnamese are coming!" But such fears proved unfounded. South Vietnamese and American officials soon established that the F-5 pilot, First Lieutenant Nguyen Thanh Trung, had taken off from Bien Hoa Air Base that morning with orders to bomb Communist positions in Binh Thuan Province, some 120 kilometers to the east. But after reporting engine trouble he split off from his formation and headed, undetected, straight for the heart of Saigon. Although Liberation Radio later boasted that Trung had long been a Communist agent and had been ordered to carry out the raid, American intelligence officers were skeptical. They were instead persuaded that he was either a disgruntled pilot trying to do Ky an unsolicited favor or a defector who decided to join the Communists at the last minute.

While the bombing underscored the vulnerability of the capital and temporarily traumatized its inhabitants, the presidential palace suffered only minimal damage and the president himself emerged unscathed. Three hours after the attack Thieu went on the radio to assure the nation that he and his family were unharmed, that there had been no coup, and that he still retained the loyalty of the South Vietnamese armed forces. "I am determined to continue the leadership of this country," he vowed.

Xuan Loc

In the face of the growing military threat to Saigon, however, Thieu's reassurances amounted to little more than posturing. By the second week in April no less than nine Communist Main Force divisions were bearing down on the capital from three directions—northwest in the area surrounding Tay Ninh, south along Route 4 leading from the delta, and east along Route 1—and it seemed likely that as further reinforcements arrived from the north and the coast the North Vietnamese would attempt to encircle the city entirely. But if the main outlines of the enemy's

grand strategy seemed clear, a number of crucial questions were still unresolved. Where and when would the principal thrust come? Would ARVN hold? Would the NVA strike Saigon itself or simply tighten its noose until the GVN surrendered? Was there still a chance for a negotiated solution, if Thieu agreed to yield power? Part of an answer to these questions came on April 9, when the 341st, 6th, and 7th Divisions of the NVA's 4th Army Corps launched the long-anticipated attack on the ARVN stronghold at Xuan Loc. By coincidence or design, it had been precisely eight days since the French communicated Hanoi's "ultimatum" to Tran Van Don.

The 341st NVA Division spearheaded the assault on Xuan Loc, penetrating from the northwest following a 4,000-round barrage of artillery, rocket, and mortar fire that set half the town aflame. As thick columns of smoke billowed into the night sky, Soviet-made T54 tanks clanked forward, firing, with waves of infantrymen close behind. Savage hand-to-hand fighting ensued as the North Vietnamese pushed toward the heart of the city, seizing a number of key installations along the way. By dawn the NLF flag flew over the police station, the CIA compound, the railway station, and the local Ranger base.

But the soldiers of the 18th ARVN Division, commanded by General Le Minh Dao, refused to fold. Though outnumbered and outgunned, the 43d Infantry Regiment launched counterattack after counterattack throughout the morning of April 10 and ultimately forced the invaders to yield ground. The North Vietnamese responded by hurling into the battle two additional regiments from their 6th and 7th Divisions and by pounding ARVN positions with unremitting artillery fire. Still, the Communists could not dislodge the defenders.

As the fighting raged on, reducing much of the town to a heap of burning rubble, the civilian residents of Xuan Loc desperately tried to escape. Although helicopters were brought in to evacuate ARVN dependents, most of the population had to flee on foot and bicycle. Thousands headed north toward enemy lines. The majority, however, trudged west toward Route 1, the main road leading to Saigon.

Theirs was not an easy journey. To prevent the South Vietnamese from reinforcing Xuan Loc from the west, the North Vietnamese had established a blockade along a sixteen-kilometer stretch of Route 1 between the town of Hung Loc and the city's perimeter. Throughout the day VNAF fighter-bombers and helicopter gunships hammered at NVA entrenchments, hoping to punch a hole wide enough to allow an armor- and artillery-supported task force to reach Xuan Loc. But the Communists held on, stalling the recently dispatched reinforcements near the junction of Routes 1 and 20.

Despite their failure to break the NVA blockade west of Xuan Loc, the South Vietnamese military command had reason to be pleased with the performance of their troops

Preceding page. *Former residents of Xuan Loc wait to be lifted out by CH-47s which ferry ARVN reinforcements into the embattled city and the refugees out.*

on the first full day of battle. Not only had General Dao's forces successfully resisted a multidivisional enemy assault, but they had inflicted heavy casualties on the North Vietnamese while suffering comparatively few. They had also captured twenty prisoners, most of whom, according to General Vien, "were newly recruited conscripts ... about 17 years old." Unfamiliar with the terrain and frightened by artillery fire, many had been found hiding in sewers with their rifles fully loaded. The youth and inexperience of the soldiers of the 341st NVA Division suggested that the Communists were willing to pay whatever price was necessary to take Xuan Loc. If so, the South Vietnamese had no choice but to match them.

On April 11 the North Vietnamese resumed their attacks, this time striking the rear base of the 52d Infantry northwest of Xuan Loc on Route 20 as well as the 43d Infantry and the 82d Ranger Battalion inside the town. Fearful that the Communists might attempt to surround the city entirely, the South Vietnamese ordered a second task force from Cu Chi to join the fight to open Route 1 and helolifted two battalions of the 1st Airborne Brigade to an area just south of Xuan Loc. To neutralize the firepower of the enemy's tanks, each of the paratroopers carried a LAW (light antitank weapon) in addition to his usual battlefield equipment. Morale was high. "Airborne No. 1," one grinning officer told an American reporter. "Everything be okay now because Airborne is here."

With the arrival of the Airborne, 25,000 troops, nearly a third of what remained of the Army of the Republic of Vietnam, were committed to the defense of Xuan Loc. In addition, for the first time since the onset of the North Vietnamese offensive the Vietnamese Air Force was consistently providing effective air support for the ground troops. Flying out of Bien Hoa and Tan Son Nhut airfields, prop-driven A-1 Skyraiders and F-5 fighter-bombers repeatedly hit enemy troop concentrations around the city. Even C-130 transport planes were used in an attack role. Armed with 750-pound bombs strapped to wooden pallets that the crews rolled out of the rear cargo hatches, they served as makeshift substitutes for the absent B-52s.

On April 8, government soldiers stand ready to enforce the twenty-four-hour curfew imposed after an F-5 aircraft bombed the presidential palace that day.

Largely as a result of the close coordination between air and ground forces, by April 12 the battle seemed to be turning in ARVN's favor. Although the North Vietnamese maintained their tight grip on Route 1 west of the town and continued to pin down the 52d Infantry to the north, the 43d Regiment had regained control of the city itself and the Airborne was slowly but steadily closing in from the south. Moreover, the reinforced task force fighting to reopen Route 1 was finally beginning to make some headway against the entrenched North Vietnamese.

Encouraged by the RVNAF's determined resistance, General Smith shot off a telegram to General George Brown, chairman of the Joint Chiefs of Staff, declaring that the South Vietnamese "had won round one" of the crucial battle for Xuan Loc. "The valor and aggressiveness of GVN troops," he concluded, "appears to settle for the time being the question, 'Will ARVN fight?'"

"The State of the World"

Smith hoped that the news of ARVN's brave stand would convince the U.S. Congress that South Vietnam could still be saved, provided that additional military aid were immediately forthcoming. But the prospect was not encouraging. When Congress reconvened on April 7, resistance to the administration's Indochina aid package seemed stronger than ever. During the twelve-day Easter break most representatives had ascertained little support among their constituents for the president's proposal, and their impressions were confirmed by the latest public opinion polls. A Gallup survey conducted in late March and early April showed that three out of every four respondents opposed a comparatively modest $300 million supplement to South Vietnam, while opposition to a $222 Cambodia aid bill was running at two to one. "The feeling is," said Republican Garner Shriver of Kansas, "that we have made a considerable contribution to Vietnam and Cambodia, and that we've done enough." Even more telling were the remarks of Democrat Joseph Gaydos, whose district encompassed the formerly prowar steel towns of western Pennsylvania. Like some newspaper editorialists, Gaydos had already begun to speak of America's role in Southeast Asia in the past tense. "Most people realize," he commented, "that regardless of how much we might have spent in lives or dollars, we couldn't have changed the outcome."

Many congressmen, moreover, returned to Washington angry at the administration's intimations that they were to blame for the failure of U.S. policy. Particularly disturbing was President Ford's suggestion at an April 3 press conference that 55,000 American lives had been wasted because Congress refused to honor commitments made under the terms of the Paris agreement. Secretary of State Kissinger's contention that a continuation of American aid to the GVN was "inherent" in the structure of the cease-

fire pact also stirred resentment, as did his attempt to validate past policy on the grounds that Congress had never directly challenged his decisions. "Some commitments are invented where no commitments exist," snapped Senator Robert Byrd, "and then Congress is blamed for not living up to those commitments."

The furor over the nature of the U.S. obligation intensified after Senator Henry Jackson (D-Washington) took the floor on April 8 and charged that the Nixon administration had made "secret agreements . . . in writing" with the South Vietnamese without consulting Congress. Since administration officials had repeatedly stressed in recent weeks that the United States had a "moral . . . but no legal commitment" to support South Vietnam, Jackson called upon Kissinger to disclose the substance of those agreements to Congress under oath. The White House responded with the claim that President Nixon had promised nothing in private to the South Vietnamese that he had not reiterated many times in public. While in one sense this was true, it was also a fact that Congress had never been apprised of the contents of the former president's letters of assurance to Nguyen Van Thieu.

Nor did Congress know that the Ford administration was actively considering a new, and much larger, Vietnam aid package in place of the $300 million bill already on the table. Although Defense Secretary Schlesinger and the president's political advisers continued to oppose the $722 million Weyand proposal, Kissinger remained adamantly in favor of it. Ultimately it was the secretary of state who prevailed. In a series of meetings of the Washington Special Action Group and the National Security Council on April 8 and 9, he convinced Ford that the future interests of American foreign policy required the strongest possible demonstration of U.S. resolve. If the United States were to withdraw its support from South Vietnam now, he argued, the nation's other allies around the world would surely begin to doubt the value of an American commitment, with severe repercussions for the entire global balance of power.

Other members of the WSAG and NSC, however, were less concerned about the long-range implications of the aid question than the more immediate need to protect some 6,000 American lives in Saigon. Prompted by General Weyand's remarks about the need to "plan now for a mass evacuation," Schlesinger, CIA Director Colby, and JCS Chairman Brown all began to press for a rapid acceleration of the U.S. withdrawal. Colby also urged that "high risk" Vietnamese be included in the evacuation effort. Kissinger took a middle position. Although he agreed that an effort should be made to reduce the size of the U.S. community in Vietnam as soon as possible, he also shared Ambassador Martin's fear that a hasty withdrawal might trigger the collapse of the GVN and provoke a violent backlash against those Americans who remained.

Again Kissinger's views prevailed. At the conclusion of

ARVN troops made a defiant stand at Xuan Loc in late March and early April despite the crushing advance of Communist troops. Above. III Corps gunners, supporting the task force advancing on Xuan Loc, at an artillery position. Left. ARVN soldiers brandish captured Communist flags after they had won "round one" at Xuan Loc.

the WSAG/NSC sessions it was decided that preparations for a total evacuation were to be expanded, but the final "hard pull" would be postponed until Congress reached a decision on the aid issue. In the meantime, Ambassador Martin was to step up the "thinning out" process already under way, reducing the American presence to 1,100 over a period of two weeks so that a fleet of helicopters would be sufficient for the final pullout. The estimation of naval and combat force requirements for a full-scale evacuation was assigned to Admiral Gayler, while administration officials agreed to seek a relaxation of U.S. immigration rules to facilitate the extraction of large numbers of Vietnamese. All evacuation planning was to be completed within ten days—by April 19.

On April 10 President Ford revealed his decisions in a nationally televised address on "The State of the World" before a joint session of Congress. Many legislators had been hoping that the president would use the occasion to look beyond Vietnam and chart a new bipartisan course in U.S. foreign policy. Instead they sat in stony silence as an unusually nervous Ford sounded the same themes they had heard so often in the recent past, including the implication that the failure of Congress to provide "adequate support" to South Vietnam had invited aggression from the North. In a dramatic breach of legislative etiquette, two freshmen congressmen stalked out of the chamber while the president spelled out his latest requests.

In addition to asking for the full $722 million in military aid recommended by General Weyand, Ford called upon Congress to provide $250 million for emergency refugee relief, food, and medicine. He also requested an amendment of existing law to permit the evacuation of "tens of thousands" of South Vietnamese "to whom we have a profound moral obligation" as well as clarification of Congressional restrictions on his authority to use U.S. military forces "if necessary" to protect American lives. Apparently rejecting any compromise on the aid issue, Ford warned that "half-hearted action would be worse than none," while "drift and indecision" would only invite "far deeper disaster." He asked Congress to complete action on all of these measures no later than April 19.

Operation Eagle Pull

The president said little in his speech about the parallel crisis in Cambodia. He expressed regret that Congress had not approved the $222 million aid bill he had submitted in January and quoted in full a moving appeal from acting Cambodian President Saukham Khoy. "For a number of years now the Cambodian people have placed their trust in America," the letter read in part. "I cannot

A South Vietnamese soldier guards North Vietnamese prisoners captured during the fighting at Xuan Loc, the keystone of the GVN's final defense line.

believe that this confidence was misplaced and that suddenly America will deny us the means which might give us a chance to find an acceptable solution to our conflict." Ford made no mention, however, of his own unwillingness to compromise with Congress by accepting a mandatory June 30 cutoff date in exchange for the authorization of aid. Nor did he present a new aid proposal for Cambodia as he had for South Vietnam. In fact, he conceded, "as of this evening, it may be too late."

It *was* too late. Two hours before the president went on the air, the White House received a flash cable from Ambassador Dean renewing his request for the initiation of Operation Eagle Pull, the final phase of the American evacuation from Phnom Penh. He sent the message shortly after Khmer Rouge gunners, now within mortar range of Pochentong airport, hit an American DC-8 as it taxied along the runway, killing four members of the crew and bringing the U.S. airlift to a halt. With the capital's sole remaining life line to the outside world now cut off, and time running out, Dean wanted the helicopters brought in to extract the remaining Americans.

Preparations for Eagle Pull had been made long before. Since early March Amphibious Ready Group (ARG) Alfa, a group of American ships that included the navy helicopter carrier U.S.S. *Okinawa*, had cruised off the Cambodian coast in the Gulf of Thailand. Aboard the *Okinawa* were some 800 men of the 2d Battalion, 4th Marines, newly designated as the 31st Marine Amphibious Unit, as well as two dozen CH-53 helicopters. Another carrier, the U.S.S. *Hancock*, was steaming toward the group with twelve more helicopters when Dean's cable reached Washington, while in Thailand a dozen strike aircraft and ten other support planes of the U.S. 7th Air Force were standing by to provide air cover.

Although the administration promptly authorized the evacuation, they informed Dean that there would be a twenty-four-hour delay. They wanted to allow enough time for the *Hancock* to join the other ships, and Secretary Kissinger wanted to make one final bid for a "controlled solution." L-hour, the time when the first marine helicopters would land in the Cambodian capital, was therefore set for 9:00 A.M., April 12, Phnom Penh time—9:00 P.M., April 11, Washington time.

In the meantime Kissinger, who in the past week had made no headway in his attempts to cajole Prince Sihanouk into negotiations, launched his eleventh-hour peace initiative. Dropping an earlier demand that Sihanouk first agree to share power with other leaders of the Khmer Republic, he instructed George Bush, the U.S. liaison chief in Peking, to contact the prince directly and invite him to take over the Cambodian government. Not surprisingly, Sihanouk flatly refused the offer. Having already accepted a figurehead role as "head of state" under a Khmer Rouge regime while conceding all internal governmental responsibilities, he stood to gain nothing by breaking with his

Communist allies on the eve of their military triumph. "I will remain until the end on the side of the Red Khmers," he asserted in a written reply to Bush's message, "my allies whom I would never betray."

Several hours later, and six minutes ahead of schedule, Operation Eagle Pull was under way. It proceeded flawlessly. As the first wave of three Sea Stallion helicopters set down on Landing Zone Hotel, a soccer field half a kilometer southwest of the U.S. Embassy, 90 marines charged out and established a defense perimeter. Armed with M16 rifles and M79 grenade launchers, they had expected to meet threatening mobs and hostile enemy fire; instead they found only a few hundred passive onlookers and the distant sound of Khmer Rouge guns. Soon helicopters were arriving every ten minutes, touching down only long enough to board evacuees before shuttling back to the decks of the *Okinawa* and the *Hancock*. At 10:15 A.M. a somber Ambassador Dean departed, carrying under his arm the folded American flag that had flown over the embassy until the previous night. By eleven o'clock all of the civilians were safely on their way to the ships of the U.S. 7th Fleet, and only part of the 360-man marine security detachment remained. Although Khmer Rouge rockets and mortar rounds were now beginning to fall among the surrounding crowd, Communist gunners did not zero in on the landing zone itself until 11:15, moments after the last contingent of marines had lifted off.

All told, 276 people were evacuated during the operation. Eighty-two were American, 159

Carrying the flag from the embassy in Phnom Penh, Ambassador John Gunther Dean arrives at U Tapao, Thailand.

Cambodian, and 35 other nationalities. More could have gone, since the thirty-six helicopters used in the evacuation were capable of carrying a total of 780 passengers in addition to the marines. Yet most Cambodian government officials, including Prime Minister Long Boret, his adviser Sirik Matak, and others on the Khmer Rouge death list, declined Ambassador Dean's offer of escape. As Matak explained in a poignant letter to Dean that arrived shortly after the first helicopters landed:

I thank you very sincerely for your letter and for your offer to transport me towards freedom. I cannot, alas, leave in such a cowardly fashion. As for you and in particular for your great country, I never believed for a moment that you would have this sentiment of abandoning a people which has chosen liberty. You have refused us your protection and we can do nothing about it. ... But mark it well that, if I shall die here on the spot and in my country that I love, it is too bad because we are all born and must die one day. I have only committed this mistake of believing in you, the Americans.

Among the highest-ranking members of the Khmer government, only Saukham Khoy requested evacuation. Long Boret and Sirik Matak were later executed by the Khmer Rouge.

After five years of fitful, often clandestine, effort and the expenditure of more than a billion dollars in aid, the American attempt to prevent a Communist takeover in Cambodia had come to an end. The Khmer Republic nevertheless limped along for five more days. The mood in Phnom Penh was festive when the end finally came on the morning of April 17. Buoyed by the prospect of peace after so many years of bloodshed, crowds lined the streets waving white flags in anticipation of the arrival of their new rulers. Spirits rose even higher when a group of black-clad soldiers marched down one of the capital's central boulevards and smilingly told government soldiers to put down their weapons and go home. Only later did the citizens of Phnom Penh realize that this initial contingent of cheerful "liberators" was but a group of local students attempting to associate themselves with the revolution before the Khmer Rouge arrived.

Jubilation gave way to silence and dread when the real conquerors entered the city. "Grim, robotlike, brutal," wrote Sydney Schanberg of the *New York Times*. The Khmer Rouge troops, many of them teen-age boys and girls, marched into the capital with weapons "[dripping] from them like fruit from trees." Speaking in the name of an entity identified only as *Angka Loeu*—"Organization on High"—they immediately began ordering everyone to leave the city. The Americans, they said, were going to bomb Phnom Penh. Their leaders knew better; they had other purposes for the evacuation.

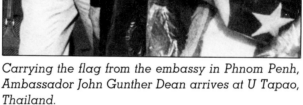

Operation Eagle Pull. Cambodian civilians watch as evacuation helicopters pull some of the last Americans out of Phnom Penh on April 12.

A Khmer Rouge guerrilla commands shop owners into the street as the evacuation of the capital begins.

Under the Khmer Rouge: Day One

On the morning of April 17, 1975, peace came to Phnom Penh, albeit temporarily. Although most government soldiers had not received formal orders to surrender, the Khmer Rouge entering the Cambodian capital met with no resistance. The more than 2 million civilians cramming the city were to receive no respite; the victors immediately ordered all people out of Phnom Penh, beginning Pol Pot's reign of terror.

Right. *The first Khmer Rouge arrivals are welcomed with white flags and applause.* Above. *Heavily laden with weapons, young Khmer Rouge soldiers march down one of Phnom Penh's central boulevards.*

Conflicting signals

The American pullout from Cambodia only reinforced the mood of grim foreboding that had gripped Saigon since the first days of April. Convinced that the United States was preparing to abandon them as well, many South Vietnamese now began to direct their energies toward getting themselves and their families out before it was too late. The obstacles to departure, however, remained formidable. In the past two weeks the standard bribe for a passport and exit visa had risen from $500 to $3,000, while for those who sought to escape by sea the price of a modest junk had tripled to $10,000 or more. To meet these escalating costs, family heirlooms and even luxurious villas were placed on the market at bargain basement prices. But there were few takers. Those who had the means to pay their way out tended to hoard their money or tried to exchange it for gold, already valued at $725 an ounce and destined to appreciate even further.

Fueling the growing sense of desperation were numerous stories of Communist atrocities in the "liberated" provinces of the north, graphically embellished and widely publicized by the GVN and the local press. South Vietnamese Roman Catholics were especially fearful of a Communist blood bath, as were those Vietnamese who had any association with the Americans. Not only "high risk" intelligence operatives but even chauffeurs, laundresses, and other menial laborers at U.S. installations viewed themselves as primary targets of Communist retribution. Along Tu Do Street, bar girls began approaching every foreigner who passed in search of a deal that would get them out of the country, while the mistresses of Americans beseeched their lovers to take them along when they left. "He says wait, wait, wait," lamented one Vietnamese girl who wanted her American boyfriend to marry her. "You don't understand. They will not just kill me. They will torture me before."

If many Saigonese felt betrayed, however, it was not so much the Americans as their own government that they held responsible. When President Thieu at last announced the make-up of his new "government of war and national union" on April 14, dissatisfaction with his leadership was so widespread that the only remaining question seemed to be when, not whether, he would be forced to step down. Barricaded inside his third-floor office in Doc Lap Palace, he could no longer silence his critics in the press or command the personal loyalty of his troops. In open defiance of government censorship laws, newspapers now printed full accounts of the worsening military situation, while some senior ARVN officers spoke freely of the need to be rid of their leader. "As commander in chief Thieu has presided over one of the worst defeats in recent military history," one general told an American reporter. "He must resign." A young ARVN officer was even more blunt. "Thieu," he said, "has done more for Communism in the past two weeks than General Giap did in two decades. He is a traitor."

The Americans, too, were beginning to waver in their support for the South Vietnamese president. Although Ambassador Martin continued to believe that any extra-constitutional change in government could prove disastrous, he also knew that any hope for a negotiated settlement hinged on Thieu's removal from power. Despite the expiration of the alleged "eight-day ultimatum," the Provisional Revolutionary Government was still sending out signals that a political solution was possible. "It depends on our adversaries whether we use military measures," Madame Binh told two Western reporters on April 9. "We do not want our compatriots to die if we can obtain our objectives by other means." Four days later Pierre Brochand, the head of French intelligence in Saigon, approached CIA Station Chief Polgar at Le Cercle Sportif with a more detailed version of the Communists' ostensible offer. While the French agreed with Polgar that the military situation was irretrievable, Brochand said, they had reason to believe that Hanoi was "not in a hurry" and would agree to an interim "neutralist" government as a bridge to eventual Communist rule. "Big" Minh was considered the most likely candidate to head such a coalition, but former Prime Minister Khiem, Tran Van Don, former Foreign Minister Tran Van Do, and Senate Chairman Tran Van Lam might prove acceptable alternatives. Further confirmation of Brochand's information was provided by Tran Van Don, who claimed to have been in contact with a PRG representative. In a meeting with Ambassador Martin at the U.S. Embassy on April 14, the day after Brochand's tête-à-tête with Polgar, the new GVN defense minister passed along three specific points made by his contact: that Don himself was acceptable as a replacement for Thieu; that Communists would not interfere with the evacuation of "select" South Vietnamese; and that the United States could still maintain a small embassy presence in Saigon provided that all other "official Americans" left the country.

However encouraging these hints may have seemed, other evidence indicated that the Communists had something far different in mind than a political settlement. Not only did the North Vietnamese Army continue to press its advantage on every front, but official Communist pronouncements took on an increasingly hard-line tone. Whereas previously the PRG had called only for Thieu's ouster and the cessation of American "military involvement and intervention" as the price of peace, by mid-April they were demanding the withdrawal of all "25,000 US military advisers disguised as civilians" and threatening a "mass uprising" in Saigon unless the South Vietnamese president and his "clique" resigned. To encourage the prompt departure of the Americans, the North Vietnamese Foreign Ministry publicly announced on April 16 that "liberation forces" would create "no difficulty or obstacle

whatsoever" to a U.S. evacuation if it were carried out "immediately."

ARVN *soldiers pour rifle fire into a house on the outskirts of Saigon to root out suspected Communists, April 11.*

Congress, aid, and evacuation

The North Vietnamese were not the only ones interested in hastening the pace of the American withdrawal from Saigon. By the end of the second week of April many U.S. congressmen were becoming convinced that the Ford administration was deliberately stalling the evacuation effort in order to force a positive vote on the $722 million aid bill. The administration did not help matters by shifting its rationale for the request. In his "State of the World" speech Ford had contended that the funds would give the South Vietnamese a chance to defend their remaining territory and thus open the way to a political solution. But when that line of reasoning failed to sway Congress, a different and, in the view of some legislators, more cynical justification surfaced. In off-the-record comments to reporters, White House officials intimated that they no longer believed that additional arms could make a difference but

sought passage of the aid bill in order to prevent a violent anti-American backlash in the event of a full-scale U.S. pullout. The clear implication was that the Americans still in Saigon were hostages and the supplemental aid package their ransom.

The issue came to a head during a meeting at the White House between senior administration officials and the Senate Foreign Relations Committee on April 14, when the president himself advanced the ransom argument. "The quickest way to put them in jeopardy is not to vote the assistance money," Ford said. "I can't guarantee that if we say 'no more money' Thieu . . . won't do something totally irrational." Yet if that were true, several senators responded, why hadn't the administration done more to get the Americans out as soon as possible?

As the senators queried the president about the administration's plans, they had in their hands a report filed earlier that day by two staff investigators, Richard Moose and

Charles Miessner, who had accompanied General Weyand on his fact-finding visit to Vietnam. Asserting that "no one including the Vietnamese military believes that more aid could reverse the flow of events," Moose and Miessner reported a "consensus" among U.S. officials in Saigon urgently favoring evacuation. Yet, "this sense of urgency is not shared, and indeed is being actively resisted, by Ambassador Martin and a few of his senior officers." Martin did not "perceive or acknowledge" the gravity of the situation, they charged, and had declined to step up planning for an evacuation for fear of weakening the resolve of the South Vietnamese government. Although the two investigators conceded that there were grounds for the ambassador's fear of a backlash, they saw this as reason to accelerate rather than delay the U.S. withdrawal.

After the meeting Senators Hubert Humphrey (D-Minnesota) and Dick Clark (D-Iowa) told reporters that final approval of the president's request for humanitarian aid, as distinguished from military aid, would be granted once the committee was certain that Ambassador Martin had begun to expedite the evacuation of Americans from Saigon. They also said the bill would authorize the extraction of some Vietnamese, though far fewer than the 175,000 to 200,000 mentioned by the administration. Two days later, after the committee tentatively approved emergency legislation providing the president with a $200 million contingency fund to use during an evacuation, Senator Frank Church (D-Idaho) reiterated the conditions for final approval. "Before acting," he said, "we want to make certain that a plan for the withdrawal of nonessential American citizens from Saigon . . . is being effectuated."

In response to the insinuation that he was needlessly delaying the American withdrawal, Martin shot off an acerbic cable to the White House on April 15. "The relatively few people about whose opinion I really care," he asserted, "will not change their opinion of me."

Even the sly, anonymous insertion of the perfumed ice-pick into the kidneys in the form of quotes from my colleagues in the Department are only a peculiar form of acupuncture, indigenous to Foggy Bottom, against which I was immunized long ago.

"There are only two important considerations I keep in mind," he went on, "the safety of the people under my charge and the integrity of US policy. Both of these objectives . . . seem to me to demand that we not be diverted by any kind of pressure, press or Congressional, from coolly pursuing a course best designed to achieve them." That course, as Martin later put it, involved "walking a tightrope of judgement" above a host of contingencies—the growing possibility that the generals might turn on Thieu and mount a coup, the likely prospect of a Congressional denial of military aid, the growing need to push ahead with the American withdrawal—any one of which could set off a "mass panic" that would endanger the very people Congress was so concerned about.

According to Martin, moreover, the charge that he did not "perceive or acknowledge" the seriousness of the situation was preposterous and directly contradicted what Moose had told him just before leaving Saigon. Two years later, in response to a Congressional request for declassification of the Moose/Miessner report, Martin challenged Moose to deny under oath that he had told the ambassador "he would report that [Martin's] handling of things had been 'brilliant,' and that the only thing preventing thousands of deaths had been the ambassador's adamant resistance to the reintroduction of American military forces to protect any immediate mass evacuation." But Moose declined, Martin recalled, and Congress promptly withdrew its request.

Nor did the American ambassador take kindly to the claim that he was "actively resisting" the evacuation effort. Not only had he set in motion the original U.S. "drawdown" plan, but after receiving the WSAG's directives of April 9 he had organized a missionwide task force to coordinate all contingency preparations for a full-scale pullout. The new planning team had updated the embassy's standing four evacuation options to accommodate varying numbers of "high risk" Vietnamese. Although Options I and II still envisaged a step-by-step withdrawal by fixed-wing aircraft, Option III, a combined air- and sealift scheme, was now expanded to allow for the extraction of up to 200,000 Vietnamese by ship from the Newport Harbor complex in northeast Saigon and the port city of Vung Tau. A new and more detailed blueprint for Option IV, the "worst case" alternative, was also drawn up. Under the revised plan, bus convoys and small Air America UH-1 helicopters were to collect passengers at twenty-nine designated assembly points around Saigon and shuttle them to Newport or the DAO complex at Tan Son Nhut. From there the evacuees would be transported by helicopter to the U.S. fleet anchored offshore.

In the meantime General Smith tried to speed up the "voluntary" departure of nonessential personnel by canceling PX privileges for army retirees living in Saigon and by ordering a revised estimate of the number of contract and staff employees who could be released without shutting down the DAO. His efforts were frustrated, however, by the same emigration and immigration restrictions that had hampered the American withdrawal from the start. Although C-141 transports were bringing fresh military supplies into Tan Son Nhut daily, most of them returned empty to Clark Air Base in the Philippines. By April 13, nearly two weeks after the inauguration of the "drawdown" plan, only 1,285 Americans and 1,837 Vietnamese had departed on outbound airlift planes.

On April 14 the red tape finally began to unravel when U.S. immigration authorities and the GVN both agreed to relax restrictions for Vietnamese dependents of American citizens. Henceforth, the South Vietnamese Interior Ministry announced, any Vietnamese who could demonstrate that he or she was an American dependent would be issued a special document known as a *laissez passer* in lieu of the standard exit visa and passport. Yet while the new rules greatly facilitated the departure of one large category of Vietnamese, it had a number of consequences that further complicated the American withdrawal. Since the U.S. "parole" applied only to Vietnamese with American relatives actually resident in Vietnam, it encouraged an influx of several hundred U.S. citizens who had been living in Hong Kong, Bangkok, Singapore, and elsewhere and now saw a chance to rescue their Vietnamese friends or lovers. At the same time, an unspecified number of U.S. military deserters suddenly surfaced with their Vietnamese wives and families in tow. As a result, at the very moment when Congress was insisting that the evacuation effort be accelerated, the list of potential American evacuees in Saigon grew by over 1,000 names.

A decision to delay

While the Americans contemplated how they were going to get out of Saigon, their North Vietnamese adversaries were reconsidering how they were going to get in. Since their initial conference on April 8, the three Politburo members in the South, now known as Group A75—General Dung, Pham Hung, and Le Duc Tho—had been forced

to reevaluate their plan for the final assault on Saigon. Not only had the NVA run into much stiffer resistance than anticipated at Xuan Loc, but General Nghi's ARVN forces at Phan Rang had posed unexpected difficulties for Communist Main Force units assigned to finish off MR 2. When Dung learned that the three reserve divisions dispatched from the DRV had also been delayed and would not arrive at their appointed positions north of Saigon until April 25, he concluded that there was no choice but to postpone the original timetable for victory.

The other members of the Politburo agreed. Aside from Dung's strictly tactical considerations, it is possible that the leaders in Hanoi wanted to allow more time for the Americans to proceed with their withdrawal, as evidenced by their repeated promises not to "interfere" with a U.S. evacuation if carried out "immediately." In any case, a series of directives issued on April 14 authorized Dung to delay launching the "general offensive on Saigon" pending the arrival of the bulk of the 1st and 2d Army Corps, but only until "the last week of April . . . at the very latest." In the meantime those forces already in place were gradually to intensify pressure on the South Vietnamese capital. To the south and southwest, the four divisions of the recently organized 232d Tactical Force would accelerate their drive up from the delta, cut Route 4, and force the GVN to spread out its defenders. The three

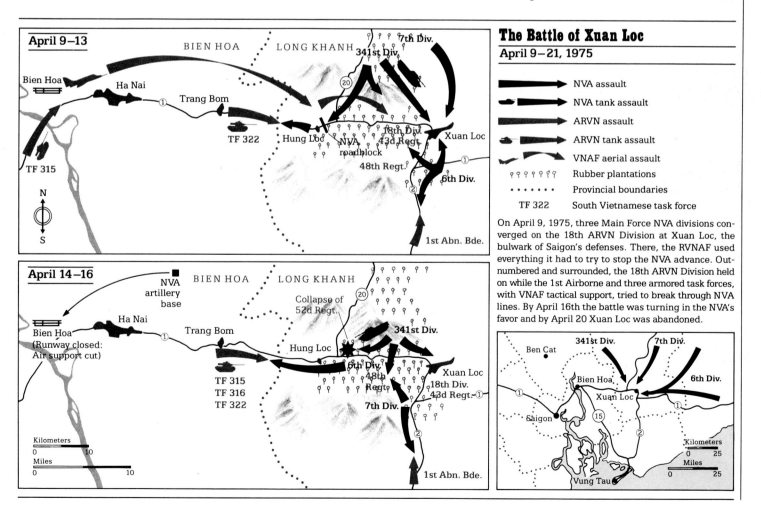

April 9–13

BIEN HOA · LONG KHANH · 7th Div. · 341st Div. · Bien Hoa · Ha Nai · Trang Bom · TF 322 · Hung Loc · NVA roadblock · 18th Div. · 43d Regt. · Xuan Loc · 48th Regt. · 6th Div. · TF 315 · N · S · 1st Abn. Bde.

April 14–16

NVA artillery base · BIEN HOA · LONG KHANH · Collapse of 52d Regt. · 341st Div. · Ha Nai · Bien Hoa (Runway closed: Air support cut) · Trang Bom · Hung Loc · 6th Div. · 48th Regt. · Xuan Loc · 18th Div. · 43d Regt. · 7th Div. · TF 315 · TF 316 · TF 322 · 1st Abn. Bde.
Kilometers 0 10 · Miles 0 10

The Battle of Xuan Loc
April 9–21, 1975

➤	NVA assault
➤	NVA tank assault
➤	ARVN assault
➤	ARVN tank assault
➤	VNAF aerial assault
♀♀♀♀♀♀	Rubber plantations
⋯⋯⋯	Provincial boundaries
TF 322	South Vietnamese task force

On April 9, 1975, three Main Force NVA divisions converged on the 18th ARVN Division at Xuan Loc, the bulwark of Saigon's defenses. There, the RVNAF used everything it had to try to stop the NVA advance. Outnumbered and surrounded, the 18th ARVN Division held on while the 1st Airborne and three armored task forces, with VNAF tactical support, tried to break through NVA lines. By April 16th the battle was turning in the NVA's favor and by April 20 Xuan Loc was abandoned.

Ben Cat · 341st Div. · 7th Div. · Bien Hoa · 6th Div. · Xuan Loc · Saigon · Vung Tau · Kilometers 0 25 · Miles 0 25

divisions of the 3d Army Corps deployed northwest of the city were also to step up their attacks around Tay Ninh, tying down the 25th ARVN Division and diverting attention away from the eastern front. In addition, sappers and special action teams were to enter Saigon, link up with underground units inside the capital, and prepare the way for the "general uprising" that would accompany the final Communist offensive.

Several hours later party First Secretary Le Duan cabled Group A75 to inform them that the Central Executive Committee had approved yet another of their recommendations. As of 1900 on April 14, message number 37/TK read, the campaign to "liberate" Saigon was to be officially known as the "Ho Chi Minh Campaign." Although the resolution was intended to honor the memory of the late North Vietnamese leader, its more practical implications were not lost on the southern commanders. "We must be in Saigon to celebrate Ho Chi Minh's birthday," Pham Hung observed. The deadline, May 19, was only a month away.

After receiving Hanoi's orders General Dung called together members of his senior staff to hammer out a new plan of operation on the eastern front. Having failed to take Xuan Loc by frontal assault as originally planned, they decided to by-pass the town itself in order to accelerate the movement of troops and equipment toward Saigon. Although elements of the 341st, 6th, and 7th NVA Divisions would remain in place to pin down the 43d ARVN Regiment inside Xuan Loc, the rest of those forces were now committed to the methodical elimination of the city's outlying defenses. To solidify control over the vital intersection of Routes 1 and 20 and thus open the principal pathway leading south, Dung ordered two regiments of the 6th Division to "annihilate" the 52d ARVN Regiment's base on Route 20 and deployed the armor-supported 95B Regiment just north of Route 1 between Xuan Loc and Bien Hoa. Even more crucial to the North Vietnamese general's plan, he directed the recently arrived Artillery Group 75 to train its long-range 130MM guns on Bien Hoa Air Base to "paralyze" the South Vietnamese air force. Meanwhile, farther north and east, the three divisions of the 2d Army Corps, reinforced by the 3d NVA Division from Binh Dinh Province, were to overrun the ARVN forward command at Phan Rang, continue south along the coast and seize Phan Thiet, then swing westward and complete the conquest of Xuan Loc.

Dung wasted no time putting his new strategy into effect. Beginning with a series of heavy assaults on the 52d ARVN Regiment on April 14, the NVA systematically isolated and outflanked the South Vietnamese defenders at Xuan Loc. As shellfire poured down on ARVN positions inside the city and the 95B Regiment struck the government task force along Route 1, elements of the 6th NVA Division began quietly slipping westward through the rubber plantations toward the village of Trang Bom. On the

morning of April 15 North Vietnamese artillery shells slammed into Bien Hoa for the first time in the war, temporarily shutting down the runway. That night NVA commandos penetrated the air base and blew up part of its giant ammunition dump, setting off an explosion so powerful that it rattled windows in downtown Saigon, twenty-five kilometers to the south.

Despite General Dao's well-publicized vow to "hold Xuan Loc" no matter "how many regiments they throw against me," by nightfall on April 15 the ARVN commander was compelled to withdraw some of his troops. Decisively outnumbered, lacking air support, and thoroughly exhausted, his soldiers no longer stood a chance of

successfully resisting the onrushing North Vietnamese Army. "It's like running a twenty mile race with one contestant going the distance while the other runs a four-man relay," one Western military analyst observed at the time. "There's simply no way ARVN can win."

The following day, as helicopters set down amid the smoldering rubble that was once Xuan Loc to extract elements of the 43d Regiment, the North Vietnamese finally overran the base camp of the stubborn 52d Regiment. Breaking ranks only after 70 percent of their unit had been killed or wounded, the survivors fled toward the shattered armored task force along Route 1, which was itself in retreat west of Trang Bom. In the meantime, 130MM shells

At Xuan Loc on April 14, with NVA troops beginning to outflank the ARVN defenders, townspeople race to climb aboard the back end of a CH–47 Chinook helicopter.

continued to pound Bien Hoa with ever-increasing accuracy, damaging six F–5 Freedom Fighters and fourteen A–37 Dragonflies and all but immobilizing what remained of the Vietnamese Air Force.

That same day, April 16, the "eastern column" of General Dung's army broke through the makeshift ARVN defense line outside Phan Rang and rushed into the city. In addition to seizing nearly forty combat-ready South Vietnamese aircraft, the North Vietnamese captured MR 3 commander General Nghi, 6th Air Division commander General Pham Ngoc Sang, and an American CIA agent who had been serving as a liaison with Nghi's staff. What became of the two Vietnamese generals remains unknown. The American was released seven months later after undergoing intensive interrogation.

Pulling the plug

For the Ford administration, the collapse of ARVN's forward defense line could hardly have come at a worse time. With the April 19 deadline for Congressional action fast approaching, the president and his top advisers were engaged in a final, desperate bid to win approval of their $722 million aid proposal. No longer able to sustain the claim that additional aid could lead to a stabilization of the military situation, administration officials now introduced some new arguments on behalf of the request. Secretary Kissinger, for instance, intimated to members of the Senate Appropriations Committee on April 15 that the funds would enhance the prospects for a political solution. "The sum we have requested," he testified, "would enable the government of South Vietnam ... to negotiate under conditions more consistent with self-determination." Taking a different tack, Secretary Schlesinger warned the same committee that a Communist takeover would likely mean the execution of over 200,000 South Vietnamese.

When these pleas failed to move Congress, the president went on the attack. In a speech before the American Society of Newspaper Editors on April 16, Ford once again accused Congress of reneging on the U.S. obligation to support South Vietnam. Drawing an unfavorable contrast between American behavior toward Saigon and Chinese and Russian backing of Hanoi, he noted that "it appears that they have maintained [their] commitment. Unfortunately the US did not carry out its commitment. ... It just makes me sick," he later added, invoking a football metaphor, "that at the last minute of the last quarter the country would not make that special effort, [that] small, additional commitment in economic and military aid" needed to avert "this tragic situation." Rather than gaining fresh support for the administration's cause, however, the president's remarks only revived the controversy over the meaning of the word "commitment" and the undisclosed contents of President Nixon's letters to President Thieu.

The aid debate finally came to an end the following day when the Senate Armed Services Committee, which had previously rejected a series of compromise proposals by identical eight to seven margins, voted not to approve any additional military aid to South Vietnam. Though several other committees were still to be heard from and the question of humanitarian aid remained unsettled, the administration conceded defeat. "The time has come for restraint and compassion," Kissinger declared. "The administration

has made its case. Let all now abide by the verdict of Congress—without recrimination or vindictiveness."

As the focus of Congressional attention shifted from aid to evacuation, Kissinger redirected his own energies toward the possibility of a negotiated settlement. Earlier in the month the secretary of state had refused to pursue the prospect as long as Thieu's removal remained a precondition. But by mid-April it had become apparent that the South Vietnamese president's days were numbered. In fact, the most recent information from Ambassador Martin indicated that members of the Joint General Staff might move against Thieu once it became clear that Congress was not going to approve any additional military aid. Believing that "the essential process of negotiations [could] not be started with Thieu in power," Martin informed Kissinger on April 17 that he intended to go to Thieu "unless instructed to the contrary" and tell the South Vietnamese president that "his place in history would be better assured with the recording of all the truly significant things he has accomplished, if he does not, by staying in power too long, be remembered for failing to permit the attempt to be made to save what is left of Vietnam as a reasonably free state." The ambassador told Kissinger he would make it "absolutely crystal clear" that he was speaking only for himself, "as a friend who has always told him the whole truth." He would further say that it was his "dispassionate and objective conclusion that if he does not do this, his generals will force him to depart."

I would say that it would seem to most of the world a much more honorable way to go, if his departure was at his own volition, telling his country he did so to preserve the legitimacy of the Constitution and the successor administration which would help them negotiate from a greater position of strength to preserve a free Vietnam.

In the meantime, Martin suggested to Kissinger "perhaps some way could be found to make the Soviet Union and China believe it would be to their advantage in their future dealings with us to exercise the most massive restraint on Hanoi to back away from Saigon and resume the negotiating track."

In the same message Martin reiterated his adamant opposition to the introduction of U.S. military forces to protect the American pullout. Noting that it could "trigger a hell of a mess ... if some God-damned fool persuades any of you in senior positions to send in the Marines until I send for them," he urged Washington to "play it cool" so that he could "get our people out alive in a way that will not add a rather ghastly mistake to the thousands the Americans have already made in and about Vietnam." The ambassador promised to reduce the American community in Saigon to "2000 or less" by the end of the following week, April 26.

Kissinger made his first direct peace overture on April 18, when he met with Soviet Ambassador to the U.S. Ana-

Government soliders wounded at Xuan Loc await evacuation from a town nineteen kilometers west, Hung Loc.

toly Dobrynin and passed along a note from President Ford to Premier Leonid Brezhnev. The message stated that the "overriding concern" of the United States was to achieve "controlled conditions" for the evacuation of American citizens and select Vietnamese nationals from South Vietnam. In exchange for Hanoi's acceptance of a cease-fire, the U.S. was prepared to convene talks in Paris, stop supplying the RVN, and proceed with its withdrawal from Saigon. At the same time, Kissinger warned that any interference with the evacuation effort, including attacks against the capital, Tan Son Nhut airfield, or U.S. aircraft, would create a "most dangerous situation" for the North Vietnamese. Emphasizing that the U.S. was dealing only with Moscow, not Hanoi or Peking, the secretary of state requested a prompt reply. Dobrynin agreed. Several hours later the *New York Times* Moscow bureau reported that "Soviet diplomats" had recently assured "well-placed sources" that the North Vietnamese did not intend to attack Saigon during "the current campaign."

Unbeknownst to Kissinger, however, the day before his meeting with Dobrynin intelligence officials in Saigon had received the hardest evidence to date that Hanoi had no

interest in any form of political accommodation. A "long-range penetration" agent inside COSVN came in from the field on April 17 and reported that since late March the North Vietnamese had been committed to total military victory. He recounted the recent decision to delay the final attack until the last week of April, listed the primary targets in Saigon, and even told of preparations for an air attack on the capital. Any talk of negotiations or coalition governments, with or without Thieu, he stressed, was simply a ruse. The Communist high command had vowed to be in Saigon to celebrate Ho Chi Minh's birthday.

Since the agent "had long been a wellspring of extraordinarily accurate intelligence," CIA analyst Snepp recalled, most American and South Vietnamese intelligence officers were convinced that they now had a "complete blueprint" of Hanoi's plan. But the chief of the CIA station, Thomas Polgar, was skeptical. "Nothing new in that," Snepp remembered him saying, "we've heard it all before." Nor did Polgar change his mind when the chief

PRG delegate to the Joint Military Team two days later raised the price of a political agreement by demanding the immediate departure of Ambassador Martin. "He's cloaked as an American diplomat," Colonel Vo Dong Giang declared at a press conference on April 19, "but actively directs all military, political, and economic policies and is responsible for all criminal acts of the Thieu regime." Instead, with the encouragement of his Hungarian contacts, Polgar continued to believe that there was still time to work out an acceptable political arrangement.

Polgar's superiors back in Washington did not share his optimism. By April 19 CIA Director Colby had already concluded that "Saigon faces total defeat—and soon," and most White House officials had become preoccupied with the task of evacuation. In response to the negative Congressional verdict on the aid question, the administration had taken a number of steps in recent days to prepare for an accelerated withdrawal. In addition to expanding the fleet of U.S. evacuation ships stationed off the South Vietnamese coast near Vung Tau, the WSAG directed the State Department on April 17 to establish an interagency task force to coordinate overall planning for refugees. Under the direction of L. Dean Brown, a retired foreign service officer, the group concentrated on resolving problems involved in the prospective extraction of large numbers of Vietnamese nationals, including the determination of possible relocation sites.

Meanwhile, Admiral Gayler left his CINCPAC headquarters in Honolulu to confer with Ambassador Martin in Saigon and inform him that the time had come to "pull the plug" on the evacuation effort. Arriving on April 19, Gayler told the ambassador that Washington wanted the American community in Saigon reduced to 1,100 as quickly as possible and all Vietnamese slated for evacuation sent out by freighter to the U.S. ships off Vung Tau. But Martin balked. In the first place, he told Gayler, there was no need to cut back the U.S. presence so drastically since a final Option IV helilift could accommodate up to 2,000 Americans. Moreover, to attempt to board thousands of Vietnamese on boats anchored at Newport in full view of the Saigonese would likely plunge the city into chaos.

Admiral Gayler suggested an alternative. If the embassy were to issue a simple "affidavit of support," signed by a U.S. citizen and listing the names of those Vietnamese for whom he agreed to take financial responsibility after their departure from the RVN, large numbers of Vietnamese nationals could leave as American "dependents." It would not require much in the way of paperwork, Gayler reasoned—a piece of paper with the embassy consular seal would suffice. And since U.S. immigration authorities had just agreed to extend their "parole" to dependents of Americans not residing in the RVN, such an arrangement would allow long-distance "sponsorship" of Vietnamese evacuees. Martin quickly endorsed the idea, and before the meeting ended a draft of the affidavit was drawn up.

The new scheme removed the last major obstacle hindering an accelerated withdrawal. From April 20 on, the total number of evacuees leaving Tan Son Nhut on outbound C-130s and C-141s grew dramatically. Within forty-eight hours of the issuance of the first "affidavit of support," in fact, Vietnamese departures rose from an average of some 200 per day to more than 3,000. In addition, beginning on April 19 a series of ultrasecret "black flights" were initiated to ensure that the most "sensitive" Vietnamese, such as intelligence operatives, could get out without having to deal with GVN emigration authorities.

President Thieu was not unaware of the American decision to begin the "hard pull," but he did nothing to obstruct it. Realizing that additional military aid would probably not be forthcoming, he had finally begun to accept the inevitability of a full-scale U.S. pullout or, as he preferred to see it, U.S. abandonment. He also reconciled himself to the fact that there was no longer any hope that his army could hold back the inexorable enemy advance toward Saigon. On April 18, shortly after a Communist commando squad struck Phu Lam radar installation on the western edge of the capital, MR 3 commander General Toan had called Thieu from his headquarters at Bien Hoa to tell him that the war was in effect already lost. The last remnants of the ARVN defense force at Xuan Loc were about to collapse, the NVA 2d Corps was on the verge of seizing Phan Thiet, and on every front government forces were hopelessly outnumbered, Toan said. He also confirmed the fall of Phan Rang and the capture of General Nghi. Then, in what must have been the cruelest blow of all, the ARVN commander informed the president that government soldiers had "bulldozed and leveled" Thieu's ancestral grave site outside Phan Rang. In a culture steeped in reverence for one's forbears, there could be no greater gesture of contempt.

Later that same day a group of leading political moderates and opposition figures confronted Thieu and told him that they would publicly demand his resignation in six days if he did not agree to step down. Rather than yield to the mounting pressure, however, the president responded by ordering the arrest of several high-ranking military officers, including General Phu, who he insisted were far more responsible than he for the military debacle. Nevertheless, Thieu must have sensed that the end was drawing near. The government he ruled no longer supported him, his generals were threatening to depose him, the North Vietnamese Army surrounded him, and the Americans seemed unwilling to rescue him. By the time U.S. Ambassador Graham Martin mounted the steps of Doc Lap Palace on April 20 to call on the South Vietnamese president, Thieu was, in the words of one senior ARVN officer, "probably the most hated man in Vietnam."

A distraught mother joins other refugees at Bien Hoa. Several members of her family are missing in the battle zone.

The Saigon Redoubt

"I told President Thieu the actual military order of battle and the analysis of the comparative forces each side could bring to bear provided a very grim picture," Ambassador Martin later recalled in testimony before the House International Relations Committee. "I said it was my conclusion that almost all of his generals, although they would continue to fight, believed defense was hopeless unless a respite could be gained through the beginning of the negotiating process. And they did not believe such a process could begin unless the President left or took steps to see that the process began immediately. I said it was my feeling that if he did not move soon, his generals would ask him to go."

The fateful meeting between Martin and Thieu began shortly after ten o'clock on Sunday morning, April 20, and lasted for an hour and a half. Emphasizing that he was speaking "only as an individual, not for the President or for the Secretary of State, or even as the American Ambassa-

dor," Martin tried to convey to the South Vietnamese president "as candidly and as accurately and objectively as I could, the situation as we perceived it." At no point, Martin stressed, did he recommend or even suggest, "directly or indirectly," that Thieu should resign. Instead he made it clear that this was a decision Thieu, and Thieu alone, would have to make. He did tell Thieu, however, that most Vietnamese held him responsible for the military debacle, that they no longer thought him capable of leading the country out of its crisis, and that they believed that his departure would facilitate negotiations with the Communists. Personally, Martin said, he thought it would make little difference, but Thieu's "colleagues felt it might buy time which was now the essential commodity for South Vietnam."

Vainly, the South Vietnamese leader asked whether his resignation would have a positive effect on the aid vote in Congress. Martin replied that while it "might have changed some votes some months ago," it was a "bargain whose day had passed." Besides, the ambassador pointed out, even if additional aid were now approved, it could not arrive in time to alter the military balance sheet. After listening intently to all that Martin had to say, Thieu assured the ambassador that he would do what he thought "best for the country."

"Destiny has come to me"

Martin was not the only foreign emissary who visited Thieu that day. Shortly before Martin's black Cadillac limousine pulled up in front of Independence Palace, French Ambassador Jean-Marie Merillon met with the South Vietnamese leader and impressed upon him the same message: If Thieu did not voluntarily step down soon, the military was prepared to oust him. General Vien, the JGS chairman, later maintained that the two diplomats were mistaken. "I am certain that on our side there was absolutely no pressure from any general to force [Thieu] to resign." Yet according to some American officials, earlier that same day Vien himself joined a cabal against the president that included Defense Minister Tran Van Don, Prime Minister Nguyen Ba Can, and Economics Minister Nguyen Van Hao. Recognizing that Thieu's removal represented an unalterable precondition for any fruitful negotiations with the enemy, the four men agreed to call on the president the next day and demand his resignation. If he refused, they would tell him he had no choice.

Whatever the truth of the matter, Thieu pre-empted any direct move against him by deciding on his own to resign.

Preceding page. *An ARVN soldier waves an M79 grenade launcher to hold back civilians at a roadblock twenty-five kilometers east of Saigon on April 27. Fearful that refugees swarming into the city might trigger mass panic, the GVN sealed off all major roads into the capital on April 3.*

The first to learn of his decision were former Prime Minister Khiem and Vice President Tran Van Huong, whom the president summoned to his office just before noon on April 21. Recounting his conversations with Merillon and Martin the previous morning, Thieu emphasized that neither ambassador had advised or urged him to leave. It was rather the "hopelessness" of the military situation that had convinced him he could no longer serve a useful purpose. In relinquishing his power, however, he added one stipulation. In order to preserve the principle of constitutional legitimacy, Vice President Huong would be designated as his successor.

That evening Thieu announced his decision in a ninety-minute address to the National Assembly and a national television audience. Often rambling and at times choked with tears, the president of the Republic of Vietnam devoted most of his speech to an acerbic attack on "our great ally" and "leader of the free world," the United States. He described how he had resisted signing the Paris agreement and relented only after receiving assurances of continued military aid as well as President Nixon's "solemn pledge" that the U.S. "would actively and strongly intervene ... if North Vietnam renewed its aggression." But the Americans, Thieu charged, had failed to honor Nixon's commitments, and in the process they had dishonored themselves. "The United States has not respected its promises," he declared. "It is inhumane. It is not trustworthy. It is irresponsible." Likening the recent Congressional aid debate to "bargaining at the fish market," he added bitterly, "I could not afford to let other people bargain over the bodies of our soldiers."

Only after he finished his tirade did Thieu unveil his decision to turn over the government to Vice President Huong. "I depart today," he announced. "I ask my countrymen, the armed forces, and religious groups to forgive me my past mistakes I made while in power. The country and I will be grateful to you. I am very undeserving. I am resigning, but I am not deserting."

Immediately following the speech Tran Van Huong was formally installed as Thieu's successor. Seventy-one years old, enfeebled by asthma and arthritis, and nearly blind, the new president of the GVN inspired even less confidence as a leader than he had during his brief reign as prime minister in the mid-1960s. It was nonetheless widely hoped that Huong would quickly agree to transfer power to someone more capable of dealing with the Communists. "He is a very old and very tired man," one Western diplomat observed. "Much will depend on how well he recognizes that."

Initially, however, Huong showed little inclination to yield his newly gained power or to bargain with the enemy. "Thieu has fled destiny," he told French Ambassador Merillon. "Destiny has come to me." In his brief inauguration speech he made no mention of peace talks but instead exhorted his already defeated army to stand firm

Ambassador Martin

By Graham Anderson Martin's own admission he had always been "controversial." As U.S. ambassador to Thailand from 1963 to 1967 he had waged a fierce battle with the American military to keep U.S. ground troops out of the country. As ambassador to Rome from 1968 to 1972 he built a reputation as an imperious mission leader who demanded total loyalty from subordinates. And from the moment Martin arrived in Saigon in June 1973 as ambassador to South Vietnam—a post he accepted with great reluctance—the ambassador made it clear that he, and he alone, was running the show.

Outspoken, at times abrasive, and ever-conscious of protocol and power, Martin liked to refer to himself as "the representative of the President of the United States of America." He insisted on reading all cable traffic between the mission and the White House—a task that kept him at his desk long into the night and afforded him few opportunities to leave the embassy. This practice led one secretary in the embassy to compare Martin half jokingly to God: "I know he exists, but I haven't seen him." General John E. Murray, head of the DAO, described the workaholic ambassador as "a man of infinite mental energy."

Raised by a Baptist minister in a small town in North Carolina, Martin learned at an early age the value of hard work. After graduating from Wake Forest College in 1932, he worked briefly as a Washington correspondent for several southern newspapers before joining FDR's National Recovery Administration. In 1947 he entered the Foreign Service as Averell Harriman's protégé and was appointed administrative counselor to the U.S. Embassy in Paris. There, he was impressed by the effectiveness of Vietminh propaganda, which he felt turned French popular opinion against the Indochinese war. Eventually he reached the rank of career minister and was subsequently assigned to Bangkok as U.S. ambassador to Thailand. By 1973, when Martin was sworn in as ambassador to South Vietnam, he was a well-established Indochina hand.

Tall, poised, and soft-spoken, Martin gave the impression of a gracious southern gentleman, but he was a man of overwhelming self-confidence who seldom, if ever, doubted the wisdom or accuracy of his own views. As Martin once reminded a U.S. senator, "The one asset I have prized most highly is a reputation for complete and total integrity. . . . This fact is too widely known to be open to serious question."

Although Martin unquestionably adopted a hard line, he was far from a typical Indochina hawk. As ambassador to Thailand he strongly urged that no U.S. combat troops be introduced into the country because, as he put it, "you may have some American boys over there in Vietnam who can tell the difference between a good (anticommunist) Vietnamese and a bad one, but I doubt it. In any case, I can guarantee that there aren't any kids who can tell the difference between a good Thai and a bad one." Even during Vietnam's final days, when the Ford administration wanted to send in the U.S. Marines to secure the American evacuation, Martin vehemently lobbied against such a move.

His hawkish reputation largely derived from his crusade against the press corps and liberals. Martin branded Senator McGovern and the peace movement pawns of a great conspiracy to subvert American opinion. And in one of his many outbursts against newsmen he castigated the editors of the *New York Times* charging that their "emotional involvement in a North Vietnamese victory was transparent."

At no point in his career, however, did Martin generate more controversy than during South Vietnam's final weeks. The main charge leveled against him was that he was out of touch with the situation, that he had misread Hanoi's intentions, overestimated Saigon's chances for survival, and therefore needlessly, perhaps dangerously, delayed the American withdrawal. The ambassador's detractors pointed to such evidence as his statement on April 3 that "there is no danger to Saigon," as well as his claim on April 9 that South Vietnam could survive as a truncated nation. As journalist H. D. S. Greenway recalled, "Some of us thought that Martin might just find a way to stay and die in Saigon like Gordon at Khartoum."

Others, like Lieutenant Colonel Harry G. Summers of the DAO, were more sympathetic to Martin's situation. He believed Martin was given two virtually contradictory tasks: to preserve order in Saigon and at the same time accelerate the evacuation of the American community. President Ford and Secretary of State Kissinger also acknowledged the difficulties of their ambassador's position and publicly praised his performance.

Despite this public support, Martin sensed that he was being set up as a fall guy. In an April 19, 1975, cable to Henry Kissinger, Martin wrote that the intelligence community, the Defense Department, and the State Department had all taken steps to ensure that if something went wrong they would not be blamed. "The only one whose ass isn't covered is me," Martin wrote. Kissinger replied, "My ass isn't covered. I can assure you it will be hanging several yards higher than you when this is all over."

Martin had his own explanation for his conduct during the last weeks of April 1975: He was determined "to play it cool" and avoid any action that might trigger a repetition of the horror of Da Nang. To keep a lid on things, Martin argued, required sustaining the "legitimacy" of the GVN while effecting a "gradual drawdown" of Americans. The appearance of business as usual, Martin maintained, was intentional—a manifestation of the "sense of theater" which he claimed was an essential part of any good diplomat's "baggage."

The question was whether Martin's "sense of theater" ultimately deceived himself as much as his audience. As late as April 27, 1975, Martin cabled to Kissinger, "It is the unanimous opinion of the senior personnel here that there will be no direct or serious attack on Saigon."

In the end history would determine whether Martin was to be vilified or venerated for his performance in Vietnam. In June 1976 he told a Congressional committee, "I believe future dispassionate historians will record that we did what we set out to do in April, 1975. . . . If I could relive that month I would change almost nothing in the way the Saigon Mission reacted to the realities of the unfolding situation."

Neither Huong's futile bellicosity nor the Communists' growing intransigence, however, deterred those who still thought that a negotiated settlement was possible. The day after Thieu resigned, CIA station Chief Polgar again met with Colonel Toth, the head of the Hungarian ICCS team, to find out whether the fulfillment of the PRG's principal demand—Thieu's ouster—had in fact softened their stance. The Hungarian was cryptic. "If you play gin rummy," he said, "you know that when you put down a card your opponent picks it up to determine whether to keep or discard it. We have picked up your card." At the same time, French officials began promoting the "Big Minh solution" more actively than ever. By the morning of April 22, according to CIA analyst Frank Snepp, French intelligence Chief Brochand was "spending every waking minute with ["Big"] Minh, coaching and encouraging him, and warding off all potential challengers."

The effort to push Minh to the fore quickly ran into problems. To begin with, Minh insisted that he could "strike a bargain" with the Communists only if he were first invested with full presidential powers. President Huong, however, would agree only to offer Minh the post of prime minister on the grounds that he was not empowered to relinquish his own authority to someone else. "The power which I possess has been granted to me by the constitution," he told the National Assembly. "This power is not like a handkerchief or a banknote that I can take out of my pocket, hand over to the general and tell him: Here you are. I cannot do that." Nor was he convinced that the Communists were any more willing to deal with Minh. "I shall believe it," Huong said, "only after I have proof."

Instead Huong launched a peace initiative of his own, calling for an immediate cease-fire and the establishment of a National Council of Reconciliation, announcing the dismissal of Prime Minister Can's nine-day-old "government of national union," and proposing to send the outgoing information minister, Brigadier General Phan Hoa Hiep, as a special emissary to Hanoi. The Communists reacted contemptuously to all three gestures, particularly the offer of a cease-fire. It "fools no one," a spokesman for the PRG delegation in Saigon asserted, "and will hardly help the Americans out of their defeat."

Yet just as the quest for a political solution began to look utterly hopeless, an apparent breakthrough occurred. On April 23 the White House received Brezhnev's reply to President Ford's note of April 18. The Soviet leader reportedly made several points: that the "Vietnamese side" had assured Moscow that it had no intention of interfering with the American evacuation, that they did not want to humiliate the United States, and that they were willing "to proceed from the Paris accords" with respect to political issues. In return, it was expected that the U.S. would take "no action," presumably meaning military action, that might exacerbate the situation.

Despite the ambiguity of the message, Secretary Kissinger interpreted it to mean that the withdrawal of the Americans and "select" Vietnamese could continue without fear of Communist attack, that Hanoi might agree to a residual American presence in Saigon after the evacuation, and that the PRG was willing to negotiate a coalition arrangement as envisioned in the Paris agreement. Moreover, since Kissinger had originally proposed to the Soviets that two weeks be allowed for the U.S. pullout, he now assumed that that timetable had proved acceptable to Hanoi even though Brezhnev made no specific mention of it. The secretary of state immediately cabled the text of the Soviet reply as well as his interpretation of it to Ambassador Martin in Saigon.

To General Dung, the various "shrewd diplomatic maneuvers" of those who sought "to halt our advancing troops and save themselves from defeat" were meaningless. By April 22 the North Vietnamese commander and his staff had already put the finishing touches on their plan for the "Ho Chi Minh Campaign," and "the resolution for attack" had been approved and signed. A variation on the "blossoming lotus" tactic employed at Ban Me Thuot, the blueprint for the assault on Saigon called for lightning thrusts by mechanized units against five principal targets inside the capital: Independence Palace, the Joint General Staff headquarters, the Special Capital Zone headquarters, the General Police Directorate, and Tan Son Nhut airfield. Once these vital "nerve centers" of the GVN were "smashed," Dung reasoned, "the Saigon army and administration would be like a snake without a head. What remained of their system of defense and repression would fall apart, the masses would rise up . . . and Saigon would be quickly liberated." Countless lives would be spared, the general added, and material destruction would be kept to a minimum.

Dung also realized that to pull off his plan he could not rely on the same methods of diversion and evasion that had proved so successful in the highlands campaign. At Ban Me Thuot most ARVN Main Force units had been lured away from the central target in advance of the attack, leaving only two battalions of regular troops and a collection of Regional Forces to defend the city's perimeter. Saigon, by contrast, was protected by five infantry divisions deployed in a ring thirty to fifty kilometers from the center of the city. If the NVA were to attempt to slip around the capital's defenses, the South Vietnamese were almost certain to pull back to Saigon and dig in for a prolonged last stand. Yet if they committed themselves to destroying ARVN's outlying forces before turning toward the capital, the cost in lives, destruction, and above all time would be unacceptably high.

To resolve the problem and maximize the chances for a quick, "decisive" victory, Dung decided to take the risk of dividing his forces. Rather than attempt to overrun the government units on the outskirts, he would use only those forces necessary to encircle them, isolate them, and prevent them from retreating to Saigon. The bulk of his forces would meanwhile move in rapidly to secure the major roads, bridges, and other key positions leading into Saigon, thus opening the way for the mechanized assault units assigned to seize the five chosen objectives inside the city. As they approached their targets, sappers, special action teams, and "self-defense units" would serve as guides, "neutralize traitors, and mobilize the masses for an uprising." Even more crucial support would be provided by long-range artillery, a battery of SA-2 antiaircraft missiles, and a group of captured A-37 light bombers. Whether the North Vietnamese ever intended to use the SA-2s Dung would not say. The purpose of the 130MM guns and the A-37s, however, was clear: to shut down Tan Son Nhut airfield before the final attack.

After poring over their maps and charts, Dung, Le Duc Tho, and Pham Hung ultimately set two tentative springboard dates: April 27 for the attacks on the perimeter, April 29 for the final drive. It was further decided that Nhon Trach, a marshland southeast of Saigon that had been selected as the site for the antiaircraft batteries, would have to be occupied by "28 April at the latest," the same day that Dung hoped to launch the first North Vietnamese air strike of the war.

In the days that followed, the eighteen divisions and approximately 130,000 troops under Dung's command moved methodically into position for the final attack. East of Sai-

Corpses at Long Thanh on the road to Saigon lie amid wreckage of a bus destroyed by an NVA tank shell, April 27.

gon, the 4th Army Corps, after seizing Trang Bom, edged along Route 1 toward Bien Hoa, while the 2d Army Corps moved down Route 2 toward Ba Ria and Vung Tau. To the southwest, the 232d Tactical Force and several independent regiments closed in on South Vietnamese defensive positions along Route 4 and prepared to cut off all access to Saigon from the delta. To the northwest, the 3d Army Corps began to encircle the 25th ARVN Division, stretched out along Routes 1 and 20. Due north of the capital, meanwhile, the long-awaited reserve divisions of the 1st Army Corps moved into assembly areas east of Ben Cat.

The scramble to get out

As the North Vietnamese Army tightened its grip on the capital, as the politicians bickered over who should run the government, and the hope for a peaceful settlement faded with each passing day, the desperate scramble to

Americans and South Vietnamese await evacuation from Tan Son Nhut airfield in Saigon on April 27.

escape from Saigon intensified. Aware that the pace of the American withdrawal was accelerating, thousands of Saigonese converged on the U.S. Embassy and the DAO compound in a frantic search for some way out of the country. Everywhere Americans were besieged by Vietnamese waving letters postmarked from the States, missionary school diplomas, and U.S. Army discharges—any document that established some slender connection to the United States. Outside the American embassy a young Vietnamese woman clutched a telegram with the words "Phuong, I love you. I want to marry you, Tom," and tried to convince a consular official to issue her a visa. Others searched for sponsors who would agree to sign an "affidavit of support" in their behalf. "Fairly pretty high school girl, 18, of well-to-do family," read one classified advertisement in the *Saigon Post*, "seeks adoption by or marriage with foreigner of American, French, British, German or other nationality who would take her abroad legally to enable her to continue her college studies outside Vietnam at her own expense. Please telephone 45470." When a CBS correspondent trying to reach Hong Kong kept typing

over the wire, "Can you get me Hong Kong?" the Vietnamese operator repeatedly tapped back, "Can you get me out?"

To accommodate the growing crush of applicants for evacuation, General Smith ordered all processing moved from the cramped movie theater at the DAO compound to the more spacious annex a half a mile away. Field kitchens were set up, the bowling alley converted into a makeshift nursery, and the gymnasium established as the new processing center. At first U.S. officials tried to screen prospective evacuees for proper documentation and then assign them to flights according to preset quotas for each U.S. agency. But as the crowds grew, at times swelling to as many as 10,000 people, the formal procedures quickly broke down. "Sometimes I was facing families of fifty or sixty members," recalled Ken Moorefield, a former aide to Ambassador Martin who was assigned to man the screening desk, "all of them supposedly the 'immediate relatives' of an American sponsor."

At first I tried to restrict each group to ten or fifteen on the theory I had to make space for others. But how do you explain to a Vietnamese that he is going to have to leave a half dozen of his loved ones behind? Many of them wanted me to make the selection for them, since they couldn't face up to it themselves. I tried to do the best I could, with all the compassion I could muster. But God, it was impossible! Imagine, hundreds of people sliding before you every few minutes, tears running down their faces, beseeching you to recognize their particular problems.

Moorefield bent the rules when he could. When it became apparent that South Vietnamese authorities and black marketeers were profiting handsomely from the sale of phony "dependent status" papers, he began issuing his own bogus forms that said simply, "I've lost my paperwork, but I'm an American dependent" or "This is my legally adopted child." Although South Vietnamese consular officials initially objected, once assured that they and their families would be evacuated they became more cooperative.

Moorefield's personal improvisations received some measure of endorsement when the Senate Judiciary Committee, at the urging of Secretary Kissinger, unanimously approved a proposal on April 22 to waive entry restrictions for 130,000 "aliens from Indochina," including 50,000 "high risk" Vietnamese. Although the new ruling did not officially go into effect for three more days, it had an immediate impact on the Saigon evacuation. In addition to easing concern about where the Vietnamese departees might ultimately be placed, the "high risk" provision in effect eliminated the need to pair each evacuee with an American sponsor. Anyone without an "affidavit of support" or other proof of dependent status could now simply be declared "high risk" and sent off under the 50,000-person quota. "Using the John Marshall broad construction approach," Ambassador Martin later told Congress, "we stretched the authority to cover the problem."

What the Americans could not stretch any further, however, was the capacity of the airlift itself. By April 22 evacuation planes were flying in and out of Tan Son Nhut round-the-clock, huge C-141s by day and smaller C-130s at night. Every half-hour on the average another plane would arrive, board up to 200 passengers, and then take off for the Philippines or Andersen Air Force Base on the island of Guam. U.S. officials also continued to organize one or more "black flights" each day to ensure that especially "sensitive" Vietnamese, many of them intelligence operatives who had worked for the Americans, could get out without the knowledge of the GVN. To prevent South Vietnamese police and security personnel from obstructing the secret exodus, the embassy and the DAO were ultimately forced to pay out substantial bribes.

As a result of the expanded American evacuation effort, the numbers of departing Vietnamese rose steadily throughout the last week of April—2,781 on the twenty-second; 3,824 on the twenty-third; 5,574 on the twenty-fourth. The American "drawdown" also proceeded apace until, by April 24, virtually all "non-essential" government personnel had been evacuated. That same day the West German, Dutch, Canadian, Thai, Japanese, and Australian embassies all shut down, leaving only the French, the Belgians, and the Americans with official diplomatic missions in Saigon.

In Washington, the stepped-up pace of the American withdrawal still did not satisfy many members of Congress. Convinced that any further postponement of a total U.S. pullout was pointless, the sizable antiwar bloc in the House and Senate insisted that the Ford administration immediately reduce the American presence in South Vietnam to a bare minimum. As Senator Dick Clark of Iowa put it: "We don't want any more Americans in Saigon than can be removed in one swoop of a helicopter." Nor did Congress show much sympathy for the administration's argument that the United States had an obligation to rescue as many "endangered" Vietnamese as possible. "They can do what they did in Cambodia," said one Senate Democrat, "bring out as many as they can at the same time that they bring out Americans. But we're not going to let them go beyond that." In response to Ford's request for authority to use U.S. troops if necessary to assist in the evacuation of Vietnamese nationals, several prominent liberals voiced fears that any such legislation might provide a pretext for renewed military intervention. "We could bomb Cambodia and Laos and North Vietnam if the president determined that it was necessary to evacuate all foreign nationals," Representative Elizabeth Holtzman (D-NY) warned. Fellow New Yorker Bella Abzug was even more alarmist: "This legislation is just an excuse to enable the United States to remain in Vietnam and to use military force if necessary to maintain control. . . . It borders on a new Gulf of Tonkin resolution."

In an effort to allay Congressional suspicions about his

145

Struggle to Get Out

On April 22 the American evacuation effort went into high gear; around the clock, C–130 and C–141 transports touched down at Tan Son Nhut airport, loaded the passengers, and took off. Thousands of Vietnamese desperate to secure a flight out of South Vietnam to Guam or the Philippines lined up in front of the U.S. Embassy and DAO complex. But even with the accelerated airlift and the loosening of immigration restrictions, too many Vietnamese wanted to leave on too few flights. According to one U.S. intelligence report, a Vietnamese without an American sponsor faced a "fifty to one" chance of getting out.

Above. *Vietnamese anxiously wait in line in front of the U.S. Embassy hoping to guarantee a seat on an evacuation flight.* Right. *At Tan Son Nhut airport on April 22, South Vietnamese children are led off buses onto a C–130 transport.*

intentions, President Ford astonished the nation on April 23 by declaring, in effect, the end of the Vietnam War. Yielding to the advice of his domestic political advisers and, in view of some, his own better instincts, the president seized the occasion of a long-scheduled speech at Tulane University in New Orleans to urge the American people to forget the past and to begin thinking about the future. Drafted by Robert Hartmann and speechwriter Milt Friedman without the knowledge of Secretary Kissinger, the speech compared America's travail in Vietnam to the humiliation of the British capture of Washington in the War of 1812. Just as the Battle of New Orleans had subsequently restored the nation's self-esteem, the president asserted, "America can regain the sense of pride that existed before Vietnam. But it cannot be achieved by refighting a war that is finished as far as America is concerned." As soon as Ford uttered the word "finished," the primarily student audience of 4,500 erupted into a thunderous roar of shouts and applause that went on for several minutes. "It was one of those moments that seemed to crystallize the whole nation's mood," wrote journalist Arnold Isaacs. "America wanted to forget the war, not argue about the blame."

Two days later, following a stormy fourteen-hour debate, House and Senate conferees finally agreed to authorize the use of U.S. military forces in the evacuation but only within narrowly prescribed limits. American troops could be employed "only in numbers, areas and for the length of time" required to complete the withdrawal of U.S. citizens and their dependents, the congressmen stipulated. No provision was made for the evacuation of Vietnamese nationals. Yet when some House members objected that even these restrictions were not stringent enough, the final vote on the measure was postponed until April 29 or 30.

"Nothing historic"

Half a world away, American officials in Saigon seemed less concerned about the outcome of the legislative debate over the limits of presidential authority than by the possibility that a full-scale U.S. pullout might yet prove unnecessary. On the morning of April 25, a fresh series of signals once again fanned hopes that the Communists might be willing to accept a "controlled solution." First came another approach to Polgar by the Hungarian ICCS representative, Colonel Toth, who told the CIA station chief that the PRG delegation wanted to meet with him on Sunday, the twenty-seventh, to discuss "political problems." The Hungarian also made it clear, however, that fruitful talks now required a "clear break" with the South Vietnamese

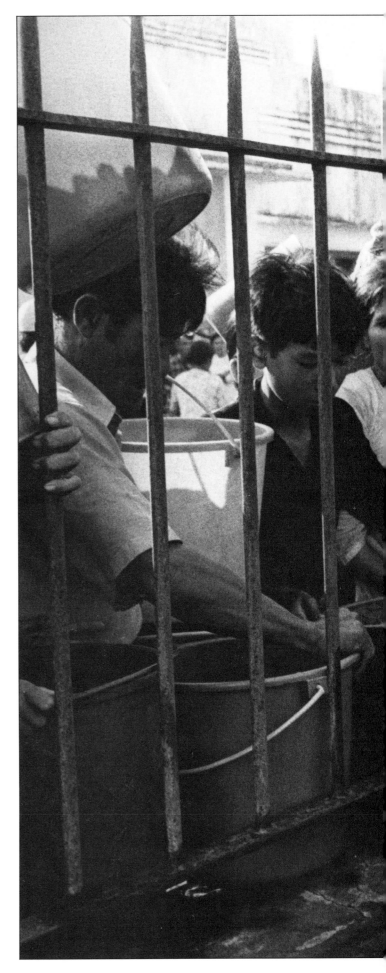

South Vietnamese relief workers supply water to refugees at a camp near Vung Tau. The refugees have been detained at the camp to keep them out of Saigon.

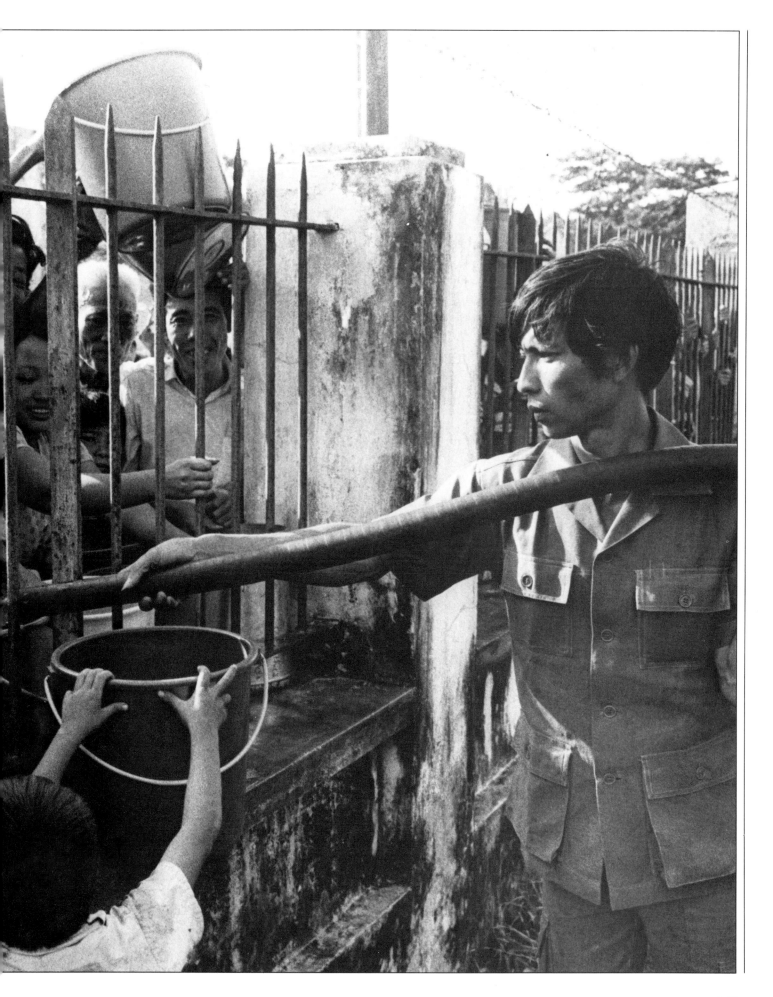

constitution, presumably meaning that Huong would have to be deposed and replaced by Minh, as well as a pledge from the U.S. that it would not intervene militarily.

Several hours later a more direct, and hence more credible, indication of Hanoi's intentions was communicated to Lieutenant Colonel Harry Summers of the Joint Military Team delegation. After flying into Hanoi on what proved to be the last of the JMT's weekly liaison flights, Summers was taken aside by his North Vietnamese escort, Major Huyen, who "went to great pains to make the point that there was no reason friendly relations could not be quickly established between the US and the DRV." "Why are all you Americans leaving?" Huyen asked in an excited voice. "You know that we have told you that we mean you no harm." Rather, the major asserted, it was only the DAO staff of "military advisers" that "must go." The American delegation to the Joint Military Team should stay on to accomplish its humanitarian tasks, while the embassy would be allowed to work out its future with the new government. When Summers suggested that future relations between the two countries largely depended upon how the war ended, Huyen assured him that there would be no "blood-bath." "I tell you honestly," he said, "there will be no reprisals—we need these people to rebuild Vietnam."

On the return flight to Saigon several other North Vietnamese officers reiterated the same message, thus indicating that Huyen was not just offering his personal views but conveying an official line. Although the subject of a negotiated settlement was never directly broached, Summers inferred from the conversation that Hanoi preferred a political solution to the conflict. After reading the colonel's report, Ambassador Martin and other senior embassy officials agreed. Even more heartening in the ambassador's view were Huyen's remarks about the Joint Military Team and the U.S. Embassy, which seemed to confirm Kissinger's assumption that the North Vietnamese were willing to permit a gradual American withdrawal as well as a residual U.S. presence in Saigon.

Whether Major Huyen and his comrades were deliberately deceiving the Americans or, as Colonel Summers later speculated, whether they may have been presenting the view of only one faction of the DRV leadership, remains unknown. Postwar Communist accounts contain only a few scattered references to the diplomatic by-play and political maneuvering that went on during the war's final days. Most are derisive. The rest are at best ambiguous. For example, in *Great Spring Victory*, General Dung's memoir of the 1975 offensive, the North Vietnamese commander noted that Group A75 decided to split up just prior to launching the attack on Saigon, with Dung going to a new forward headquarters at Ben Cat while Le Duc Tho and Pham Hung remained behind to coordinate "diplomatic, political, and military activities." Dung offered no clue, however, as to whether those diplomatic and political activities might potentially have included a last-minute settlement. He also observed at one point that the Americans played the "Duong Van Minh card ... far too late," thereby implying that Hanoi might have been willing to accept the "Minh solution" at an earlier date. But again, he gave no indication when that date had passed.

What is clear, however, is that by April 25 any chance for a peaceful solution had become exceedingly remote. Despite increasingly insistent calls for Huong's resignation by leading South Vietnamese political figures, the aged new president of the GVN still refused to surrender his power to Minh or anyone else. General Dung, meanwhile, was locking the final details in place for the "Ho Chi Minh Campaign," now scheduled to begin at precisely 1700 hours the following day with a series of major attacks on the eastern front. And the Americans, though still hopeful that a deal with the Communists might be worked out by the GVN, were proceeding with their preparations for a "worst case" Option IV evacuation. That day a platoon of marines was brought in from the offshore fleet to bolster security at the DAO compound and a new emergency warning system devised to alert all Americans if and when a final helolift was mounted. On E-Day (Evacuation Day), the DAO radio station would transmit the code phrase "the temperature is 105 degrees and rising," followed by Bing Crosby's "White Christmas."

Shortly after 9:30 P.M. that evening, a small caravan of cars attached to the U.S. Embassy slowly approached the front gate at Tan Son Nhut airfield. In the back of one of the cars, a big Chevrolet driven by the CIA's Frank Snepp, sat embassy military liaison General Charles Timmes, a minor Vietnamese official, and, sandwiched between them, the former president of the Republic of Vietnam, Nguyen Van Thieu. As the car reached the military checkpoint at the main gate, Timmes turned to Thieu and warned him to stay down. But it was unnecessary. Once the guards identified the diplomatic license plates they simply waved the convoy through. Moments later Snepp wheeled the car onto the tarmac, extinguished the headlights, and then braked to a halt near the Air America terminal. Dimly visible a short distance away was an American C–118 transport plane, guarded by several plainclothes marines. Next to them, at the foot of the boarding ramp, stood Ambassador Martin. Snepp recalled that Thieu, fighting back tears, briefly thanked him, slid out of the car, and scurried up the ramp accompanied by his aides and by former Prime Minister Khiem. Martin followed. A short time later the ambassador descended the steps and the plane took off for Taiwan. Later asked what he had said to Thieu in their final meeting aboard the plane, the ambassador replied, "I just told him goodbye. Nothing historic. Just goodbye."

Refugees from the Mekong Delta, with their personal belongings, head by truck for Saigon—the last GVN enclave.

The End

On Saturday morning, April 26, 125 members of the South Vietnamese National Assembly sat in hushed anticipation as President Tran Van Huong rose to speak. Many of the legislators hoped, some even assumed, that Huong had called them together to announce his resignation. At first it seemed that he would not disappoint them. Conceding that "we are lost" and "have no choice but to negotiate," the aged president declared himself ready to yield power to General Duong Van Minh. There was, however, one condition. He would relinquish the presidency, he stipulated, only if the legislature formally directed him to do so; he would not give up power unless the assembly first voted to take it away. "If you cannot decide to replace me with General Minh," he warned, "and if we cannot successfully and happily negotiate, then Saigon must be turned into a mountain of bones and a river of blood." For the one thing he would not do, Huong affirmed, was capitulate. "The term 'negotiation'

does not mean surrender," he pointed out, logically if unrealistically. "If negotiation meant surrender, why would we have to negotiate? . . . If God no longer wants Vietnam to exist, we shall die with our country, but we cannot surrender."

After Huong finished his speech, a heated debate erupted on the floor of the assembly over whether, and in what way, the government ought to be altered to meet Communist demands. Some of the legislators, primarily those formerly allied to President Thieu, opposed Minh's elevation for fear of reprisals at his hands. Others, on the right, proposed that Air Vice Marshal Nguyen Cao Ky be chosen as Huong's successor to carry on the fight against the enemy. Still others argued in favor of a "clear break" with the constitution since this was what the "other side" had most recently specified.

In the meantime, as if to underscore the meaninglessness, the almost hallucinatory nature, of this eleventh-hour dispute, the Communists made it unmistakably clear that the only "settlement" they would now accept was total capitulation. Dropping any pretense that they might enter into negotiations, and further abandoning the oft-repeated claim that they were fighting to uphold the terms of the Paris agreement, the Provisional Revolutionary Government demanded the dismantlement of the entire structure of the GVN, including the army and police, as agencies of American "neo-colonialism." Furthermore, in a statement apparently directed at General Minh and his "neutralist" supporters, they called upon the "Third Force" to "see through . . . the pernicious scheme of the US and its henchmen" and help "reduce to a minimum the sacrifices and losses of our people" by joining in the "general uprising."

If there were any lingering doubts about the intent of that message, they were soon erased. At precisely 5:00 P.M., right on schedule, the seven divisions of the 2d and 4th North Vietnamese Army Corps launched the "Ho Chi Minh Campaign" with a series of major attacks along Saigon's eastern defense line. Operating on what General Dung called the "Xuan Loc-Bien Hoa front," the 6th, 7th, and 341st NVA Divisions advanced toward Bien Hoa Air Base and the former U.S. base at Long Binh behind a torrent of artillery fire. Farther to the south, the 304th and 325th NVA Divisions attacked ARVN defensive positions at Long Thanh and attempted to cut Route 15, the sole remaining overland link between Saigon and Vung Tau, while the 3d "Gold Star" Division assaulted Ba Ria at the base of the Vung Tau Peninsula.

Neither the Communists' words nor their actions, however, seemed to have any effect on the Saigon politicians. Throughout the day and well on into the evening, the members of the National Assembly remained at loggerheads, unable to reach agreement on Huong's successor. To break the deadlock, after ten hours of debate they finally decided to hand the choice back to the president. By a 123-2 vote, the legislators resolved to support Huong "in the mission of seeking ways and means to restore peace to South Vietnam on the basis of the Paris agreement." A corollary proviso authorized Huong, if it became necessary, to select a replacement "to carry out the above mission" with the assembly's approval. Then, after a moment of silent prayer for peace, the assembly adjourned.

April 27

Hours later, early on the morning of April 27, the first attack on the capital in more than five years shattered the predawn stillness. Four heavy Communist rockets slammed into downtown Saigon and the populous district of Cholon. The blasts killed 10 people, wounded more than 200, and ignited a raging fire that left some 5,000 people homeless. All around the city heavy fighting erupted as North Vietnamese forces rushed forward on five fronts toward their appointed objectives.

At his command post in an abandoned government Ranger camp near Ben Cat, General Dung closely monitored the movement of his troops, watching for any signs of unanticipated ARVN resistance. Although the South Vietnamese fought "stubbornly," the general later reported, his NVA forces "attacked like a hurricane" and made rapid progress. Southwest of the capital, just as Dung had planned, the 232d Tactical Force permanently severed Route 4 nineteen kilometers from the city's edge and engaged elements of ARVN's 7th, 9th, and 22d Divisions. To the north and northwest, the 3d Army Corps blocked Route 1 at several points between Saigon and Tay Ninh and surrounded the 25th ARVN Division at Cu Chi. To the east the 4th Army Corps closed in on Bien Hoa, while the two divisions assigned to take Long Thanh overran government defenders following one of the fiercest tank battles of the war. And to the southeast, the 3d NVA Division drove the rebuilt 3d ARVN Division and remnants of the 1st Airborne Brigade out of Ba Ria and tightened the ring around Vung Tau.

As soon as the news of the latest Communist advances reached Washington, President Ford convened an emergency meeting of the Washington Special Action Group to reconsider the available options. With the Saigon-Vung Tau highway now sealed off, the administration quickly ruled out the possibility of mounting a large-scale sea lift (the expanded version of Option III, also known as Option V) from the beaches at Vung Tau. Also discarded were contingency plans to move out as many as 30,000 Saigonese on U.S. cargo ships docked at Newport Harbor. The ships, it was decided, would have to set sail at once—without passengers—before the entire Saigon River corridor

---

Preceding page. *On April 29, the day before Saigon fell, evacuees board an Air America helicopter at one of several downtown Saigon evacuation points.*

fell prey to North Vietnamese artillery, which would effectively block any passage to sea.

Having in effect abandoned any hope of evacuating large numbers of Vietnamese from Saigon, the White House planners contacted Admiral Gayler at his Honolulu headquarters and instructed him to prepare for a total U.S. pullout, perhaps Option IV. But Ambassador Martin objected. There was no need to resort to "extraordinary measures," he informed Secretary Kissinger, since no more than 1,000 Americans remained in Saigon and he "could get a maximum number of Vietnamese and Americans out by the thirtieth" by means of the ongoing airlift. Yielding to their "man on the scene," the members of the WSAG agreed to delay. That day 7,578 more people left Tan Son Nhut on outbound planes, the largest single daily exodus since the airlift began. Only 219 of the evacuees, however, were Americans.

Retreating ARVN soldiers were already appearing on the city's streets when President Huong, on the afternoon of the twenty-seventh, finally stopped vacillating. After conferring one last time with his chief advisers, he asked Senate President Tran Van Lam to notify the members of the National Assembly that he would resign as soon as they could gather together. Stressing that "action must be taken as soon as possible," he further recommended that the legislators name Duong Van Minh as his successor

Buildings burn after the rocket attack on Saigon on Sunday, April 27. Five rockets exploded in the Central Market area of the South Vietnamese capital in the predawn hours.

and put an end to the pointless bickering that had paralyzed them the preceding day. At 6:45 that evening the assembly reconvened. An hour and a half later it reached a decision. With one-third of the representatives abstaining, the assembly voted to elevate General Minh to the presidency to "carry out the mission of seeking ways and means to restore peace to South Vietnam." Minh's inauguration was tentatively scheduled for nine o'clock the following morning, Monday, April 28.

April 28

Shortly after daybreak, just a few kilometers north of downtown Saigon, North Vietnamese commandos overran two government outposts at the far end of the Newport Bridge. Setting up a machine-gun nest they immediately began firing at anything that moved within range. Repeated attempts by South Vietnamese soldiers and helicopter gunships to dislodge the attackers failed. The Saigon-Bien Hoa highway, the last major artery leading into the capital, was closed.

As General Dung's forces edged ever closer to their fi-

nal objectives, the new president-designate of the Republic of Vietnam remained at his villa near the presidential palace interviewing prospective cabinet members. Throughout the day Minh repeatedly postponed his inauguration as one candidate after another filed into his garden to chat amid the general's prize orchids and tropical fish. Dissatisfied with most of the choices, he ultimately decided to delay naming a full cabinet until after he was sworn in. Only Vu Van Mau, a long-time associate of Minh's who headed the Buddhist National Reconciliation Force, and Nguyen Van Huyen, a liberal Catholic and former Senate president, would join the government immediately—Mau as prime minister, Huyen as vice president.

It was shortly before 5:00 P.M. when Minh and his entourage arrived at Independence Palace, where some 200 notables had been gathering for several hours. At 5:15 President Huong hobbled up to the podium to deliver his farewell address. Thunderclaps signaling the approach of the summer monsoons boomed outside as Huong spoke. "General, your mission is very heavy, [but] if you wholeheartedly serve the country . . . and strive to restore peace and ensure that the bloodshed stops, the meritorious service you render will be remembered forever by younger generations." After Huong finished, one of Minh's aides walked up to the podium, removed the plaque bearing the national seal of the RVN, and replaced it with a yin-and-yang sign enclosed by an apricot blossom—a symbol of the reconciliation of opposites.

Convinced that the Communists would negotiate with him, President Minh began his brief acceptance speech by calling for an immediate cease-fire and the commencement of formal talks in accordance with the principles of the Paris accords. Noting that his choices for vice president and prime minister were both long-standing opponents of President Thieu, he pledged to assemble an administration drawn from all parts of the "Third Force" political spectrum. And to show his good faith, he promised to free all political prisoners and lift restrictions on the press. At the same time, however, he ordered all government soldiers to "protect the remaining territory" and refuse to surrender until a cease-fire was in place. Lightning flashed above Saigon and it was raining heavily when Minh concluded his speech with an appeal to those attempting to flee abroad to "remain here to join us and all those with good will in building a new South for our future generations." It was 5:50 P.M.

Ten minutes later, air controllers at Tan Son Nhut spotted five A-37 aircraft approaching the airfield at an altitude of approximately 5,000 feet. "A-37s!" one of them radioed as the jets dropped into steep dives. "What group do you belong to? What group?" But the only reply he re-

The April 27 rocket attack destroyed hundreds of homes in the center of town. Here, some of the 5,000 newly homeless douse flames and search for missing family members.

157

ceived was, "These are American-made aircraft." Moments later the pilots released their bombs over a line of Vietnamese Air Force planes parked along the main runway, destroying three AC-119 gunships and several C-47s. After pulling out of their runs, the jets veered northward toward the captured airfield at Phan Rang, strafing Route 1 along the way.

Out in the rain-washed streets, the concussive shock of the explosions brought traffic to a dead halt and sent people scurrying for shelter. For a time, the entire city seemed to erupt in gunfire as soldiers and police fired wildly into the darkening sky. At Tan Son Nhut, meanwhile, several South Vietnamese F-5s scrambled into the air in the hope of intercepting the attackers. But it was far too late. The first and only Communist air strike of the war, with the code name "Determined to Win," had been flawlessly executed.

At first it was widely believed that the air attack had been launched in response to Minh's accession to power. In fact it had been planned weeks before. Since his defection to the Communists after the bombing of Independence Palace on April 8, former South Vietnamese Lieutenant, now North Vietnamese Captain, Nguyen Thanh Trung had been training a small group of MiG pilots to fly several relatively simple A-37 "Dragonfly" jets captured from the South Vietnamese earlier during the offensive. General Dung had told them that they would be given "only one day, only one time" to make the strike. It was merely coincidence that when the flight group took off from Phan Rang at 5:15, with Trung leading the way, President Huong was delivering his resignation speech.

To the Americans, however, the timing of the air strike was of far less consequence than its impact on the continuing airlift. Within minutes of the first pass, General Smith had put two inbound C-130s into a holding pattern and ordered a temporary suspension of the evacuation. The planes were still circling far to the east of Tan Son Nhut an hour later when Ambassador Martin called the defense attaché for a damage assessment. Told that the runways were still in serviceable condition despite the destruction of the VNAF planes, Martin was relieved. The fixed-wing airlift would continue as planned. At 8:00 P.M. the two C-130s landed, boarded 360 passengers, and departed without incident. A short time later, Ambassador Martin told Smith that a "maximum practicable" schedule of sixty C-130 flights would be flown the following day, April 29, to evacuate all remaining DAO personnel and some 9,000 "high risk" Vietnamese. In an effort to placate the Communists, President Minh had asked the U.S. ambassador to order all American military personnel to leave the country within twenty-four hours. Martin had agreed but also requested that he and some twenty members of his staff be allowed to remain to give "dignity" to the U.S. departure. Two helicopters, Martin said, would suffice to extract this residual group in the event of an emergency.

April 29

Marine Lance Corporal Darwin Judge of Marshalltown, Iowa, and Corporal Charles McMahon, Jr., of Woburn, Massachusetts, were both recent arrivals to Vietnam, part of the U.S. Embassy security force that had been called in to protect the evacuation airlift at Tan Son Nhut. For ten days the two young men had performed a variety of duties at the sprawling DAO complex, directing traffic, verifying papers, maintaining order among the thousands of Vietnamese trying to get into the evacuation processing center. In the dark morning hours of April 29, Judge and McMahon were standing guard at a checkpoint just beyond the airfield's front gate when the final battle of the Vietnam War began.

It was 3:58 A.M. when the first rockets hit. One exploded just under the wing of a taxiing C-130, rupturing a fuel tank that minutes later burst into flame. Another hit just outside the DAO command billet, bouncing General Smith and several other officers to the floor but without injuring anyone. A third, and then a fourth, slammed into the guard post where McMahon and Judge were standing. They were killed instantly, the first American victims of the "Ho Chi Minh Campaign" and last U.S. casualties of the war.

Another salvo of rockets landed in the area of the evacuation processing center, scattering 1,500 Vietnamese who were waiting in the open for the airlift to resume. One round ripped into the roof of the DAO gymnasium, sending shards of metal boomeranging through the air and terrorizing the 300 to 400 evacuees inside. Miraculously no one was hurt.

Barely had the rocket fire subsided when General Dung's long-range artillery guns joined the attack. Fired from Nhon Trach, the 130MM shells passed directly over the DAO compound and crashed into the runways and flight line with deadly accuracy. As the shelling intensified to a rate of nearly one round per minute, pandemonium broke out. Vietnamese soldiers and airmen, some firing weapons, swarmed over the parking area and even onto the tarmac in a desperate attempt to board any aircraft that might take them out of the country. As one C-130 labored to reach air speed along a parallel taxi way, crewmen pushed soldiers off the plane's loading ramps. Another C-130 barely cleared an old control tower as it climbed into the sky. Still another plane, a twin-engine C-7 Caribou transport, spun off the runway and burned on the grass. "It appeared that most of the passengers got out," recalled one U.S. Air Force officer at the scene, "but nobody bothered to check." As it began to get light, South Vietnamese air force pilots fired up their A-37s and F-5s

Smoke billows from Tan Son Nhut airfield on April 29 after artillery and rocket attacks convinced U.S. officials to halt their fixed-wing airlift.

and took off for U Tapao Air Base in Thailand, where they joined several dozen VNAF aircraft that had been flown out the day before.

According to Ambassador Martin, the premature exodus of the South Vietnamese air force on the twenty-eighth had been encouraged by Deputy Assistant Secretary of State Erich Von Marbod, who had returned to Saigon on April 24 under orders from the Pentagon to coordinate the removal of American military equipment. In his testimony before Congress, Martin accused Von Marbod of having violated an understanding that none of the VNAF aircraft would be flown out until the ambassador gave the order. Instead, Martin asserted, "after the bombing run on the air base [Von Marbod] went to see Air Marshal Ky and persuaded him to influence the commander of the Vietnamese air force to fly out a considerable portion of serviceable planes that afternoon [April 28]." The net result of Von Marbod's actions, the ambassador contended, was not only a breakdown of discipline at Tan Son Nhut, but the decision on the part of the North Vietnamese to shell the runways. Ten years later, Martin still maintained that the NVA would not have attacked Tan Son Nhut on the twenty-ninth had they not been "enraged" by the attempt to extract some of South Vietnam's most valuable military assets.

North Vietnamese shells were still falling on Tan Son Nhut when President Ford convened a meeting of the National Security Council shortly before 7:30 A.M. Saigon time to reassess the situation. Secretary Kissinger was the first to speak. Urging caution, and appealing to the judgment of Ambassador Martin, he noted that it might yet be possible to continue the fixed-wing airlift. Defense Secretary Schlesinger and Joint Chiefs Chairman General Brown disagreed. Option IV, they argued, was already overdue. In the end it was Brown who suggested a compromise: a test run of seven C-130s from the Philippines and Thailand. If they could land in Saigon, the airlift was on; if not, Option IV would be implemented. The other members of the NSC promptly agreed.

While the president and his top advisers temporized, DAO officials at Tan Son Nhut reached their own conclusions about the feasibility of continuing the fixed-wing airlift. Shortly after 7:00 A.M. Colonel Earl Mickler, the airlift supervisor, told General Smith that the runways were no longer usable. Jettisoned fuel tanks and live bombs, dozens of trucks, and other pieces of equipment littered the tarmac, and hundreds of rioting Vietnamese troops were still chasing any aircraft that moved. Even if the C-130s could land, Mickler pointed out, the planes were sure to be mobbed before they could load any of the 2,800 evacuees waiting in the processing center. In his opinion, it would require several thousand marines to make the airfield secure enough to permit a resumption of the airlift.

The disintegration of the South Vietnamese air force became complete several minutes later, when some thirty senior VNAF officers, most of them carrying side arms, burst into the DAO compound and insisted that they be evacuated immediately. Apprised of the demands, General Smith told the assistant air attaché, Lieutenant Colonel Dick Mitchell, to inform the officers that they would be shot on the spot unless they surrendered their weapons. Mitchell complied. So did the Vietnamese officers who, once disarmed, were temporarily placed under lock and key. They were later evacuated. "This incident," the authors of the DAO Final Assessment later wrote, "signalled the complete loss of command and control" of the air force "and magnified the continued deterioration of an already volatile situation."

Convinced that he had no choice but to go to Option IV, Smith ordered his staff to prepare the three designated landing zones in the DAO complex—one at the annex, one at the ball field, and one adjacent to the theater near the tennis court—for a full-scale helolift. Then he called Ambassador Martin, informing him of the condition of the runways and requesting authorization to call in the helicopters. But Martin was unconvinced. Refusing to accept the defense attaché's assessment of the situation, he left standing the previous night's orders to proceed with a "maximum" schedule of C-130 flights.

An hour or so later, shortly after nine o'clock, the ambassador's bulletproof limousine pulled up to the DAO compound. He had decided to inspect the runways firsthand. When Smith and other DAO staffers reiterated their collective opinion that the airfield was no longer usable, Martin responded by affirming his determination to move out as many "high risk" Vietnamese as possible. Then he called the White House from Smith's office to ask for a reconfirmation of the orders to continue the airlift. Assured that this was what had been decided, Martin stalked out and returned to the embassy.

Though frustrated by his inability to carry out his orders, Smith waited another hour before taking any further action. Then, shortly before 10:30, he called Admiral Gayler in Honolulu and persuaded him that there was simply no way the C-130 flights could continue. Gayler promised to contact the Joint Chiefs of Staff immediately and recommend Option IV. Smith then decided to make one final plea to Martin. This time the ambassador relented. Minutes later Martin was on the telephone to Kissinger, who in turn contacted President Ford. It took the president only a moment to decide. At 10:51 A.M. Saigon time, the "execute" order for Operation Frequent Wind flashed over command channels from USSAG headquarters in Thailand to the U.S. fleet off the South Vietnamese coast. In hot and steamy Saigon, operators at the American radio station began playing a tape of "(I'm Dreaming of a) White Christmas," signaling Americans throughout the city that the final pullout had begun.

Anchored some sixty-four kilometers out to sea, the largest naval armada assembled by the U.S. since the

Christmas bombings of 1972 rolled gently in calm waters. Stretched out in a crescent nearly 160 kilometers long, five carriers, the guided missile cruiser *Long Beach*, and more than two dozen support ships had been anticipating orders to commence Operation Frequent Wind for nearly a week. Especially anxious were the pilots of three marine helicopter squadrons and ten additional air force helicopters who would carry the marine ground security force into Saigon and bring out a still undetermined number of evacuees. Though placed on "one-hour alert" the previous day, the pilots had not yet received orders to "cross-deck" from ship to ship to pick up the 800 marines of Battalion Landing Team 2/4, a complicated operation that required a minimum of three hours to complete. Admiral Gayler, CINCPAC, believed that the "cross-decking" had already been accomplished and, on that basis, had assured the U.S. Embassy that the first helicopters would land at Tan Son Nhut within an hour of the order to "execute" Option IV. Instead, when the order finally did come through shortly before 11:00 A.M., a delay until midafternoon was unavoidable. The pilots would have only four or five hours of daylight in which to carry out their mission.

In Saigon, meanwhile, convoys of olive-drab buses began moving through the city's streets to pick up evacuees and shuttle them to Tan Son Nhut. Under the DAO's standing "surface extraction" plan, the buses were to follow prescribed routes that would take them past several designated "assembly points," board forty passengers each, and then carry them to the DAO compound. Yet as the drivers soon discovered, the number of people waiting to board the buses in most cases far exceeded their assigned capacity. As soon as the evacuees began to gather at their prearranged assembly points, crowds of Saigonese began milling around them in the hope of being taken along. "If the idea was to assemble discreetly so as not to draw a potentially panicky crowd," recalled Arnold Isaacs, the Saigon correspondent for the *Baltimore Sun*, "then something was very wrong. We might as well have announced the evacuation with movie marquee lights over our heads." By limiting the amount of luggage each passenger could carry, or by eliminating baggage entirely, some drivers managed to cram as many as seventy people onto their buses. But even then there were many who were stranded. Recalling his own harrowing journey that day, journalist Keyes Beech of the *Chicago Daily News* wrote: "At every stop Vietnamese beat on the doors and windows pleading to be let inside. . . . Every time we opened the door we had to beat and kick them back."

Even those Vietnamese who had been promised evacuation by their American employers were sometimes lost in the mad rush to get out of Saigon. Some 70 CIA translators and their families waited in vain throughout the day

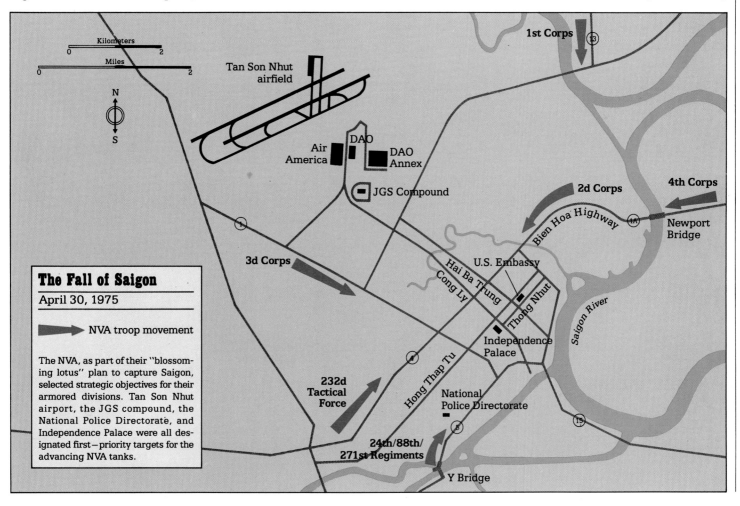

The Fall of Saigon

April 30, 1975

➤ NVA troop movement

The NVA, as part of their "blossoming lotus" plan to capture Saigon, selected strategic objectives for their armored divisions. Tan Son Nhut airport, the JGS compound, the National Police Directorate, and Independence Palace were all designated first-priority targets for the advancing NVA tanks.

The First Boat People

During the final stages of the American evacuation from Saigon, thousands of privileged Vietnamese waved good-by to their homeland from the cargo holds of U.S. military helicopters. Others were not so fortunate. Pursued by nightmarish visions of retribution at the hands of the Communist victors, tens of thousands of refugees abandoned their homes and their possessions, scrambled over the beaches at Vung Tau, and jammed into a motley assortment of craft in a desperate attempt to reach the American evacuation fleet standing offshore.

Since mid-April, Ambassador Martin had been advocating an evacuation from Vung Tau as the best means of bringing out a maximum number of Vietnamese. Martin cabled Washington on the eighteenth to propose this "over the beach" plan. Pentagon analysts deemed the scheme impractical, but the ambassador pushed ahead anyway. In the days that followed, embassy officials encouraged local Vietnamese to make their way overland to designated spots on the coast. A Military Sealift Command task force drew up comprehensive guidelines, and a half-dozen merchant ships moved into position offshore on the twenty-eighth. Unfortunately, military planners had underestimated the scope of the operation. As North Vietnamese troops closed in on Vung Tau, hundreds of boats fled the dying city in the last days of April, fanning out across the sea in search of the evacuation armada.

On the morning of April 28, one of the ships attached to the Sealift Command, USNS *Greenville Victory*, was anchored five kilometers south of the Vung Tau sea buoy. At 10:00 A.M. the first few boats laden with refugees pulled up alongside the ship. Soon after boarding this group, the *Greenville*'s crew discerned a flotilla of approximately 200 boats leaving a small village north of Vung Tau. Although most of the craft were detained by Vietnamese navy gunships, several boats slipped through the attempted blockade and arrived at the evacuation fleet sporadically throughout the afternoon.

By early evening, North Vietnamese artillery shells rained down upon the city of Vung Tau, sparking a mass exodus out to sea. As enemy troops drew to within twenty-four kilometers of the city limits, a determined bombardment drove the remaining Vietnamese out of their homes. Captain Raymond Iacobacci of the *Greenville* followed the battle with increasing concern. Shell bursts erupting along the shoreline told him all he needed to know. Fearing for the safety of his ship, the captain decided to move another five kilometers out to sea early on April 29. The ship towed four fishing boats as she steamed and others followed under their own power.

At the new anchorage, beyond range of encroaching NVA guns, the crew recommenced loading. Security personnel screened the Vietnamese and confiscated weapons as they boarded. As the craft arrived in increasing numbers, seamen

dropped ladders over the sides to bring people aboard. Eventually, the crew resorted to suspending huge cargo nets from booms to handle the overflow. As many as twenty refugees were hoisted in a net at one time, while others clung desperately to the outside. Women with small babies in their arms grabbed at the netting and older children in turn clasped onto their mothers. Driven on by the relentless military assault, the trickle of boats became a veritable torrent, discharging hundreds of frightened, exhausted refugees. Many wept as they watched their abandoned boats, repre-

senting one final link to Vietnam, drift beyond the horizon.

By late afternoon, the *Greenville Victory* had reached its assigned capacity of 6,000. Though the sea was still swarming with vessels, the captain was forced to cut boats loose and steam away. As if drawn by a powerful magnet, the Vietnamese boats followed. A short time later, Iacobacci received permission to continue loading. Eventually over 10,000 refugees pressed aboard, spilling out of the hold onto the decks and into every corner of the ship. On the evening of the thirtieth, the captain was compelled to abandon

seventy to eighty boats still drifting alongside. Others in the distance raced futilely to reach the departing ship. "It's a sight that will be impressed in everyone's memory for a long time," wrote Iacobacci in his ship's log. "We did our best and yet it seemed so inadequate."

The ordeal of the *Greenville Victory* was only one among many that marked the last few days of April 1975. One group of approximately 150 refugees departed in a dilapidated Saigon ferryboat, which they had purchased for 46 million piasters—$60,000 at the official exchange rate. A convoy of tugs and barges that had been stationed at Newport Harbor dodged rocket and small-arms fire along the Saigon River as they made their way to safety in international waters.

Officers commanding the American evacuation ships listened to terrified pleas for assistance over their radios. An intelligence officer named Khanh tied up the ship-to-ship radio frequency for hours demanding to be taken aboard. Again and again he repeated the names of Americans he had known, recited the address of a sister married to a U.S. officer living in America, and recalled the U.S. training courses he had attended. "Sorry, sir," Khanh apologized to a sympathetic radioman trying to ease his fears, "please understand. Frankly I am very excited after this hell trip. ... I don't know that you people can understand our case or not." Perhaps the toughest Vietnamese unit in the war, the 1st Airborne Brigade, made up of streetwise kids from the Saigon slums, now appealed with frightened voices: "We can't go home. ... We will be caught. ... We like to go to America now so we need your help."

In the end, according to official estimates, more than 60,000 Vietnamese refugees fled the beaches at Vung Tau and were picked up by carrier ships. Yet when the task force was ordered home on the afternoon of May 2, many stragglers still bobbed on the horizon, hoping to be rescued. No longer authorized to take on more passengers, the evacuation ships turned away, steaming eastward toward the Philippines. In their wake they left hundreds of vessels, abandoned and drifting, like so much flotsam upon the sea.

Some of the first "boat people" leave Vietnam in early May 1975.

at their compound for the Americans to arrive and take them away, as did 100 or so Vietnamese employees of the agency who gathered at the CIA billet just a few blocks away from the embassy. There were others as well.

In the USIS offices at 8 Le Qui Don Street, 185 Vietnamese waited throughout the morning for transportation to Tan Son Nhut. Among them was a thirty-year-old Chinese woman named Trai Quoc Quang, who had worked as a secretary for the Americans for eight years. During the past few days Quang had seen all but five of the USIS headquarters employees leave Vietnam, while she stayed on at the request of her boss. Convinced that her long association with the Americans would mean death if she were left behind, she was frightened. But she also believed in the repeated assurances she had received that she would not be abandoned. Even when she learned that morning that her employers had already departed, she did not despair. Nor, seemingly, did any of the others waiting with her at the assembly point.

Finally, shortly after noon, two buses pulled up and began loading passengers. Since there was not enough room for everyone, half of the people in the crowd, mostly senior Vietnamese employees and their families, were told to go to the villa of USIA Chief Alan Carter and await further instructions. The others, Quang among them, climbed onto the bus and headed toward Tan Son Nhut. Once they reached the airfield, however, armed Vietnamese security guards refused to let them enter. Forced to turn back, the driver headed toward the Newport docks where, someone suggested, there were boats waiting to carry people down river. The bus was within a half-mile of the harbor when milling crowds and congested traffic prevented it from proceeding any farther. A subsequent stop at the USAID headquarters also proved futile; the building was empty except for looters. The driver then steered the bus toward the U.S. Embassy but was again halted by mobs a block short of his destination. Although at that point several passengers got off the bus, presumably in the hope of finding some other way out of the city, Quang stayed aboard and eventually found herself back where she had started: at the USIS headquarters. Now desperate, she left the bus and accosted several UPI newsmen, who listened sympathetically but could offer no suggestions. They themselves were planning to stay behind to cover the Communist takeover. No one knew if she ever got out.

The other part of the surface extraction plan, which called for small UH-1 Air America helicopters to pick up high-priority evacuees from designated rooftops around Saigon, also ran into problems. To begin with, Communist shells and rockets heavily damaged the Air America buildings across from the DAO compound and delayed the arrival of the twenty-four pilots who had volunteered to undertake the mission. When the pilots finally did make their way to the airfield, moreover, they discovered that four of their twenty-two Hueys had been hijacked earlier

in the morning by Vietnamese paratroopers. Once under way, the operation was further plagued by a loss of refueling capability, since the Air America terminal was still taking occasional rockets and the lone fuel truck at the DAO compound was not working. As a result, pilots began dropping off their passengers at the U.S. Embassy rather than the airfield in order to save flying time and fuel. When they did run low, they flew with full passenger loads directly out to the evacuation fleet and refueled on the ships.

As the buses bulldozed their way through the city's crowded streets and the UH-1s shuttled from rooftop to rooftop, the growing throngs of evacuees at Tan Son Nhut stared expectantly into the sky, searching for some sign of the huge CH-53 helicopters that would whisk them away to safety. Because of further delays, it was nearly 3:00 P.M. when the first wave of twelve helicopters, flying in four Vs of three aircraft each, appeared overhead. One after another the Sea Stallions descended into the fires that still blazed on the airfield. After dropping off marines of Battalion Landing Team 2/4, the first of the helicopters loaded up with evacuees and lifted off only six minutes after touchdown, setting a course parallel to the Vung Tau highway, en route to the fleet. As the aircraft passed over ARVN dependent housing just southwest of the DAO annex, they drew several rounds of M16 fire. But the harassment proved to be minor, necessitating only a small adjustment in flight plans.

Although flying conditions were hazardous, with pilots reporting visibility of only one mile as they approached Tan Son Nhut, the operation went like clockwork. During the next hour thirty-six helicopters arrived, boarded more than fifty passengers each, and returned safely to the offshore ships. By 5:00 P.M., the lines of evacuees at the three DAO helicopter landing zones were thinning rapidly. But some 1,300 potential evacuees, including the 800-man marine security force, still remained. DAO officials estimated that it would require at least two more hours to pull everyone out. By then it would be dark.

By late afternoon the entire city of Saigon seemed to dissolve into chaos. Huge angry mobs roamed the streets, overturning abandoned cars and setting fire to buildings. Looters were everywhere, pawing through the former residences of Americans and carrying away furniture, bathroom fixtures, anything that might be of the remotest value. Thousands of others converged on the U.S. Embassy compound either in the hope of finding a means of escape or simply to vent their rage. Scattered atop the compound walls, marine security guards used boots and rifle butts to fend off those trying to climb over, while at the same time helping stranded Americans and "third country nationals"

As a helicopter lifts off from the U.S. Embassy on April 29, Saigonese still hoping to be evacuated gather nearby. Many have been promised a ride out by Americans.

get in. Journalist Keyes Beech, whose bus never made it to Tan Son Nhut but instead dropped him off at the embassy's side gate, recorded the frenzied scene there:

Once we moved into that seething mass we ceased to be correspondents. We were only men fighting for our lives, scratching, clawing, pushing ever closer to that wall. ... Now, I thought, I know what it's like to be a Vietnamese. I am one of them. But if I could get over that wall, I would be an American again. ... Somebody grabbed my sleeve and wouldn't let go. I turned my head and looked into the face of a Vietnamese youth. "You adopt me and take me with you and I'll help you," he screamed. ... Suddenly my arm was free and I edged closer to the wall. There was a pair of marines on the wall. They were trying to help us and kicked the Vietnamese down. One of them looked down at me. "Help me," I pleaded. "Please help me." ... He reached down with his long, muscular arm and pulled me up as if I were a helpless child. I lay on a tin roof, gasping for breath like a landed fish.

To American evacuation planners, however, the 3,000 or so Saigonese outside the compound walls were of less concern than the 2,000 to 3,000 people inside. Frequent Wind operation plans had anticipated "a total not to exceed 100 evacuees" from the embassy on the final day, including the ambassador himself, the embassy's marine guards, and a small number of senior officials whose presence was deemed essential until the very end. No one had foreseen the possibility that some of the buses might fail to reach Tan Son Nhut or that the Air America pilots would be forced to unload their passengers at the embassy in order to save fuel.

The marine commander in charge of the evacuation, General Richard Carey, was not apprised of the situation until four o'clock in the afternoon. Before then he had been under the impression that the operation was running perfectly smoothly. He had further calculated that his mission was nearing completion. Now, suddenly, Carey had to find a way to divert an undetermined number of helicopters to the embassy to haul out an unspecified number of people. Making matters worse, the only two possible landing sites inside the embassy compound—the rooftop helipad and the parking lot—could accommodate only one helicopter at a time. At the DAO compound, he could extract up to 2,000 people in an hour. At the embassy, the pace would be far slower.

During the next several hours the flow of helicopters alighting on the embassy roof was sporadic, as Carey and General Smith focused their energies on completing the airlift from Tan Son Nhut. To bolster security inside the compound and prevent those outside from getting in, the first helicopters brought in 130 more marines. In the meantime U.S. officials, led by Deputy Chief of Mission Wolf-

gang Lehmann and Colonel John H. Madison, Jr., chief of the U.S. delegation to the four-party Joint Military Team, tried to organize the impending evacuation. Assisted by other members of the JMT and by Reverend Thomas Stebbins, a local missionary, Madison marshaled the evacuees into two holding areas, a courtyard next to the parking lot and another courtyard adjacent to the embassy swimming pool. Separating the two courtyards was a building that housed the embassy's fire trucks. The passage between them was blocked off by a chain-link fence with a gate. Once the airlift began, Madison and his team would funnel passengers through the gate and direct them either to the parking lot or up the stairs inside the chancery to the roof. In the interim, however, they concentrated on keeping the increasingly impatient crowd calm. Everyone, they repeated again and again, would get out. Nobody would be abandoned.

It was already nightfall when the helicopters began arriving frequently enough to justify the use of both landing zones. With the darkness came heavy gusts of wind and rain, which thinned the mobs surrounding the embassy but also created hazardous flying conditions. Until then, the CH-53s descending into the cramped embassy parking lot had been guided by hand signals, but as visibility dropped this was no longer feasible. To solve the problem, an embassy staffer rigged a 35MM slide projector on the roof overlooking the landing zone. As the helicopters began to drop down, the projector was switched on, illuminating the area in a sharp rectangle of white light.

Darkness and rapidly deteriorating weather conditions also hampered operations at Tan Son Nhut, where the evacuation was now almost complete. Although at first DAO landing zone controllers tried to "talk" the remaining inbound helicopters down by radio, repeated interruptions by hysterical Vietnamese breaking in on their frequencies quickly made this impossible. Strobe lights were also abandoned once it became clear that pilots could not distinguish these signals from the myriad other flashes and

Left. *Atop the fence of the embassy compound, Vietnamese try to cross into the American sanctuary.* Right. *Vietnamese plead with a guard to be let in.*

aimless tracer rounds that streaked over the base. In the end, the pilots resorted to flashing their landing lights as they approached, although this risked attracting ground fire. "The efforts of both the Marine and USAF pilots flying into that hazardous environment at night in the rain," reported one DAO official, "were the most outstanding feats of airmanship that I could imagine."

By seven o'clock only some thirty DAO officials and the marine ground security force remained at Tan Son Nhut. Although orders had already come through for General Smith to evacuate the remaining members of his staff, the defense attaché was reluctant to leave. He had intended to stay as long as Ambassador Martin needed him, and it was clear that the embassy evacuation was far from over. Other members of the DAO planning team believed, however, that it was pointless, and potentially dangerous, to delay any longer. No one knew how long it would take to complete the embassy pullout since estimates of the number of evacuees remaining in the compound had not varied for hours. Whenever DAO officials inquired, air force historians later wrote, the embassy's answer "was always the same—2,000 to go. . . . Everyone in the evacuation con-

trol center believed that if the evacuation had continued for days, the estimate would have remained 2,000."

In the end, the deciding factor was neither Smith's conscience nor Gayler's orders, but a loss of electrical power. Around 7:15 the lights in the operations center at DAO headquarters blinked out. A saboteur had shorted an incoming power line with a wooden pole, and the surge of current on the circuits knocked out a satellite terminal that supported the DAO's communications with the outside world.

At eight o'clock General Smith gave the final order, and the remaining members of the staff filed out to the tennis court where two CH-53s stood waiting. As they prepared to lift off, a bus packed with Vietnamese pulled up outside the gate. In a final gesture of generosity, Smith stood aside and let the late arrivals on board. One of the helicopters departed with over ninety passengers. The general himself was finally airborne by 8:15, leaving the DAO compound in the hands of the marines.

Some of the 2,000 evacuees who had gathered at the embassy compound board a CH-53 helicopter.

In Washington it was now the morning of April 30. At 9:30 A.M. Secretary Kissinger informed the president that the evacuation out of the DAO compound was all but complete. Over 6,000 people, more than 5,000 of them Vietnamese, had been safely extracted by eighty-one helicopters flying more than 100 sorties under Option IV of Operation Frequent Wind. Only the marines remained, plus an undetermined number of American and Vietnamese civilians who were still being pulled out of the U.S. Embassy.

With the airlift now approximately six hours old, the weather poor, and visibility diminishing, Ford pondered the possibility of suspending the operation until morning. Though he apparently favored this option, there were other pressing considerations. Hanoi could easily interpret a temporary delay as a sign that the Americans were deceitfully stalling for any number of political or military reasons. Moreover, the understanding with the North Vietnamese that they would not interfere with evacuation was tenuous enough as it was.

Defense Secretary Schlesinger, however, strongly opposed any continuation of the helolift beyond what was absolutely necessary. Not only were the flying conditions hazardous, he pointed out, but nearly half of the helicopters used in the evacuation were down for maintenance and pilot fatigue was becoming a serious problem. Schlesinger also expressed concern that too many of the evacuees coming out of the embassy were Vietnamese; Ambassador Martin did not seem to understand priorities. He therefore suggested that the entire operation cease by midnight, Saigon time, and resume the following morning. In the interim, a period of about two hours, nineteen additional helicopters would be ordered in to pick up the remaining Americans.

Informed of the possibility that the helolift might be discontinued, Martin replied that he "damn well didn't want to spend another night here." By his own estimate, thirty CH-53 sorties, as opposed to the nineteen proposed by Schlesinger, would allow him to clear the entire compound. "I REPEAT, I NEED 30 CH-53s AND I NEED THEM NOW," the ambassador cabled. Forty minutes later, at around 10:45 P.M. Saigon time, Washington agreed.

In the meantime, all available helicopters were dispatched to Tan Son Nhut to extract the marine ground security force. Since the departure of the DAO staff, the marines had spent much of their time preparing for the systematic destruction of the entire DAO complex. The former headquarters of the United States Military Command, Vietnam (USMACV), it had served for more than ten years as a symbol of the American commitment to prevent a Communist takeover in South Vietnam. Now, as midnight approached on April 29, 1975, marine demolition teams placed high-powered explosives around the DAO's sophisticated communications equipment and scattered thermite bombs on the floor of the headquarters building. At approximately 11:40 P.M., the marines triggered the delayed-action fuses on the bottom floor of the DAO compound and dashed for the helicopters. As they ascended, they looked down and watched the structure crumple like a cheap toy, destroying millions of dollars of secret equipment along with barrels containing more than $3.5 million in U.S. currency.

For America, the Vietnam War was over. Almost.

April 30

After the marines returned to their ships, the task force command ordered a temporary grounding of all helicopters to allow the weary pilots, many of whom had been flying for ten hours or more, a chance to rest. But General Carey vehemently objected. Saigon would likely be in North Vietnamese hands by morning, he pointed out, and besides, he was confident that his pilots could keep flying. He had also been assured by Ambassador Martin that once the helicopter flow resumed, the embassy compound could be cleared "in a relatively short time." Carey's superiors yielded. The pilots climbed back into their helicopters and headed back to Saigon.

At the embassy, the temporary break in the flow of incoming helicopters planted a seed of panic among the several hundred evacuees still anxiously waiting to be rescued. A rumor rippled through the crowd that the North Vietnamese were about to attack and they were to be abandoned. Suddenly everyone in the recreation courtyard began surging toward the chain-link gate, where several marines had established a cordon. The marines at first tried to push them back, then resorted to jabbing at them with rifle butts. Flailing arms and fists exploded. Captain Stuart Herrington of the Joint Military Team grabbed a bullhorn and waded into the crowd, trying to calm everyone down. "Don't worry," he shouted in Vietnamese, "you will all be evacuated. No one is abandoning you." But his assurances seemed to have little effect.

Finally, Herrington, Colonel Harry Summers, and Master Sergeant Bill Herron linked arms and managed to push the front ranks of the mob back. The crowd suddenly quieted and obeyed orders to line up. The three Americans then led the group through the gate and up a stairway to the roof of the fire station, where they could see the landing zone that previously had been blocked from their view. When everyone was through, the gate was closed and locked. The evacuees discarded their remaining luggage and anxiously scanned the skies for helicopters.

When the helicopters finally did arrive, however, they were not the promised CH-53s but much smaller CH-46s—amounting to the nineteen sorties suggested by Schlesinger rather than the thirty demanded by Martin. Pointing out that the CH-46s "carry about 2/5ths of CH-53 capacity," Martin reiterated his earlier request for thirty more

Sea Stallions. At 1:30 A.M. Secretary Kissinger called and asked Martin how many people still remained in the compound. Though it was impossible to determine precisely, the ambassador gave him a figure off the top of his head: 726. Based on this estimate, planners in Washington worked out a new schedule to bring out everyone at the embassy by 3:45 A.M., April 30. The ambassador himself was to board the next to last helicopter.

At 2:17 A.M. two CH–53s and two CH–46s left the fleet for the embassy, with other flights following at ten–minute intervals. The first helicopter touched down at approximately 3:00 A.M. Colonel Madison and his team were busily forming passenger loads among the Vietnamese in the courtyard and leading them either to the roof to board the smaller CH–46s or out to the CH–53s in the parking lot. It was a laborious process, complicated by the ambassador's underestimation of the number of people to be evacuated and by Washington's refusal to send the full complement of helicopters previously promised.

As a result of these miscalculations, when the helolift reached its scheduled termination point at 3:45 A.M., more than 400 people remained at the embassy. Colonel Madison estimated that only six more CH–53s were needed to lift all of them out. At 4:20 A.M. a lone CH–53 set down in the parking lot and loaded up with evacuees. Then the skies fell silent. Convinced that the embassy was a "bottomless pit of refugees," Admiral Gayler, CINCPAC, and Rear Admiral Donald Whitmire, the fleet commander, had decided to shut down the operation in accordance with White House instructions. Pilots flying over Vietnam received the following transmission over their VHS radios:

The following message is from the President of the United States and should be passed on by the first helicopter in contact with Ambassador Martin. Americans only will be transported. Ambassador Martin will board the first available helicopter and that helicopter will broadcast "Tiger, Tiger, Tiger," once it is airborne and en route.

Just before 5:00 A.M. a CH–46 with the call sign "Lady Ace 09" set down on the rooftop landing pad. Captain Jerry Berry refused to take on the load of evacuees led out by the marines, insisting he was under strict orders to evacuate only Ambassador Martin and members of his

On April 30, thousands of GVN soldiers were too frightened of retribution merely to "stop fighting, and stay put," as ordered by President Minh. Instead, they opted for anonymity by abandoning their uniforms and weapons. Right. Soldiers strip off their uniforms. Far right. Abandoned uniforms and equipment lie in heaps along a Saigon street.

staff. A few minutes later, Martin appeared and climbed aboard "Lady Ace 09," assisted by Ken Moorefield. At 4:58 the helicopter lifted off into the dark sky and headed for the fleet. A second CH-46 arrived and swooped down minutes afterward to board the rest of the officials.

Only after the ambassador was on his way did the other Americans in the compound learn that there would be no more evacuation flights for the remaining Vietnamese and "third country nationals." Colonel Madison was furious. A half-hour before he had been assured by embassy officials that there would be enough helicopters coming in to get everyone out. Insisting that he would not leave until the task was accomplished, he urged the marine commander, Major Jim Kean, to do likewise. But Kean refused. The orders had come from the president himself. He would not defy them. Since Madison had only two army officers, two army NCOs, and one marine NCO with him, far too few to secure the embassy grounds, he conceded. Quietly, his men withdrew into the building.

Still standing in the parking lot landing zone were approximately 420 people, including South Korean embassy officials, a German priest who had spent much of the day helping to organize the evacuation, embassy firemen who had volunteered to stay on duty until the end, and various other U.S. Embassy employees and their families. Among the South Koreans was General Dai Yong Rhee, who had once commanded 50,000 Korean troops in Vietnam and would later be imprisoned by the conquerors of Saigon. Looking down on the crowd as he lifted off at 5:30 A.M., Captain Herrington could think "of no word in any language adequate to describe the sense of shame that swept over me. . . . If I had tried to talk, I would have cried."

With the departure of the members of the Joint Military Team, the only Americans remaining at the embassy were Major Kean's marines. To avoid arousing the suspicions of those who would be left behind, Kean and Master Sergeant Juan Valdez, the head of the embassy security detachment, quietly passed the word to their men to withdraw into the courtyard. Once everyone was inside the compound, some of the men formed a perimeter in front of the lobby entrance. Others then set up a second, tighter circle inside the first, and those in the outer ring then

Frequent Wind

Operation Frequent Wind, the final U.S. evacuation from Saigon, began on the morning of April 29. By the end of the operation, more than forty ships of the Seventh Fleet had picked up 1,373 Americans and 5,595 Vietnamese in U.S. helicopters and some 60,000 Vietnamese from boats, as well as a number of South Vietnamese aircraft, including dozens of UH-1 helicopters and two 0-1 spotter planes.

Left. *A South Vietnamese helicopter pilot and his wife and child arrive on the Hancock.* Above. *Two RVNAF lieutenant generals are searched for weapons aboard the USS Blue Ridge.* Opposite above. *On the Blue Ridge, American sailors push a UH-1 helicopter into the sea to make room for others waiting to land.* Opposite below. *Ambassador Graham Martin, flanked by Rear Admiral Donald B. Whitmire (right) and press aide John Hogan, strides aboard the Blue Ridge, April 30.*

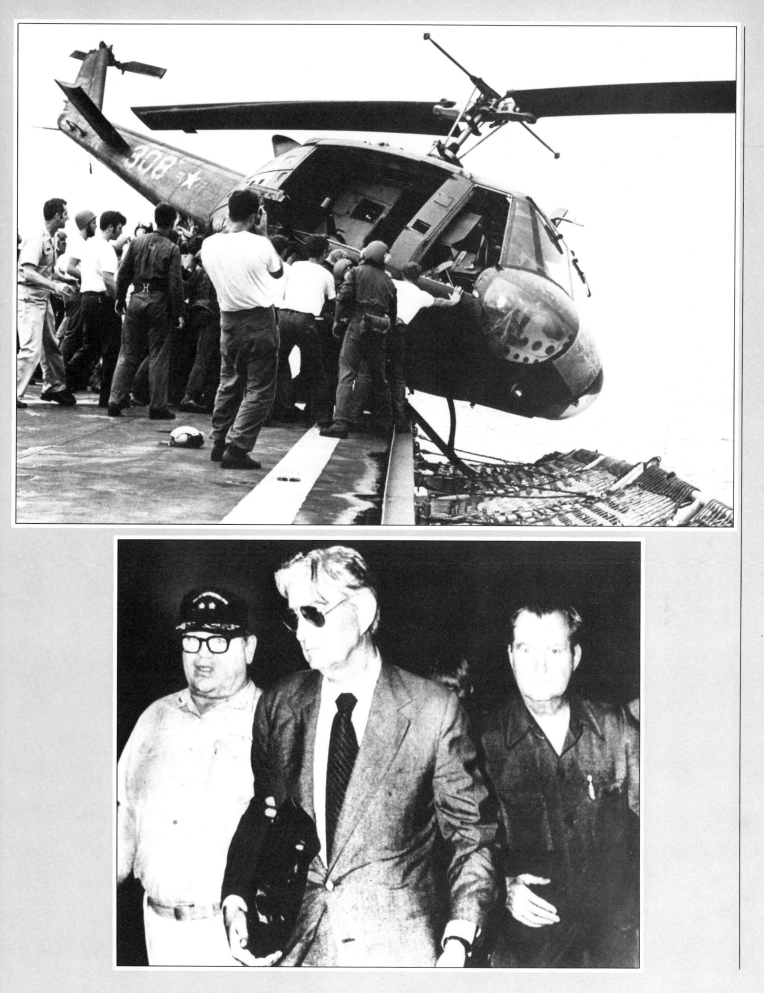

pulled through. By the time the marines began forming yet a third interior perimeter, the evacuees finally grasped what was happening and immediately started to race toward the lobby, while other Vietnamese clambered over the unguarded walls. The last marines wrestled with a few people in the surging crowd and then slammed and barred its huge double door. But, Sergeant Valdez later recalled, "We were only able to get the bar halfway on."

While the abandoned evacuees tried to push their way in, the marines took the chancery elevator up to the sixth floor. Just as the last man got on the elevator, Valdez remembered, "we heard the bar drop off the main door." Filing up to the roof, the marines barricaded the door behind them with anything they could find: heavy lockers, carts piled up with fire extinguishers, and their own packs. Then they waited. Nearly an hour passed before the first helicopters appeared over the brightening eastern horizon. While waiting the marines periodically sprayed Mace through the broken glass of the rooftop door to fend off the Vietnamese trying to get through. At one point a sniper in an apartment building across the street took a few shots at them. But no one dared return fire for fear of setting off a firefight that might make it impossible for the helicopters to land. Other random rifle shots popped in the distance. The streets below were full of roaming ARVN soldiers and looters carrying away their bounty.

At last the helicopters arrived. One by one the CH–46s bumped down, loaded, and took off. It took nine helicopters to get all the marines out, the last lagging well behind the rest. As he climbed aboard the final helicopter, Sergeant Valdez could still see Vietnamese evacuees trying to push their way through the rooftop door, waving papers to prove that they, too, should be taken along.

The end

As the last American helicopter disappeared over the eastern horizon on the morning of April 30, 1975, an eerie quiet settled over Saigon. With the exception of the docks, where crowds still converged in a last attempt to board a few small coastal freighters heading out to sea, and the streets around the U.S. Embassy, which were filled with looters, there was little activity. In the distance, random artillery sounds seemed not out of place in a country that for so long had known only war. Tan Son Nhut was relatively quiet, too. On the sides of the runways lay wrecked or abandoned planes, twisted into useless, hulking heaps of metal. Fires crackled in the fuel and munitions dumps.

At 10:24 A.M. the voice of President Duong Van Minh reached out to the defeated country over the airwaves. Expressing his commitment to "national reconciliation and

April 30. The GVN police officer lying dead in front of Saigon's war memorial statue minutes before had walked up to the memorial, saluted it, then shot himself.

concord to save the lives of our compatriots," he called "on all [Republic of Vietnam] soldiers to remain calm, to stop fighting, and stay put." He then made the same plea to "our brother combatants" of the PRGRSV (Provisional Revolutionary Government of the Republic of South Vietnam). "We are waiting to meet the PRGRSV in order to discuss the formal handing over of power in an orderly manner, with a view to avoiding useless bloodshed." After Minh finished, General Nguyen Huu Hanh, the acting chief of the JGS, directed "all generals and military men of all ranks" to obey the order "absolutely."

Across the nation, the last vestiges of resistance wilted. The Army of the Republic of Vietnam began to disappear, and with it died the last strains of South Vietnam's national anthem, "Tieng Goi Thanh Nien" ("Young People Stand Up for Your Country"). Originally it had been a rallying song against the French. In the streets, without shame, thousands of soldiers discarded their weapons and uniforms, transforming themselves into taxi drivers and peasants to avoid retribution from the victors. Others chose honor in death over defeat. In Lam Son Square, shortly after Minh's speech, a South Vietnamese colonel walked up to the huge soldier's monument facing the National Assembly and saluted. For several moments he stood at attention before the memorial commemorating South Vietnam's war dead and then reached for his holster. As Associated Press newsmen George Esper and Matt Franjola watched in horror, the officer pointed his .45 automatic directly at his head and pulled the trigger.

At midday, General Dung's II Corps tanks appeared on the edge of Saigon. Dusty roads into the capital had opened up before them; no one had even bothered to blow up the bridges. The convoy rolled past the ravaged American embassy and proceeded from Thong Nhut Avenue across Cong Ly Boulevard toward Independence Palace. Fluttering atop tall radio aerials, a bright Liberation star signified to 3 million Saigonese a new and uncertain future. Open trucks rolled alongside the caravan, jammed with young soldiers in green uniforms. A harsh sunlight glinted off steel AK47s as victorious troops advanced into the heart of the city.

Without slowing down, the lead tank roared straight into the high steel front gate, which buckled and collapsed under the powerful impact. Close behind, a second tank crashed through, then swerved around to guard the rear while the rest of the tanks swarmed onto the lawn. As the tanks formed a huge semicircle facing the steps, a lone pith-helmeted soldier, carrying a large blue-and-red flag with the yellow star of the National Liberation Front, raced across the lawn toward the steps. As he sprinted, he waved the huge flag violently above his head in a gesture of triumph. Neil Davis of Reuters asked the soldier his name. The young man looked embarrassed, then replied, "Nguyen Van Thieu." At that moment of singular irony, thirty years' war in Vietnam was over.

Final Victory

The Communist tanks arrived just before noon, accompanied by a dozen armored personnel carriers and truckloads of young, green-uniformed soldiers whose helmets bore the inscription *Tien vi Saigon*—Onward to Saigon. Minutes after the lead tank entered the grounds of the presidential palace, North Vietnamese troops hoisted the single-starred N.L.F. flag high in the air. P.R.G. officials announced over the Saigon radio station: "Saigon has been totally liberated. We accept the unconditional surrender of General Duong Van Minh, president of the former government." Half a world away in Paris, Communist representatives announced the renaming of Saigon as Ho Chi Minh City. But change did not come unopposed. Throughout the city isolated groups of government soldiers and civilians fired on the advancing columns. Barely eliciting a response from the victorious army, these acts of resistance were largely futile. For the most part, the North Vietnamese marched easily into the city.

A tank of the NVA's Huong Giang Tank Brigade smashes through the gates of the presidential palace in Saigon at noon on April 30.

Surrender

As North Vietnamese troops milled about outside the presidential palace, several of the victors entered the building to find President Minh, Prime Minister Mau, and their associates waiting quietly. When the first Communist soldier burst into the red-carpeted reception room, Minh stood formally: "We have been waiting impatiently for you since this morning to hand over power." But the president was not to be accorded the respect of his captors. "All power has passed into the hands of the revolution," said one officer derisively. "You cannot hand over what you no longer have." With this remark, the former Republic of South Vietnam's leaders were led out of the building and whisked away. A short while later, Minh broadcast his second surrender speech of the day over Saigon radio. Prime Minister Mau followed with an appeal to civil servants to return to duty and await the orders of the revolution. Soon after, Minh was released and allowed to live unmolested in his comfortable home.

Right. *North Vietnamese tanks form a defensive perimeter in front of the presidential palace.*

Opposite. *His head bowed in defeat, President Duong Van Minh accompanies Prime Minister Vu Van Mau as they are led outside the palace following their surrender.*

Left. *Communist soldiers enjoy the luxuries of the South Vietnamese presidential office following its takeover.*

The *bo doi*

Initially somber and tightly disciplined, General Dung's forces moved through the streets past the dazed population. On the whole, the NVA soldiers, or *bo doi* as they were known in North Vietnam, looked quite young, though many faces were thin and yellowed from malaria caught in the jungle. It did not take long for curiosity to break through the hardened, war-weary expressions. Glancing curiously around, the soldiers stared at sites most had never seen, including the stockpiled South Vietnamese army PX. Others fell prey to the temptations of the black market, as had generations of foreign soldiers before them. On the lips of many lingered an unasked question: Was this the oppressed world they had fought so long and hard to liberate?

North Vietnamese troops arrive in Saigon bearing their bicycles, for many years early in the war the sole means of transporting men and supplies south.

Revolution: day one

To the people of Saigon, the first few days following the surrender were a welcome relief from war, though many lived in fear of what would happen next. Tentatively they ventured out into the streets, smiling shyly and uncertainly at the Communist victors. Here and there liberation flags billowed in the doorways. The young revolutionary soldiers were gracious and polite. Some draped flowers over their rifles; others offered children rides on the tanks. But behind the smiles and seeming diffidence lurked an iron discipline. "Within hours of their arrival," remarked a French diplomat, "there was a little man in green heading into every neighborhood and every government office."

Above. A revolutionary soldier talks to Saigon youth in a downtown park. Left. Saigonese greet the PRG troops. Right. Captured South Vietnamese soldiers are led through the littered streets of Saigon on the day of capitulation.

A new beginning

The week following Saigon's "liberation" was dominated by celebrations. Each day dawned with revolutionary music blaring out over loudspeakers. Songs like "The Flowers of Victory are Blooming Everywhere" played throughout the city. Huge crowds of Communist soldiers and Saigonese citizens paraded the streets. Omnipresent were portraits of Ho Chi Minh and the North Vietnamese and P.R.G. flags. In the park in front of the presidential palace on May 8, 30,000 people gathered to cheer General Tran Van Tra, the head of the South Vietnamese caretaker government, as he spoke to celebrate the success of "the revolution."

Peace and, for some, jubilation had come to "Ho Chi Minh City." According to a French estimate, fully one-third of Saigon's citizens welcomed the Communists with genuine enthusiasm. But for the other two-thirds, indifference and apprehension would soon turn to worry as the North Vietnamese victors began rounding up a variety of Saigonese for reeducation in camps set up in the countryside. The killing was over, for now. What was to follow, only time would tell.

Saigonese gather on the grounds of the former presidential palace at the May 8 celebration of the week-old victory.

184

Bibliography

I. Books and Articles

"L'armee de Saigon abandonne un chef-lieu de province au sud-est des Hauts-Plateaux." *Le Monde,* March 22, 1975.

Austerlitz, Max. "After the Fall of Danang." *New Republic,* May 17, 1975.

Batchelder, Sydney H., Jr., and D. A. Quinlan. "Operation Eagle Pull." *Marine Corps Gazette,* May 1976.

Burchett, Wilfred. *Grasshoppers and Elephants.* Urizen Bks., 1977.

Butler, David. *The Fall of Saigon: Scenes from the Sudden End of a Long War.* Simon & Schuster, 1985.

Butterfield, Fox. "How South Vietnam Died—by the Stab in the Front." *New York Times Magazine,* May 25, 1975.

Carey, Richard E., and D. A. Quinlan. "Frequent Wind." *Marine Corps Gazette,* February, March and April 1976.

Chomsky, Noam, and Edward S. Herman. "Saigon's Corruption Crisis: The Search for an Honest Quisling." *Ramparts,* December 1974.

Dawson, Alan. *55 Days: The Fall of South Vietnam.* Prentice-Hall, 1977.

Dillard, Walter Scott. *Sixty Days to Peace: Implementing the Paris Peace Accords, Vietnam 1973.* National Defense Univ., 1982.

Donnell, J. C. "South Vietnam in 1975: The Year of Communist Victory." *Asian Survey,* January 1976.

Dornan, James E., Jr., and Peter C. Hughes. "The Scoresheet, Fall 1974." *National Review,* November 8, 1974.

Ford, Gerald R. *A Time to Heal.* Harper & Row, 1979.

G. Nguyen Tien Hung. *Economic Development of Socialist Vietnam, 1955-1980.* Praeger, 1977.

Goodman, Allen E. *The Lost Peace.* Hoover Inst. Pr., 1978.

————. "South Vietnam: War Without End?" *Asian Survey,* January 1975.

Haley, Edward P. *Congress and the Fall of South Vietnam and Cambodia.* Associated Univ. Pr., 1982.

Hartmann, Robert T. *Palace Politics: An Inside Account of the Ford Years.* McGraw-Hill, 1980.

Herring, George C. *America's Longest War: The United States and Vietnam, 1950-1975.* Wiley, 1979.

Herrington, Stuart A. *Peace with Honor? An American Reports on Vietnam, 1973-1975.* Presidio Pr., 1983.

Hosmer, Stephen T. et al., eds. *The Fall of South Vietnam: Statements by Vietnamese Military and Civilian Leaders.* Crane, Russak & Co., 1980.

Isaacs, Arnold. *Without Honor: Defeat in Vietnam and Cambodia.* Johns Hopkins Univ. Pr., 1983.

Karnow, Stanley. *Vietnam: A History.* Viking Pr., 1983.

Kenny, Henry J. *The American Role in Vietnam and East Asia.* Praeger, n.d.

Kissinger, Henry. *Years of Upheaval.* Little, Brown, 1982.

Laurie, James. "Washington Still Calls the Tune." *Far Eastern Economic Review,* February 21, 1975.

Le Kim, and Vu Thuy. "Talking with Former Puppet Officers." *Vietnam Courier,* August 1975.

Le Thi Que et al. "Why They Fled: Refugee Movement During the Spring 1975 Communist Offensive in South Vietnam." *Asian Survey,* September 1976.

Lewy, Guenter. *America in Vietnam.* Oxford Univ. Pr., 1978.

Lippman, Thomas. "The Thirty Years' War." In *A Short History of the Vietnam War,* edited by Allan R. Millett. Indiana Univ. Pr., 1978.

Maclear, Michael. *The Ten Thousand Day War: Vietnam, 1945-1975.* St. Martin's, 1981.

Martin, Earl S. *Reaching the Other Side.* Crown, 1978.

Nash, George H. "Dissolution of the Paris Accords." *National Review,* October 24, 1975.

Nessen, Ron. *It Sure Looks Different from the Inside.* Playboy Pr., 1978.

Nguyen Cao Ky. *Twenty Years and Twenty Days.* Stein & Day, 1976.

Nguyen Ngoc Ngan with E. E. Richey. *The Will of Heaven.* Dutton, 1982.

Papp, Daniel S. *Vietnam: The View from Moscow, Peking, Washington.* Macfarland & Co. Publishers, 1981.

Parker, Maynard. "Vietnam: The War That Won't End." *Foreign Affairs,* January 1975.

Pike, Douglas. *History of Vietnamese Communism, 1925-1976.* Hoover Inst. Pr., 1978.

Porter, Gareth. *A Peace Denied: The United States, Vietnam, and the Paris Agreement.* Indiana Univ. Pr., 1975.

————. "Pressing Ford to Drop Thieu." *New Republic,* February 8, 1975.

Quinn, Kenneth. "Political Change in Wartime: The Khmer Krahan Revolution in Southern Cambodia, 1970-1974." *Naval War College Review,* Spring 1976.

Reeves, Richard. *A Ford Not a Lincoln.* Harcourt Brace Jovanovich, 1975.

Robbins, Christopher. *Air America.* G. P. Putnam's Sons, 1979.

Shaplen, Robert. "Saigon Exit." *New Yorker,* May 19, 1975.

Shawcross, William. *Sideshow: Kissinger, Nixon, and the Destruction of Cambodia.* Pocket Bks., 1979.

Shipler, D. K., and D. Troute. "American Absence." *Harper Magazine,* April 1975.

Smith, Maj. Gen. H. D. "Final Report by the Defense Attaché, Saigon, May, 1975 (Extract)." In *Vietnam, the Definitive Documentation of Human Decisions,* Vol. 2, edited by Gareth Porter. E. M. Coleman, 1979.

Snepp, Frank. *Decent Interval.* Random, 1977.

Timmes, Maj. Gen. Charles J. "Vietnam Summary: Military Operations After the Cease-Fire Agreement." *Military Review,* August 1976.

Tran Van Don. *Our Endless War: Inside Vietnam.* Presidio Pr., 1978.

Turner, Robert F. *Vietnamese Communism: Its Origins and Development.* Hoover Inst. Pr., 1975.

Valdez, Juan J. Interview by Tom Bartlett. "The Last to Leave." *Leatherneck,* September 1975.

Van Dyke, Jon M. *North Vietnam's Strategy for Survival.* Pacific Bks., 1972.

Van Tien Dung, Sr. Gen. *Our Great Spring Victory.* Translated by John Spragens, Jr. Monthly Review Pr., 1977.

Vanuxem. *La mort du Vietnam: les faits, les causes externes et internes, les consequences sur le Vietnam, la France, et le Monde.* Editions de la Nouvelle Aurore, 1975.

Vo Bam. "The Legendary Ho Chi Minh Trail." *Vietnam Courier,* 1984.

II. Government and Government-Sponsored Reports

BDM Corporation. *A Study of Strategic Lessons Learned in Vietnam.* Vols. 1-8. National Technical Information Service, 1980.

Cao Van Vien, Gen. *The Final Collapse.* Indochina Monographs, U.S. Army Center of Military History, 1983.

————. *Leadership.* Indochina Monographs, U.S. Army Center of Military History, 1980.

————, and Lt. Gen. Dong Van Khuyen. *Reflections on the Vietnam War.* Indochina Monographs, U.S. Army Center of Military History, 1979.

Congressional Quarterly Service. *Almanac.* 94th Congress, 1st sess., 1975, Vol. 31. GPO, 1975.

Department of State Bulletin. October 1974-May 1975.

Dong Van Khuyen, Lt. Gen. *The RVNAF.* Indochina Monographs, U.S. Army Center of Military History, 1980.

Hoang Ngoc Lung, Col. *Intelligence.* Indochina Monographs, U.S. Army Center of Military History, 1983.

————. *Strategy and Tactics.* Indochina Monographs, U.S. Army Center of Military History, 1980.

Le Gro, Col. William E. *Vietnam from Cease-Fire to Capitulation.* U.S. Army Center of Military History, 1981.

Momyer, Gen. William W. *The Vietnamese Air Force, 1951-1975.* Vol. 3, Monograph 4, USAF Southeast Asia Monograph Series. Office of Air Force History, 1975.

Sak Sutsakhan, Lt. Gen. *The Khmer Republic at War and the Final Collapse.* Indochina Monographs, U.S. Army Center of Military History, 1980.

Tilford, Earl H., Jr. *Search and Rescue in Southeast Asia, 1961-1975.* Office of Air Force History, 1980.

Tobin, Lt. Col. Thomas G. et al. *Last Flight from Saigon.* Vol. 4, Monograph 6, USAF Southeast Asia Monograph Series. Office of Air Force History, 1978.

Tran Van Tra, Col. Gen. *Vietnam: History of the Bulwark B-2 Theatre.* Vol. 5. GPO, 1983.

U.S. Congress. House. Committee on International Relations. *The Vietnam-Cambodia Emergency, 1975.* Parts 1, 2, 3, and 4. 94th Congress, 2d sess., April 1975-May 1976.

Vietnam: The Anti-U.S. Resistance War for National Salvation 1954-1975, Military Events. People's Army Publishing House, 1982.

III. Unpublished Government and Military Documents

Defense Attaché Office, Vietnam
  Le Gro, Col. William E. "RVNAF Final Assessment, January thru April 1975, FY 1975."
  Smith, Maj. Gen. H. D. "RVNAF Quarterly Assessment, 2d Quarter, February 1975."
Gerald R. Ford Library
  Presidential Papers of Gerald R. Ford, White House File.
  Weyand, Gen. F. G. "Report to the President on the Situation in Vietnam." April 4, 1975.
Nguyen Duy Hinh, Maj. Gen. "Summary of Activities—3d Infantry Division from December 1972 to late April 1975." 1975.
U.S. Army—Center of Military History, Washington, D.C.
  Hey, E. G. "Trip Report." DAO Army Division, Final Report, Vol. 7: Transportation.
U.S. Marine Corps Historical Center—Washington, D.C.
  Oral History Program:
    Baker, Lt. Horace W.
    Batchelder, Col. S. H.
    Bohr, Lt. Col. Harper L., Jr.
    Fisher, Lt. Col. Herbert G.
    Hicks, J. B.
    Lukeman, Lt. Col. Anthony

McKinstry, Lt. Col. William
Sparks, S/Sgt. Walter
Valdez, M/Sgt. Juan
U.S. Marine Corps Command Chronology—16 March 1975 to 31 March 1975.
U.S. Navy—Operational Archives, Naval History Division, Washington, D.C.
Chung Tan Cang, Vice Admiral, Chief of Naval Operations, Navy of the Republic of Vietnam (VNN).
Ding Manh Hung, Commodore, Deputy Chief of Staff, VNN.
Ho Van Ky Thoai, Commodore, CO, 1st Coastal Zone, VNN.
Hoang Co Minh, Commander, CO, 2d Coastal Zone, VNN.
Nguyen Huu Chi, Commodore, Deputy Commander of Naval Operations, VNN.
Nguyen Xuan Son, Captain, CO, Sea Forces, VNN.

IV. Newspapers and Periodicals Consulted by Authors:
Le Monde; New York Times; Newsweek; Time; Washington Post (1974–75 issues used for all these periodicals).

V. Interviews
Colonel Hoang Ngoc Lung, JGS Intelligence; Colonel William E. Le Gro, DAO Intelligence; Colonel Le Van Me, ARVN Operations Officer, Airborne Division; Graham Martin, Ambassador to South Vietnam, June 1973–April 1975; Major General John E. Murray, Defense Attaché, South Vietnam, March 1973–August 1974; Major General Nguyen Duy Hinh, Commanding General, ARVN 3d Division; Al Rockoff, Free-lance Photographer; Dr. James Schlesinger, Secretary of Defense, August 1973–November 1975; Frank Snepp, CIA Analyst, author of *Decent Interval;* Reverend Thomas Stebbins, Missionary, Christian and Missionary Alliance; Major General Charles J. Timmes, U.S. Embassy Assistant to the Ambassador; Lt. Col. Vinh Quoc, VNAF, CO, 235th Special Operations Helicopter Squadron; General John Vogt, Commanding General, USSAG, 7th Air Force.

Picture Credits

Cover Photograph:
Vietnam News Agency—John Spragens, Jr., Collection.

Conditions So Perfect
p. 2, Courtesy of the Asia Resource Center. p. 4, top, Sovfoto; top left inset, Nihon Denpa News, Ltd.; top right inset, Alain Nogues—Sygma; bottom, UPI/Bettmann Archive; bottom insets, AP/Wide World. pp. 7–8, Vietnam News Agency. p. 12, UPI/Bettmann Archive. p. 15, AP/Wide World. p. 18, Japan Press Photos.

The Lull
p. 25, Ngo Vinh Hai—Ngo Vinh Long Collection. p. 27, top, AP/Wide World; bottom, U.S. Navy. p. 29, UPI/Bettmann Archive. p. 33, Camera Press Ltd. p. 34, Romano Cagnoni. p. 36, right, left bottom, UPI/Bettmann Archive; left top, © Al Rockoff.

Strangulation of Phnom Penh
p. 38, UPI/Bettmann Archive. p. 40, Sun Heang—Black Star. pp. 41–42, Chhor Yuthy—Camera Press Ltd. p. 43, top, Chhor Yuthy—Sygma; bottom, Camera Press Ltd. p. 44, UPI/Bettmann Archive. p. 45, © Al Rockoff.

Campaign 275
p. 47, AP/Wide World. p. 51, UPI/Bettmann Archive. p. 52, Vietnam News Agency. p. 55, UPI/Bettmann Archive. p. 56, Jean-Claude Francolon—Gamma/Liaison. pp. 59, 61, UPI/Bettmann Archive. p. 62, AP/Wide World. p. 63, UPI/Bettmann Archive.

A Glimpse of Apocalypse
p. 65, UPI/Bettmann Archive. pp. 67–68, 71, AP/Wide World. pp. 72–73, Gamma/Liaison. p. 79, AP/Wide World. p. 81, UPI/Bettmann Archive. pp. 82–83, Japan Press Photos.

Evacuation Without End
p. 84, AP/Wide World. p. 86, top, UPI/Bettmann Archive; bottom, AP/Wide World. p. 87, UPI/Bettmann Archive. p. 88, Sygma. p. 90, UPI/Bettmann Archive. p. 91, AP/Wide World.

"You Must Win"
p. 93, Gamma/Liaison. p. 96, Roger Pic. pp. 99–100, Jean-Claude Francolon—Gamma/Liaison. p. 105, top, UPI/Bettmann Archive; bottom, AP/Wide World. pp. 106–7, UPI/Bettmann Archive. pp. 109–10, Don McCullin—Magnum. p. 113, Agence Vietnamienne d'Information.

The Noose Tightens
p. 115, Hiroji Kubota—Magnum. p. 117, UPI/Bettmann Archive. p. 119, top, Hiroji Kubota—Magnum; bottom, UPI/Bettmann Archive. p. 120, Hiroji Kubota—Magnum. p. 122, AP/Wide World. p. 123, Photoreporters, Inc. p. 124, top, Sylvain Julienne—Sygma; bottom, AP/Wide World. p. 125, © Al Rockoff. p. 127, AP/Wide World. pp. 130, 133, UPI/Bettmann Archive. p. 135, Terry Fincher—Sipa.

The Saigon Redoubt
p. 137, UPI/Bettmann Archive. p. 139, Bollinger—STERN, Hamburg. p. 143, Darquenne—Sygma. p. 144, Bryn Campbell—Magnum. p. 146, Hiroji Kubota—Magnum. p. 147, J. A. Pavlovsky—Sygma. p. 148, Bollinger—STERN, Hamburg. p. 151, J. A. Pavlovsky—Sygma.

The End
p. 153, UPI/Bettmann Archive. pp. 155–56, Gamma/Liaison. p. 159, AP/Wide World. p. 162, Gamma/Liaison. p. 165, Dieter Ludwig—Gamma/Liaison. p. 166, Nik Wheeler—Black Star. p. 167, Nik Wheeler. p. 168, Nik Wheeler—Black Star. pp. 170–71, © 1975 Paul Quinn-Judge. p. 172, top, AP/Wide World; bottom, U.S. Marine Corps. p. 173, top, U.S. Navy; bottom, UPI/Bettmann Archive. p. 174, J. A. Pavlovsky—Sygma.

Final Victory
p. 176, Vietnam News Agency—John Spragens, Jr., Collection. p. 178, top, Photoreporters, Inc. p. 178, Sygma. p. 179, top, UPI/Bettmann Archive. p. 180, Dieter Ludwig—Gamma/Liaison. p. 182, top, © 1975 Paul Quinn-Judge; bottom, Vietnam News Agency—John Spragens, Jr., Collection. p. 183, Photoreporters, Inc. p. 184, Françoise Demulder—Gamma/Liaison.

Map Credits

All maps prepared by Diane McCaffery. Sources are as follows:

p. 10—"The Legendary Ho Chi Minh Trail" by General Vo Bam, *Vietnam Courier* 20, no. 5, p. 11.

p. 16—U.S. Army Center of Military History.

p. 32—U.S. Army Center of Military History.

p. 50—U.S. Army Center of Military History.

p. 69—U.S. Army Center of Military History.

p. 129—U.S. Central Intelligence Agency; Department of the Army.

p. 140—*Our Great Spring Victory* by General Van Tien Dung, Monthly Review Pr., 1977, p. 128; Department of the Army.

p. 161—Department of the Army.

Acknowledgments

Boston Publishing wishes to acknowledge the kind assistance of the following people: Bill Heimdahl, Office of Air Force History, Washington, D.C.; Vince Demma and Jeff Clark, Center of Military History, Washington, D.C.; Jack Schulimson, Major G. R. Dunham, and Benis M. Frank, Marine Corps Historical Center, Washington, D.C.; Ed Moraldo, Naval Historical Center, Washington, D.C.; Tom O'Reilly and Russ Rumney, Bell Helicopter/Textron, Fort Worth, Texas; John Corcoran, Air Force Office of Security Review, Washington, D.C.

Index

U.S. Military Units

South Vietnamese Military Units

North Vietnamese Military Units

North Vietnamese Main Force units organized for the Ho Chi Minh Campaign
(See map on page 140)

Names, Acronyms, Terms

Angka Loeu—"Organization on High," or ruling body of the Khmer Rouge.

Bo doi—uniformed NVA soldier. One of the regular Communist troops, as opposed to the southern guerrillas, or Vietcong.

Campaign 275—NVA operation to capture the central highlands.

CBU—cluster bomb unit.

CINCPAC—Commander in Chief, Pacific. Commander of American forces in the Pacific, including Southeast Asia.

COMUSMACV—Commander, U.S. Military Assistance Command, Vietnam.

Corps—South Vietnamese military forces assigned to protect a Military Region. For example, I Corps defended MR 1.

COSVN—Central Office for South Vietnam. Communist military and political headquarters for southern South Vietnam.

Daisy Cutter—15,000-pound bomb designed to clear helicopter landing zones in heavily foliated areas.

DAO—Defense Attaché Office. Part of the U.S. Embassy to South Vietnam, it replaced the Military Assistance Command, Vietnam.

DRV—Democratic Republic of Vietnam. North Vietnam.

Eagle Pull—code name of the American evacuation from Phnom Penh.

FANK—Forces Armées Nationales Khmères. The Cambodian government forces.

Frequent Wind—military plan for the U.S. evacuation of Saigon, formerly called Talon Vise.

GVN—U.S. abbreviation for the government of South Vietnam.

Ho Chi Minh Campaign—name given, on April 14, 1975, to the NVA campaign to "liberate" Saigon.

ICCS—International Commission of Control and Supervision. Representatives from Canada (later replaced by Iran), Hungary, Indonesia, and Poland whose task was to monitor the implementation of the Paris agreement.

JCS—Joint Chiefs of Staff (U.S.). Consists of chairman, army chief of staff, chief of naval operations, air force chief of staff, and marine commandant.

JGS—Joint General Staff. South Vietnamese counterpart of the JCS.

JMC—Joint Military Commission. Consisted of representatives of the DRV, the PRG, the U.S., and the RVN. Its purpose was to ensure that the concerned parties implemented and abided by the Paris agreement.

JMT—Four-Party Joint Military Team. Established in 1973. Consisting of representatives of the DRV, the PRG, the U.S., and the RVN, its purpose was to account for prisoners and MIAs on all sides.

Khmer Rouge—"Red Khmers." The forces of the Cambodian Communist party.

Lao Dong party—Vietnam Worker's party, Marxist-Leninist party of North Vietnam.

LAW—M72 light antitank weapon. Successor to bazooka, a shoulder-fired 66mm rocket with a disposable Fiberglas launcher.

LST—landing ship tank. A large, shallow-draft landing and cargo craft.

MR—Military Region. One of four geographical zones into which South Vietnam was divided for purposes of military and civil administration.

MR 1—South Vietnam's five northernmost provinces.

MR 2—central highlands and adjoining coastal lowlands.

MR 3—area from the northern Mekong Delta to the southern central highlands.

MR 4—Mekong Delta region.

National Council of National Reconciliation and Concord—institution provided for by the Paris agreement to promote implementation of the agreement, ensure democratic liberties, and organize elections.

NLF—National Liberation Front. The National Front for the Liberation of the South, it aimed to overthrow the GVN.

NSC—National Security Council (U.S.). Established in 1947 to "advise the president with respect to the integration of domestic, foreign and military policies relating to national security."

Option IV—U.S. military plan for helicopter evacuation from Saigon.

Paris agreement—Agreement on Ending the War and Restoring Peace in Vietnam, signed in Paris on January 27, 1973.

PF—Popular Forces. South Vietnamese village defense units.

POL—petroleum, oil, and lubricants.

Politburo—policymaking and executive committee of the Communist party.

PRGRSV (or PRG)—Provisional Revolutionary Government of the Republic of South Vietnam. Established in 1969 by the NLF.

RF—Regional Forces. South Vietnamese provincial defense units.

RVNAF—Republic of Vietnam Armed Forces (South).

sapper—commando raider adept at penetrating defenses.

SA-2—a Russian-built surface-to-air missile with effective altitude of 59,000 feet and speed of Mach 2.5.

Talon Vise—original name of the military contingency plan for the U.S. evacuation of Saigon. See Frequent Wind.

Third Force—GVN's non-Communist opposition. The South Vietnamese neutralists, represented in several different political and religious groups.

Truong Son Corridor—strategic supply lines paralleling the Ho Chi Minh Trail but located within South Vietnam.

USAID—United States Agency for International Development. Responsible for administering foreign aid in Vietnam.

USIA/USIS—United States Information Agency. Established for international dissemination of information about the U.S. Overseas, the agency was referred to as the USIS (United States Information Service).

USSAG/7AF—United States Support Activities Group & 7th Air Force. Located at Nakhon Phanom in northeast Thailand, it was set up after the cease-fire to plan for any re-entry of U.S. air and sea power into Indochina.

VNAF—Vietnamese Air Force (South).

VNN—Vietnamese Navy (South).

War Powers Act—law passed in November 1973 that placed a maximum ninety-day limit on the U.S. president's use of troops abroad, or on any substantial increase in the number of troops stationed abroad.